BK 759.6 L673W 1968
WORLD OF GOYA /LEWIS, DOM
1968 .00 FV

3000 188207 30011
St. Louis Community College

S0-ADE-629

759.6 L673w 1968
LEWIS   FV
THE WORLD OF GOYA
                              10.00

WITHDRAWN

JUNIOR COLLEGE DISTRICT
of St. Louis - St. Louis County
LIBRARY
7508 Forsyth Blvd.
St. Louis, Missouri 63105

The World of Goya

The World of
GOYA

D. B. Wyndham Lewis

CLARKSON N. POTTER, INC. NEW YORK

6-22-70

Designed and produced by George Rainbird Ltd,
Marble Arch House, 44 Edgware Road, London, W.2
for Clarkson N. Potter, Inc., 419 Park Avenue South,
New York, N.Y. 10016

Filmset in 'Monophoto' Ehrhardt
by Oliver Burridge Filmsetting Ltd,
Crawley, Sussex, England
Gravure by Joh. Enschedé en Zonen, Haarlem, Holland
Color and monochrome lithography by
Amilcare Pizzi S.p.A., Milan, Italy
Bound by Legatoria Editoriale
Giovanni Olivotto S.p.A., Vicenza, Italy

First published 1968

First American edition published 1968
by Clarkson N. Potter, Inc., New York

Copyright © 1968, by D. B. Wyndham Lewis

All rights reserved. This book, or parts thereof,
may not be reproduced in any form without
permission of the publishers.

Library of Congress Catalog Card Number: 67–20542

Printed in Italy and the Netherlands

To
H. V. Morton,
amicissime

Acknowledgements

With much pleasure I acknowledge my indebtedness to my friend Mr H. V. Morton, who inspired this book, and to my friend Don Xavier de Salas, Sub-Director of the Prado, Madrid, for invaluable advice and criticism; likewise to Mr John Hadfield, Editorial Director of George Rainbird Limited, for much stimulation, to Miss Mary Anne Norbury, House Editor, and to Mr George Rainbird, the 'onlie begetter'. To the late Duke of Alba I owe my introduction to one of the most fascinating women of the eighteenth century.

I owe moreover a considerable debt to my wife for a gallant feat of typing.

D.B.W.L.
Altea, Alicante, 1966–68

Contents

List of colour plates

8

Biographical notes

1746   Francisco de Paula Joseph Goya born on 30th March in Fuendetodos to Joseph Goya and Doña Engracia Lucientes
        Raymón Bayeu born

1749   Joseph Goya moves his family back to Saragossa

1757   Goya sent to school of the Píarist Order – *Escuelas Pías*; meets Martin Zapater at the school

1760   With the influence of the Conde de Fuentes, Goya is accepted as an apprentice to José Luzán y Martínez in Saragossa; meets Francisco Bayeu

1762   Maria Teresa Cayetana, Duchess of Alba, born in Madrid to Maria Teresa de Silva y Silva, Duchess of Huéscar

1763   Leaves Luzán's studio; applies to the Royal Academy of San Fernando in Madrid for a scholarship and is refused

1766   Royal Academy refuse Goya a travel-bursary for the second time
        ? Goes to Rome

1770   In Rome

1771   Leaves Rome; is awarded second prize in a competition arranged by the Academy of Fine Arts, Parma

1772   Summoned to Saragossa by Francisco Bayeu and commissioned to do fresco decorations in the Chapel of the Pilar in the basilica; starts murals for the Charterhouse of Aula Dei

1773   Marries Josefa Bayeu, sister of Francisco and Raymón; moves to Madrid

1775   Goya's son, Javier, baptised
        Maria Cayatana marries José Maria Alvarez de Toledo Gonzaga, Marquis of Villafranca

1776   Rafael Mengs commissions Goya to do cartoons for the Royal Tapestry Manufactory by the Santa Barbara gate, Madrid (*Real Fábrica de Tapices*)

1778   Begins the series of engravings after Velázquez

1780   Admitted a member to the Royal Academy of Fine Arts of San Fernando, having qualified with a painting 'Christ Crucified'
        Lives in Saragossa and works on decorations in the basilica

1781   Returns to Madrid and enters the competition for the decoration of the church of San Francisco el Grande for which he painted an altarpiece as a result (1786)

1785   Appointed Deputy Director of the Academy of San Fernando

1786   Portrait of Carlos III
        Portrait of Francisco Bayeu
        Appointed official Painter to the King: *La Vendimia* – tapestry cartoon; gains authoritative position at the *Real Fábrica*

1788   Death of Carlos III succeeded by Carlos IV
        'Self-portrait in velvet with spectacles'
        Applies unsuccessfully for the post of Director of the Royal Academy

1790   'Self-portrait with sombrero' (No. 1 of The Caprices)
        Visits Valencia with his wife

1792 Finishes tapestry cartoons
Construction of San Antonio de la Florida completed
Beginning of Goya's two year illness which results in total deafness

1793 *Los Caprichos* in progress
Applies to the King for two months sick leave

1795 Portrait of the Duchess of Alba
Posthumous portrait of Bayeu
Begins frescoes at San Antonio de la Florida
On Bayeu's death, becomes Director of Painting at the Royal Academy

1796 Death of the Duke of Alba

1797 Flying visit to Saragossa
Spends the summer with the Duchess of Alba in Andalusia; paints second portrait of the Duchess of Alba
Los Caprichos completed and published

1799 Appointed First Painter to the King
Equestrian portraits of Carlos IV and Queen Maria Luisa

1800 'The Family of Carlos IV'

1801 Official portrait of Godoy

1802 Death of the Duchess of Alba, 23rd July

1803 *Los Caprichos* reissued with eight additional plates

1805 ? 'The Nude' and 'The Clothed Maja'

1808 War of Independence breaks out with the 2nd May uprisings in Madrid; Carlos IV overthrown

1810 Begins 'Disasters of War' series

1811 Josefa Goya dies

1812 Portrait of the Duke of Wellington

1813 End of War, 7th October
'Madrid, 2nd May, 1808: Battle of the Mamelukes'
'Madrid, 3rd May, 1808: Executions at the Mountain of Prince Pius'

1814 Restoration of Fernando VII
Goya granted pardon for his affiliation with Joseph Bonaparte

1815 Finishes 'Disasters of War' series

1816 *Tauromaquia* series published

1819 Begins work on 'The Black Paintings' having bought and moved to the 'Quinta del Sordo', where Doña Leocadia Weiss becomes his housekeeper
Falls ill

1824 Granted six months leave of absence to go to Plombières-les-Bains, but instead goes to Bordeaux visiting Paris for three months

1825 French edition of the lithographs 'The Bulls of Bordeaux'

1826 Granted another extension of leave
Vicente López paints Goya's portrait

1828 Dies in Bordeaux, 16th April

1863 'Disasters of War' published

1864 *Los Proverbios* published

1878 Baron d'Erlanger displays The Black Paintings at the Paris Exhibition

1 Enigma of a skull

O N a November morning of 1888 in the cemetery of the Grande Char-
treuse, Bordeaux, the Spanish consul resident in that opulent city
received the shock of his life. Hastening to the nearest telegraph-
office he despatched a wire to Madrid: GOYA SKELETON HEADLESS.

In a less agitated condition, and able to recall the master's whimsical
etching of a seated corpse pushing up the lid of a tomb bearing the one-word
See p. 12 inscription *Nada* ('Nothing'), the consul might pardonably have begun his
telegram TYPICAL GOYAESQUE SITUATION STOP. However, within an hour
or so came the official reply: DESPATCH GOYA WITH HEAD OR WITHOUT.

Dying in self-chosen exile in 1828, at the age of eighty-two, Francisco
Joseph Goya y Lucientes had been buried in the tomb of a close friend and
fellow-expatriate, Miguel Martín Goicoichea, deceased three years previously, the memorial-tablet accurately proclaiming him *Hispaniensis Peritis-
simus Pictor*. His skull, stolen at some time unknown, has not been seen or
heard of since. The exhumation duly proceeded, and Goya's truncated
remains were returned with honour to his native land after an absence of
sixty-six years. The Regent María Cristina and her ministers had gladly
accepted an offer of repatriation from President Carnot's government, made
possible by the replanning of the principal cemetery of Bordeaux.

Any votary of the *Caprichos* will feel a natural temptation to drape this
mystery in a little pertinent melodrama. A moonless night; cloaks, masks,
dark-lanterns; a trio of professional body-snatchers with sacks and crowbars
crouching by a rifled tomb; the muffled rasp of a saw . . . only a covey of
circumambient witches and ghouls need be added. The operation, to judge
by an early engraving of the tomb showing a stout circular stone pillar
surmounted by an iron cross, the whole protected by a breast-high railing and
seemingly about as pregnable as the Bastille, would be no ploy for amateurs.

It is, however, on record that in 1875 the then Spanish consul observed the
fabric to be cracked and presenting a 'ruinous' aspect. Situated as it was in an
outlying sector of a spacious cemetery, flanked by an alley called, not in-
appropriately, Rue Coupe-Gorge, 'Cut-throat Street', the tomb may for
some time have presented little difficulty to normally-skilled practitioners.

The fog of conjecture enveloping the missing head may be said to centre
on the year 1849, when a young Navarrese artist, Dionisio Fierros, painted
for a patrician family of that province, his patrons, what its title alleges to be a

study of the skull of Goya. The canvas was next heard of in 1928, when a junk-dealer bought it at an auction in Saragossa. It was acquired for the Provincial Museum in that city and later transferred to the Ateneo in Madrid, where it remains, its authenticity still queried. Sceptics point to a curious absence from Fierros' study of the true proportions of the headpiece dominating every portrait of the master – that massive cranium, contemplation of which enables one to understand why adepts of the pseudo-science of phrenology, launched by Gall and Spurzheim at the end of the eighteenth century and claiming serious devotees all over Europe for about a century more, have been suspected of inspiring a midnight snatch.

What a head! The mysterious grey mass it enclosed had produced a harvest of genius in paint, pencil, etching, and lithography over some sixty years. The stubborn black hair thatching it had been pulled by irate Aragonese peasants in boyhood and – undoubtedly – stroked in years of maturity by Spain's most wayward duchess. The paintbrush directed by this brain had bequeathed to posterity the essence of the ardent multicoloured contemporary Spanish scene: a kaleidoscope of kings, queens, princes, grandees, soldiers, friars,

'Nothing!' That is what it says (No. 69 of The Disasters of War) etching, burnished acquatint, lavis, drypoint and burin $6\frac{1}{8} \times 7\frac{3}{4}$ in. (15.5 × 19.6 cm.) The British Museum, London

See p. 96
See PLATE XXVIII p. 153

See PLATE XXXVIII pp. 186–87

See PLATE XXIV pp. 139–40

See p. 30
See PLATE VII p. 56
See p. 96

bullfighters, highborn beauties, gypsies, pilgrims, guerillas, inquisitors, fops, intellectuals, majas, saints, tinkers, the gaily-clad fashionables lounging on the Pradera de San Isidro, revellers at proletarian fiestas, the street-combatants of 1808. In this same hand the etching-needle had given life to more nightmare chimeras than even Hieronymus Bosch had imagined: warlocks, witches, ghouls, a world of sinister fantasy. The Court painter had turned a family portrait-group of thirteen mediocre Spanish royalties into what most authorities regard as a jewel of satire. The Duchess of Alba's adorer had used her as the model for a shamelessly spectacular nude, disguising only the patrician features, and when she tired of the affair had saluted her with the most savage of caricatures. The landscapist had produced the lovely autumnal mistiness of the *Vendimia* and the delicate Watteauesque pastel-shades, pink, blue, green, of the San Isidro picnic, an ensemble which has been compared for colouring to a fruit-sherbet. The same prolific hand had portrayed for posterity some of the bloodshed and fury of the French invasion: the citizens of Madrid fighting Napoleon's troops in the Puerta del Sol, the patriots facing the execution squads, the hangings, the shootings, the reprisals, the ravages of famine, rapine, loot, and epidemic.

See PLATE XXVIII p. 153

See PLATE XXIX p. 154

An unaccustomed criticism which seems incidentally worth recording attaches to this last period. It came from Wellington, superbest of martinets, curtly waving away one of the three portraits Goya painted at Madrid. The Duke perhaps had good reason. This particular work, if it were indeed the portrait sold at Sotheby's in June, 1961, for £140,000, stolen from the National Gallery in London in August of the same year, and recovered from the left-luggage office of a Birmingham railway station in May 1965, might well be labelled 'Portrait of an Unknown Spaniard'. There is a story – now regarded as apocryphal – that the painter impulsively responded to the Duke's disapproval by flinging a plaster cast at his head, or, according to another version, grabbing a pistol.[1]

The discovery in the Bordeaux cemetery did not stagger Goya's fellow-countrymen unduly. What Gregorio Marañón has called *la visión lucida de la muerte* has been a national asset for too many centuries to permit queasy shudders over skulls and bones, whatever their destiny. In a world in which, to echo Cervantes, large numbers of fools appear to believe themselves immortal, the Spaniard continues to accept death as a normal and inevitable issue. 'Since it is the law and no punishment why should I complain?' asks Quevedo of his soul in one of his very last sonnets. The Spaniard has been familiar with mortality as a theme for native poets, dramatists, and painters from time immemorial. Indeed, he may view sudden death before his eyes any afternoon during the bullfight season. An investigator of crowd-

---

[1] To his equestrian portrait by Goya, now in Apsley House, London, the Duke had apparently no great objection, but he seems to have preferred the smoother brush of Benjamin Haydon; on learning of whose dramatic suicide, it may be recalled by enthusiasts for form, the Duke at once sent a footman round to his late portraitist's studio to retrieve his Waterloo hat. This might have amused Goya.

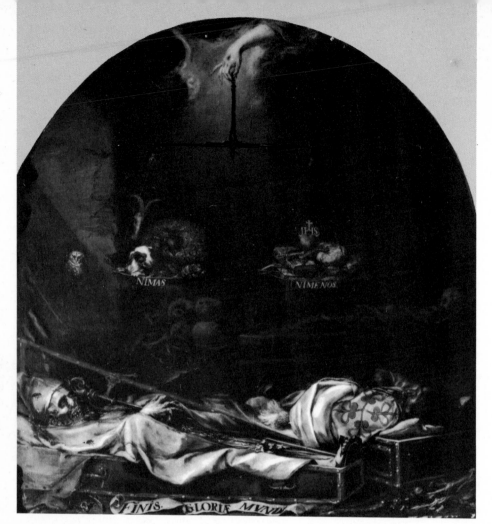

JUAN VALDES LEAL Hieroglyphs
of our last days (*Finis Gloriæ
Mundi*), 1672
oil on canvas
Hospital de la Santa Caridad,
Seville

psychology has attached the enduring spell of these near Mithraic rites to
their 'intrinsic aura', *hálito especial*, of mortality, intensified by the hierarchic
garb of the ministers and the recurring bray of the trumpets heard in Lorca's
dirge for the matador Ignacio Sánchez Mejías. 'Your appetite for death and
the taste of its mouth! The sadness incarnate in your valorous gaiety!'

Amid the galaxy of Golden Age poets the great satiric Quevedo, carrying a
rosary ever in his sword-hilt, might pre-eminently be styled Death's laureate
in verse and prose alike. His last letters to intimates orchestrate with almost
the mastery of a Bossuet the theme that for all humanity death begins at birth,
rebirth at death. Three centuries later the shade of Quevedo might well have
been imagined sardonically approving the skull-and-crossbone devices
daubed so liberally by anarchist hands on Spanish walls on the eve of the
late civil war over the slogan *'Viva la muerte!'*[1] Between such homely re-
minders and, say, Valdés Leal's celebrated painting of a bishop rotting in
his coffin, or St Teresa's cry of longing for the vision of God – 'I die because

---

[1] Normally the battlecry of the Spanish Foreign Legion.

14

I do not die!' – there is a certain gulf. They equally illustrate a national acceptance, not fatalist but realist. As some foreign observer or other has said, not too fantastically, Death is the patron saint of Spain.

Misadventure to illustrious corpses seems likewise peculiar to hispanity. In vain, when the church of San Francisco el Grande in Madrid was temporarily decreed a national pantheon in the 1860s, did commissions of archaeologists comb every possible nook and corner for the remains of Cervantes, Velázquez, Murillo, Lope de Vega, Herrera, Tirso de Molina, Mariana, and several other notables of the Golden Age. In some cases, those of Cervantes and Lope included, the body had by its dying owner's order been lowered, garbed in the rough brown habit of the Franciscan tertiary, into an anonymous and unidentifiable grave. In others, the probing of heaps of jumbled bones, skulls, and cinerary rubbish piled high in church vaults during restoration or rebuilding down the centuries was equally fruitless. Of historic Spanish dust only that of Gonzalo Fernández de Córdoba (*el Gran Capitán*), of Calderón de la Barca, Quevedo, and Garcilaso de la Vega has so far been retrieved for re-entombment.

See PLATES XXI & XXII pp. 127–28

There was no trouble in identifying what was left of Goya at Bordeaux. His remains were finally entombed in the chapel of San Antonio de la Florida at Madrid, where they rest today, accompanied once more by those of the faithful Goicoichea, under Goya's own frescoes. A curious echo of the master's loss was due much later. At the invitation of the Ayuntamiento or civic authority of Madrid, the sculptor Juan Cristóbal of Granada early in the 1920s carved in granite a head of Goya imposing in dimension and virile of aspect. Erected on a stone pedestal near San Antonio de la Florida and badly battered during the civil war, the head was found one day to have vanished altogether. There seems so far no more explanation of this disappearance than of the other.

The Poe-like mystery of the tomb at Bordeaux became, quite suddenly, a news-topic at the end of November, 1966, when the Madrid illustrated weekly *Semana* seized on the occasion of an exhibition of Dionisio Fierros' paintings to attempt what seems to be the first serious probe. Though its investigators failed to discover any trace of the illustrious skull, some interesting theories were forthcoming. That Goya's head was removed by grave-robbers from the torso and stolen at some time between 1828, the year of his burial – certified intact – and 1849, the year of Fierros' painting, now appears, however melodramatic, likely enough. Suspicion regarding the principals involved rests on at least three persons – the fifth and sixth Marqueses de San Adrián, at whose country seat at Tudela, Navarre, young Fierros painted his study, and possibly Fierros himself, their protégé. Both noblemen were ardent Goya-addicts; a faded label on the back of the picture-frame concerned bears the fifth Marqués's signature.

Exploration of the San Adrián mansion at Tudela, long since unoccupied, with archives in considerable disorder, yielded nothing, but a clue of sorts was the discovery that the skull painted by Fierros became by bequest his own property, to be thereafter enshrined behind glass in his studio. Simultaneously emerged the fact that Fierros' son and heir Nicolás, an anatomist at the University of Salamanca, is known to have devoted considerable professional attention in due course to this same skull, from which he extracted at least one of the parietal bones, believed to be now in the possession of the Faculty of Medicine at Santiago de Compostela. It might well be that excessive scientific curiosity, coupled with that of a phrenologist, Cubí y Soler, who assisted Nicolás Fierros in his research, proved disastrous.

Don Nicolás died suddenly in 1894, taking his secret with him. Don Gamallo Dionisio, the painter's grandson, an elderly literary figure now resident in Madrid, intends possibly to deal with the mystery himself at some future date, an interviewer gathered. And there, to echo a ritual cliché of the past, the matter rests.

★ ★ ★

For philosophers like Unamuno and Angel Ganivet who connect certain outstanding Spanish characteristics – asceticism, militancy, individualism, disdain for the mercantile spirit, racial consciousness, and the rest – with the isolation and sterility of large tracts of Spanish earth, Aragon supplies the absolute. Compared with rich provinces like Valencia, Murcia, Andalucia, or much more Granada, *paraíso de la tierra*, with its fruit and flowers, fountains and nightingales, its soft perfumed breezes and magical skies, Goya's native territory might seem a slice of another planet.

Its cultivated enclaves notwithstanding, the Aragonese scene is apt to linger in the memory of a foreign foot-traveller as one of almost lunar desolation, recalling the eminently Goyaesque hallucinations of a poet's dream:

> A savage place, as holy and enchanted
> As e'er beneath a waning moon was haunted
> By woman wailing for her demon-lover . . .

Wave after stony wave of high implacable sierra rising to the sky; parched tawny plains, turned blood-red by a setting sun; dried-up riverbeds and rock-strewn gullies; tall domed churches like fortresses, adorned with ancient barbaric wood-carving; inhospitable villages full of silence and watching eyes, with stone or lime-washed houses turning their backs on a narrow winding street; intolerable heat in summer; intense cold in winter under the unremitting howl of the northeast wind called the *Cierzo* – such a landscape breeds and nourishes a human fauna concordant.

Known to his fellow-Spaniards as a *baturro*, a term conveying mulish obstinacy, the essential Aragonese is the topic of agelong pleasantries. Tough, aggressive, opinionated, secretive, dogged, capable of driving nails into stone walls with his head, of devouring a bar of soap to prove it to be cheese, of disputing the railway-track with trains – the gibes levelled at him are plentiful. His regional dance is the *jota*. His nearest European affinities are probably the Tyneside 'Geordie' in England and the Auvergnat, or perhaps the Limousin, in France.

The so-called Great Schism of the West in the fourteenth century produced the Aragonese type *in excelsis* in the person of Pedro de Luna, known to history as the antipope Benedict XIII, elected at Avignon. The spectacle of this implacable old man spending his last years in self-imposed exile on the fortress-rock of Peñíscola off the Aragonese coast, ruling a handful of soldiers and retainers, doggedly claiming the Keys, daily excommunicating the dying Fernando I of Aragon, is one of the most fantastic in European annals. Those qualified to judge agree that such spectacular pigheadedness in a scholar, an ecclesiastic, and a nobleman is characteristic of his native province.

The average Aragonese is in fact not immediately recognizable as a unit of the nation styled by Maurice Barrès 'the aristocrats of Europe'. His lack of the social graces is indeed proverbial.

> *A uso de Aragón,*
> *a buen servicio, mal galardón.*

> In the manner of Aragon – for good service, poor return.

On the other hand he certainly shares with his fellow-countrymen that fundamental dignity which lends the Spanish peasant, in Unamuno's words, the air of a king dethroned. This quality may nevertheless frequently be allied, even in the case of his betters, with a notable lack of tact. There is no evidence that it ever hampered Goya to any extent; in fact a quip coined a century before him by Béroald de Verville in *Le Moyen de Parvenir* – 'hard to hold as a nice little angel of Aragon' – might well be attached to one or two recorded displays of Goyaesque temperament. In self-assurance and in pugnacity likewise he may be recognized as a true son of his province.

The combative propensity of the Aragonese has more than once been of inestimable value to Spain. Such a race, sprung from such a soil, might be expected to breed bonny men of war, and has lavishly done so. The early history of Saragossa, capital of the province, founded by Augustus Caesar, is in itself an epitome of violence down the ages. Suevi, Franks, Visigoths, and Moors took it in turn by force of numbers, and not without severe trouble, before Alfonso the Battler recaptured it after five years of war and a nine-months siege in A.D. 1118, to hold it permanently thenceforth for the crown of Aragon. Under Jaime I in the next century all Aragon became the spearhead of the Reconquest, driving the Moor back in fierce fighting, mile by mile, as far south as Murcia and expelling him from the Balearics. Juan II in the fifteenth century was backed by the Aragonese against the greater part of Catalonia, thus enabling Don Juan to marry his son Fernando to Isabella of Castile and to unite Spain permanently under one crown.

Que se fizo el rey Don Juan?
los ynfantes de Aragón
que se fizieron?

Where is the King, Don Juan? Where
Each royal prince and noble heir
of Aragon?
Jorge Manrique (1440–79)
translated by Longfellow.

General Don José de Palafox on
Horseback
oil on canvas
97⅝ × 88¼ in. (248 × 224 cm.)
Museo del Prado, Madrid

Hence the toughness of the *baturro*, like his self-sufficiency, may be assumed hereditary. That it may extend to the urban Aragonese bourgeoisie was demonstrated to an impressed Europe as late as 1808, when the citizens of Saragossa, men, women and children, with their monks and clergy, headed by Palafox roaring 'War to the knife!', fought back eighteen thousand seasoned troops of Lannes and Mortier, street by street, house by house; surrendering their city only after two months' resistance, with some fifty thousand killed in action or dying of famine and epidemic. Among the defenders of *Zaragoza la siempre heroica* are still yearly remembered and saluted the glorious curate Don Santiago Sas, killed while charging with tucked-up cassock and whirling sabre a file of Napoleon's grenadiers, and smoke-blackened old Uncle Jorge Ibert, serving his cannon to the last with Maria Agostina, Aragon's Joan of Arc, and Mariano Cerezo, to the cry of '*Viva María del Pilar!*' Of the celebrated little village of Móstoles in New Castile, which boasts on a monument that in 1808 its alcalde challenged Napoleon Bonaparte to mortal combat, one can only say that the shout deserved to hail from Aragon.

If the emergence of a genius like Goya should seem, after all this, to be a portent arising unexpected from a kind of Boeotia, the impression must swiftly be corrected. Though his native province has not so far produced another Martial, born at Augusta Bilbilis near Calatayud round about A.D. 40, Aragon has been no foe to the Muses. Her twelfth-century kings endowed Huesca with a university. The work of a notable native sixteenth-century school of ecclesiastical sculpture in stone and alabaster under the masters Damian Forment, Diego Morlanes, and Juan de Talavera is still to be admired here and in Saragossa. In the same century the brothers Argensola, Bartolomé Leonardo and Lupercio Leonardo, produced historical and lyrico-dramatic work of classic quality. From the Jesuit college at Calatayud in the seventeenth century emerged that most subtle and acid of philosophers Baltasar Gracián of the *Oráculo Manual*, which so ravished Schopenhauer. In Huesca at the same period the library and art-gallery of Gracián's patron Don Vincencio de Lastanosa was the meeting place of as erudite a group as any European coterie could show. Eighteenth-century Aragon equally boasted a cultivated stratum. José Nicolás de Azara, ambassador and connoisseur, was Winckelmann's patron in Rome. To the Conde de Fuentes of Saragossa, and to Ramón de la Cruz, the fashionable playwright of the day, their fellow-provincial young Francisco Goya of Fuendetodos was to owe his discovery and his debut.

Science has not yet been able to account for the phenomenon of geysers of genius splurging unexpectedly from rock and desert. A poet-descendant of the eminent Thomas Huxley, lately pondering the erratic chemistry of the spermatozoa, has no solution.

> And among that billion minus one
>   Might have chanced to be
> Shakespeare, another Newton, a new Donne –
>   But the One was Me . . .

(below left) Francisco Bayeu y Subias, 1786
oil on canvas
$43\frac{1}{2} \times 32\frac{1}{2}$ in. (110.4 × 82.5 cm.)
Museo Provincial de Bellas Artes, Valencia

(below right)
GIOVANNI BATTISTA TIEPOLO
St Anthony of Padua with the Infant Christ, 1767–69
oil on canvas
$88\frac{1}{2} \times 49\frac{5}{8}$ in. (225 × 126 cm.)
Museo del Prado, Madrid

That the elder Goya, no 'typical' peasant, earned a modest living as a gilder in touch with the studios of Saragossa provides a slender enough clue to his eldest son's achievement, which would doubtless have astonished him. In his age there were no theorists to explain why Francisco should become a starry phenomenon whereas his brother Tomás remained all his life a gilder. It would seem that the freaks of heredity are still inexplicable save by a *fantaisiste* fringe.

At the time of Goya's birth the springs of Spanish artistic genius appeared to have dried up with the death of Murillo sixty years before. In any case the Bourbon monarchy inclined to French and Italian taste. Van Loo was Felipe V's Court painter. Fernando VI and Carlos III favoured Tiepolo and the naturalized Danish-Bohemian Rafael Mengs. During the first half of the century art in Spain was represented chiefly by Houasse, Raul, Tiepolo, and the capable but uninspired Francisco Bayeu of the Saragossa school, under whom the prentice Goya was to work on the decoration of the Pilar basilica, and whose sister Josefa he was to marry.

See PLATE IV p. 44, p. 19

See p. 19
See p. 51, PLATE VI pp. 54–55
See PLATE I p. 33

Above all these painters the Aragonese rustic was to soar like a meteor in a long lifetime of creative brilliance, a master in every sphere of his art save (according to some critics, mainly foreign) the one in which he began.

A spiritual tone-deafness has been discerned in almost all Goya's religious painting. In the San Antonio de la Florida frescoes, for example, some of the fine ladies in the dome-gallery watching, with all Madrid, St Antony of Padua restore a corpse to momentary life might be viewing a minor carriage-accident in the Calle Mayor, lacking nothing but their lornettes. It could be that Goya was here deliberately adopting a frequent convention of the art of the Middle Ages: on the one hand the rapt immediate spectators of miracle, on the fringe of the group humanity going about its daily business. In the case of the figures of SS Justa and Rufina, painted for Seville Cathedral, there is certainly some doubt on this score. They represent, one might say, nothing more than a pair of contemporary *majas* in tearful ecstasy.

See PLATES XXI & XXII
pp. 127–128

See p. 183

There is no doubt on the other hand concerning the intense spirituality of the two masterpieces of Goya's later years, the one depicting St Joseph of Calasanz receiving his last Communion, the other – even more intense – Christ in the Garden of Olives. It has become a commonplace to remark that these two paintings might well be from the hand of an El Greco or a Rembrandt. There need be no great mystery about the spirituality of these pictures. However infrequently or languidly Goya may have practised his religion, he was evidently capable of profound inspiration by it. In the Spaniard this is normal enough, like a cognate trait. '*Tan admirablemente católico como paradójicamente anticlerical*', remarked a leading member of a recent (1966) Government commission for the revision of the Press laws, surveying the nation at large. It is a point to be remembered when we come to the *Caprichos*. To the Spaniard religion is not a strait-jacket but an easy all-weather garment like the ample national cloak which Carlos III's Italian minister Squillache tried so rashly to abolish by decree in 1766. The Spaniard reserves the right to reprehend the clergy when this seems necessary, herein following a precedent set long before by Dante, Boccaccio, Chaucer, and Rabelais – himself an acknowledged luminary of the Order of Friars Minor.[1] Nor, on the other hand, can the Spaniard most exasperated by clerical

See p. 181

See p. 183

See pp. 219–28

Sketch for SS Justa and Rufina in the Cathedral of Seville, about about 1816
oil on panel
$18\frac{1}{2} \times 11\frac{3}{8}$ in. (47 × 29 cm.)
Museo del Prado, Madrid

---

[1] See the eulogy in Luke Wadding, O.F.M., *Scriptores Ordinis Minorum*, Rome, 1650.

imperfection easily forget that the Church was the mainspring of the Reconquest.

Comprehension of Goya's approach to religious painting, of which he produced a fair amount, is therefore essential to contact with his 'this-ness'. It is misleading to assume a constitutional deafness to spiritual harmonies. Although no mystic, Goya was capable at times of putting himself perfectly *en rapport*. But his clerical employers did not invariably find him the ideal interpreter. Very early in his career the Committee of Works of the Basilica of the Pilar at Saragossa rejected two panels of his, purporting to represent Charity and Patience, on the grounds of 'certain defects therein detectable', and especially in the figure of Charity, of which his portrayal was adjudged 'less seemly (*menos decente*) than the subject demands'. Presumably he had produced a luscious charmer of a type to be recurrent in his later tapestry-cartoons of Madrilene life. Young Goya's irritable hackles rose. A hot-tempered reply was returned. This, however, was followed, on the advice of Don Felice Salzedo, a priest he much revered, by the submission and acceptance of a Charity more suitable to a cathedral.

This kind of reaction to the spiritual is nothing very remarkable, above all in the Peninsula, where it may assume aspects verging, to foreign eyes, on the bizarre. There exists a type of Spaniard capable – the case of a well-known freethinker is on record – of declaring with no apparent irony that 'thanks be to God and his blessed Mother, I am an atheist'. There is also, as Ramón Gómez de la Serna has remarked, a type of anarchist liable to make a pilgrimage to Rome. The anti-clericalism of a few of Goya's caricatures derives from a tradition common to Latin Christendom, and in one or two cases his barbs are not unjustifiable. This did not conflict with several friendships with clerics, to whose encouragement he owed something in his youth.

His degree of personal religion is not simple to define. For the most part he would seem to have maintained an easy minimum of practice. The print of Our Lady of the Pilar which he cherished for many years, according to a letter to Zapater, may have become – he was apparently punctilious in veiling it on certain occasions – little more than a souvenir of youth and Saragossa, with the intrinsic status of, say, the good-luck charm nestling in a modern scientist's waistcoat-pocket. On the other hand Goya's last will and testament, dated 1811 and registered at Bordeaux in May 1828, opens with that declaration of adherence to all the teachings of 'our holy Mother the Catholic, Apostolic, and Roman Church' normal to the will of any practising Spaniard. The much-quoted plate of the Disasters of War showing a corpse opening a tomb inscribed *Nada* ('Nothing') is obviously capable of more interpretations *See* p. 12 than one, and the recommendations to God and Our Lady ending many of his letters to Martin Zapater may or may not be formulae. Hence an interesting and (to some) important question-mark.

★　　★　　★

Marquesa de la Merced, about
1797
oil on canvas
55⅞ × 38⅛ in. (142 × 97 cm.)
Collection Mrs D. David-Weill,
Paris

See p. 200
See PLATE X p. 75
See PLATES II & XII pp. 34 & 78

Goya's challenge, by trafficking equally in beauty and horror, to a horde of pundits pontificating on the mission of Art remains a powerful one. No other fashionable portraitist, even a Gainsborough or a De Laszlo, has earned his fees more justly by transmitting contemporary pulchritude to posterity. Doña Lorenza Correa and the Condesa de Haro, Doña Antonia Zárate and the Marquesa de la Merced and Doña Isabel Cobos de Porcel, and, of course the Alba – *O deae certe*! How superbly those dazzling creatures gaze from the canvas with those Spanish eyes! What vitality! Radiating it with equal verve

23

(left) Where is Mummy going?
(No. 65 of The Caprices),
1797–99
etching, acquatint and drypoint
8¼ × 6½ in. (21 × 16.5 cm.)
The British Museum, London

(opposite left) WILLIAM
HOGARTH Credulity, Superstition
and Fanaticism, 1762
etching
14½ × 12⅝ in. (36.8 × 32 cm.)
The British Museum, London

(opposite right) WILLIAM
HOGARTH The Rake's Progress,
Scene iv, 'Bedlam', 1735
etching
12½ × 15 in. (31.7 × 38.1 cm.)
The British Museum, London

(opposite below) The Madhouse,
about 1796
oil on panel
17½ × 28¾ in. (45 × 72 cm.)
Real Academia de Bellas Artes de
San Fernando, Madrid

moreover are the hags and demons, ghouls and gargoyles of the *Caprichos*. Even the hideous Hydropic Woman borne along in state by the goblins of a nightmare is enjoying the ride. More than one of these plates is simply a rollick. No other practitioner in diabolism has handled it with such infectious gusto.

To equate Goya with his near-contemporary Hogarth as a caricaturist – it has been essayed – seems inexact. The square-toed shoes of the British genius, wherever his head might be, were planted firmly on the ground;

24

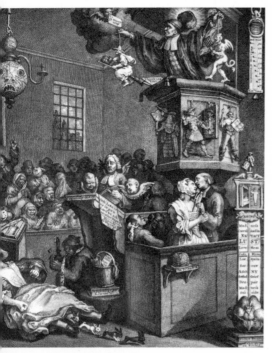

such a rare exercise of Hogarthian fantasy as the print labelled 'Credulity, *See* p. 25
Superstition and Fanaticism', that rather laborious anti-Catholic squib, is
commonplace compared with the pageant of chimeras of The Black Paintings
with which Goya in a fury of misanthropy decorated the walls of the Quinta *See* PLATES XXXIII, XXXIV & XXXV p. 175
del Sordo during the self-imposed immurement of his later years. Only
Hieronymus Bosch, Bruegel, and Grünewald had so far explored this *See* p. 125
particular kind of Freudian dreamland.

A difference in approach from Hogarth is well illustrated in the Bedlam *See* p. 25
scene in 'The Rake's Progress', a piece of brilliant reporting exhaling the
gusto, one might say, of a Leech portraying Mr Jorrocks's misadventures in
the hunting-field. Goya's colour-study 'The Madhouse', now in the Academy *See* p. 25
of San Fernando, illustrates the cleavage between the two national attitudes
to the same theme. The average eighteenth-century Londoner looked on
Bedlam as a source of entertainment, funnier than any stage-farce. Early in
the century Ned Ward described in *The London Spy* a most hilarious afternoon spent in jollying and provoking the loonies. Hogarth also saw the
diverting side of madness. This is not the Spaniard's approach. Goya's
Bedlam of desolation and despair has nothing at all to offer in the way of
amusement. 'Why, this is hell, nor am I out of it!' – the cry of Marlowe's
Mephistopheles might also serve for an epigraph.

In the field of the fantastico-horrific, again, Hogarth could no more have
conceived the vision of Saturn in The Black Paintings or the Walpurgis *See* PLATE XXX p. 163
Night gambols of the *Caprichos* than he could have conjured from his palette *See* pp. 217–28
the shimmering tints of the Pradera de San Isidro. Both geniuses have a sense *See* p. 96
of humour, but of deeply differing sheen. Out of many examples illustrating
Goya's might be selected the canvas in the National Gallery, London, called *See* p. 214
El Hechizado por Fuerza ('Bewitched Perforce'), based apparently on a
drama theme. The unfortunate village *cura* surrounded by gigantic gargoyle-
shapes of nightmare is a spectacle comic but not unsympathetic; one can feel
for him later, trying hopelessly to convince a frigid bishop. The gulf between
Goya and Hogarth is, in a word, metaphysical. Ramón Gómez de la Serna's
description of the English master as a moralist not unconnected with the
Salvation Army is, given due recognition of Hogarth's native brutality,
whimsically accurate. Goya on the other hand does not punch the pulpit
cushion. His monsters have no didactic mission. Whether or not he ever saw
Hogarth's caricatures, first published in the 1750s, they obviously had no
influence on him.

No attempt will be made in these pages to trespass on the province of the
professional art-critic. Having sufficiently pointed out an unforced pearly
quality in Goya's major portraiture which makes even Gainsborough's
brushwork look coarse, having ranked Goya next to Rembrandt for pro-
fundity of vision, having noted his immense fertility of invention and a few
shortcomings – the 'incoherent articulation' of the Nude Maja, for instance; *See* PLATE XXIV pp. 139–40
the 'ambiguity of gesture' in many of his figures, their eloquent mouths apart;

See PLATES XXI & XXII
pp. 127–28

See PLATE XL p. 205, p. 210

See PLATE I p. 33

See pp. 219–28

See p. 28

See PLATE XXVIII p. 153

See p. 196, PLATE XXVII p. 153

See p. 28

e PLATES VIII & XXXVII pp. 65
& 185

a prevalent 'absence of heroic action'; finally the furious technique which produced the frescoes in San Antonio de la Florida, if they may be correctly thus styled – having dilated on all this the expert has said practically everything the *homme moyen sensuel* needs to know. The master's verve over so many years remains unsurpassed except perhaps by Titian's. The last portraits, dated 1828, those of Don Pío de Molina and the charming 'Milkmaid', are as vital as any of his prime. The overworked adjective 'dynamic' seems here the only one possible.

Though all but one of the four or five children produced from his wife Josefa Bayeu were seemingly to die before reaching maturity, the proportion of more than three hundred and fifty portraits which fell short of obvious mastery is negligible. This applies equally to a multitude of etchings, aquatints, engravings, and performances in fresco and lithography. At the very end of his life, when overmuch brushwork has become tiring, we find Goya doodling enthusiastically at the game called *riquitillas*, in which one of the players is challenged to make a picture out of a dozen or so dots scattered haphazard on paper. The man's creative energy was in fact stupendous, though even an iron Aragonese constitution was not proof against physical setbacks such as fevers, gastric trouble, apoplectic or epileptic attacks, swoons at the easel, and the deafness which became total. His estimation of the Faculty of Medicine at large, incidentally, may be judged from the *Caprichos*. As with Molière, asses' ears are plentiful.

Goya remains the incomparable commentator on his country's emergence from the age of hairpowder, brocade, and feudalism into a more restless, complex, drab and bewildered century of tall hats, broadcloth, and what is styled progress. One of his earliest sitters, the minister Floridablanca, in the normal daily attire of the 1780s, would have seemed to a connoisseur of the 1820s as quaint a museum-piece as the Corregidor in *The Three-Cornered Hat*. Goya's own evolution is likewise arresting. The interpreter of a Spain largely remote from European contacts will display to posterity the citizens of Madrid leaping at Napoleon's troops in the Puerta del Sol. The lover (and mocker) of the most fascinating and imperious of great ladies in Europe will find himself under the bourgeois thumb of a Leocadia Weiss. The painter of the redoubtable guerrilla El Empecinado and the patriot-martyrs of 1808 will be found not long afterwards free enough from patriotic whimsies to be able to include the invader among his clients equally with the ally; what was originally a be-laurelled tribute to King Joseph Bonaparte – 'Joe Bottles' to his derisive Spanish subjects, *pro tem.* – is still conserved in its repainted state in the Ayuntamiento at Madrid.[1] 'Goya,' the saturnine Fernando VII is said to have remarked to him on regaining the throne, with the aid of British

---

[1] 'Re-painted' is somewhat inadequate. On Wellington's arrival in Madrid the word '*Constitución*' in bold capitals replaced King Joseph's features. In 1813 the portrait was restored, to be once more replaced by 'Constitución' when Joseph again left Madrid. In 1826 Vicente López, Court Painter, substituted a portrait of Fernando VII, replaced once again by 'Constitución' in 1841. After 1870 this yielded finally to the present 'Dos de Mayo'.

bayonets, half a dozen years later and restoring his Court Painter's pension, 'if we did not admire you so much you would deserve garrotting.' Another few years on and Goya would decide of his own volition to spend the remainder of his life in France. The eminent *baturro* remains fundamentally a law unto himself, recognizing no other authorities but his ego and his art.

★   ★   ★

Much of a long sequence of letters to his boyhood friend Martin Zapater of Saragossa was published forty years after Goya's death, affording evidence that the stocky figure whose eyes challenge the world so aggressively under the broadbrimmed sombrero of the self-portrait of 1790 was capable of long and sincere affection. 'My Martin', 'My best friend', 'Martin of my soul' – the faithful Zapater bulks considerably in the early career of Goya as the recipient of confidences and demands in many moods; exultant, apprehensive, boasting, depressed, abusive, exacting, always affectionate, scribbled on the spur of the moment, often misspelt, careless of style or syntax, using 'b' for 'v' in the rustic manner.

Zapater is required to co-operate on not a few occasions, including the spreading of good news ('You know the sort of club to use') to irk Goya's professional enemies, who not unexpectedly are soon active. When the newly appointed Court painter invests (what will they be saying in Saragossa?) in a

(left) Portrait of Floridablanca, 1783
oil on canvas
$10\frac{1}{8} \times 65\frac{3}{8}$ in. (262 × 166 cm.)
Banco Urquijo, Madrid

(right) The Allegory of the Town of Madrid, formerly a be-laurelled tribute to King Joseph Bonaparte – 'Joe Bottles', 1810
oil on canvas
$102\frac{1}{2} \times 76\frac{3}{4}$ in. (260 × 195 cm.)
Ayuntamiento de Madrid, Madrid

Fran.co Goya y Lucientes, Pintor

left) Self-portrait for No. 1 of
The Caprices, 1797
anguine pencil drawing
7⅞ × 5 in. (17.7 × 12.7 cm.)
Collection Walter C. Baker, New
York

right) Francisco Goya y
Lucientes, Painter (No. 1 of The
Caprices), 1797–99
tching, acquatint, drypoint and
urin
8½ × 5⅞ in. (21.5 × 15 cm.)
The British Museum, London

horse and an English gig, taking two nasty spills before deciding to exchange his purchase for a pair of mules and a *berline*, three or four letters to Zapater discuss every aspect of the matter, and Zapater is early assured moreover 'what you call my flowering doubloons are at your disposal with everything I possess'. A homespun caution in professional matters ('Don't show this to anybody') is intermittently perceptible; letters can be mislaid and may be dangerous, secretiveness is invaluable alike in palace and posada.

However, Zapater was not to be Goya's confidant in the matter of the Duchess, her spell and her treachery, the greatest event in his life. In 1797, when Goya paid a flying visit to Saragossa, the two met again, briefly, after many years, for the last time. Zapater was by now an Army contractor, a successful provincial business man, possibly a dull one. His friend was a figure in the most brilliant Madrilene high life – 'festooned with duchesses', in the French phrase; violently in love with the most dazzling and imperious of them; an intimate of royalty, a friend of the all-powerful Godoy. He had moreover just returned from a stay with the Duchess Maria Cayetana on her estate at Sanlúcar de Barrameda, near Seville. Zapater and he doubtless found little to say to each other on this occasion. On Goya's return to Madrid the correspondence began to languish, with longer and longer gaps. Within half-a-dozen years it had ceased. 'All things', as Pantagruel and his companions found inscribed on the tablet in the Temple of the Holy Bottle, 'move towards their end'. Human friendships being among them, it is useless to expatiate.

See p. 92

See p. 131

29

Publishing Goya's letters long afterwards, Zapater's family merely remark sadly that the great man had become intoxicated by fame.

Soon after this meeting Goya was to be raving with fury and advertising his ill fortune to the world at large in a celebrated couple of satires in which no informed citizen of Madrid would fail to identify the figures at a glance; namely Capricho No. 61 (*Volaverunt*) portraying a lady of quality with the Duchess's features and butterfly-wings adorning her head, poised for flight on the backs of three grotesque figures, and the more insulting 'Dream of Lies and Inconstancy'. In No. 61 the supporting figures were identified by *le tout Madrid*, rightly or wrongly, as the brilliant Pedro Romero of Ronda, pioneer of modern tauromachy, José Delgado of Seville, master of the 'flying attack', and Costillares ('Pepehillo') its inventor; all three being idols of the populace and protégés of the Duchess, whose enemy Queen Maria Luisa, a Neapolitan well versed in vendetta, must have welcomed this exposé of 'the Alba woman' (*la de Alba*) more delightedly than anyone at Court. The anonymous commentator of the *Caprichos* simply labels the supporting figures *tres toreros*.

★   ★   ★

Even at the end of the nineteenth century, when novelists of the ebullience of a Blasco Ibáñez and a Felipe Trigo were bursting into bloom, not to mention the satiric Valle-Inclán, the discovery in the Bordeaux cemetery

(opposite left) The bird has flown
('*Volaverunt*') (No. 61 of The
Caprices)
etching, aquatint and drypoint
8½ × 5⅞ in. (21.5 × 15 cm.)
The British Museum, London

(opposite right) Dream of lies and
inconstancy (Extra plate of The
Caprices), 1797–99
etching and burnished aquatint
7 × 4¾ in. (18 × 12 cm.)
Biblioteca Nacional, Madrid

Javier Goya, about 1804
oil on canvas
74¾ × 45⅝ in. (190 × 116 cm.)
Collection de Noailles, Paris

failed to inspire any native master-romancer. Doubtless the fact that the Duchess of Alba could not have had any hand in it, having died twenty-six years before Goya, robbed such a theme beforehand of many dramatic possibilities, among them the tableau of Beauty, stricken with remorse in later years, weeping over the skull of her great lover, an object lately abstracted from the grave by thugs in her own employ. The Duchess's own end emitted a faint whiff of the macabre. There were not wanting at the time rumours that she was poisoned by the Queen and Godoy, the royal favourite, who certainly had her will – in which with characteristic impulsiveness she had left most of an enormous fortune to friends and some three hundred servants – speedily revoked in legal form. Though the poisoning rumour was officially contradicted at the time, to be disposed of finally by the autopsy of 1945, which may be glanced at in its place, no romancer of spirit need handicap himself by trifles of the kind. The theme has nevertheless failed, so far as can be discovered, to attract even the five-peseta novelette industry.

See PLATES II & XII pp. 34 & 78

See PLATE XVI p. 106, p. 136

See p. 92

> Your ugly token
> My mind hath broken
> From worldly lust . . .

Whether or not the missing skull of Goya has served since 1828 to evoke in contemplation the cry of Master John Skelton, it may well, as already noted, have glutted the obscene curiosity of a nineteenth-century phrenologist. Such 'bumps' as those indicating imagination, artistic genius, doggedness, satiric power, and so forth would doubtless be obvious. Also, possibly those of misanthropy, and a trifle of sadism. Amativeness, perhaps, certainly.

What of the Affair?

Of that procession of light loves deemed essential down the ages to the practice of the graphic arts nothing – despite the remark of an old man-servant to be quoted later – is recorded in Goya's career. In the intervals of begetting scores of masterpieces and a family of perhaps four or five over nearly forty years of marriage he may not have been abnormally unfaithful to his wife Josefa, who gazes from her husband's canvas with a sort of blank resignation.

The family of twenty attributed to her and Goya is apparently a legend. Even were it fact, her husband's philoprogenitiveness would not have been anything unusual. The Spanish family is traditionally sizeable; in the previous century it was not considered remarkable for St Teresa's friend Juana de Gracián to be married at twelve to a husband of forty and to produce twenty children, of whom thirteen survived. The only known portrait extant of any of Goya's offspring is that of the survivor, Javier, painted by his father about 1804; a graceful young Brummellish buck in frilled jabot, Hessian boots, and coiffure *à la Titus*, on whom was to be lavished all the paternal affection of Goya's last years. No other of the master's progeny seems to be known to posterity, and it has never been suggested that his amour (if

See p. 31

PLATE I. Josefa de Goya (?), about 1805
oil on canvas
$31\frac{7}{8} \times 22$ in. (81 × 56 cm.)
Museo del Prado, Madrid

Plate II. The Duchess of Alba,
1795
Oil on canvas
76¾ × 51⅛ in. (195 × 130 cm.)
Collection the Duke of Alba,
Madrid

The Duchess of Alba Nursing a
Negro Child (?)
Sepia wash
Museo del Prado, Madrid
(Prado No. 426)

The Duke of Alba, 1795
Oil on canvas
77⅛ × 49⅝ in. (196 × 126 cm.)
Museo del Prado, Madrid

that could be proved the word) with Maria Teresa Cayetana, thirteenth Duchess of Alba, produced any such fruit. The Duchess, that passionate lover of children, was in fact sterile for life.

That the actual calorific content of her relationship with Goya amounts to that of a liaison is accepted by practically every Spanish authority on the artist's own evidence in paint and acid. From this view dissents a late erudite champion of the Duchess, Joaquín Ezquerra del Bayo, whose re-examination of the affair, based sternly if optimistically on 'what is really known' – *lo que realmente se sabe* – ends in a verdict of 'just friendship'.[1] If posing for a portrait in the nude is to be included among feminine gestures of 'just friendship', this could be said to mingle the absolute with the Hollywood ethos very agreeably.

It has been recognized by many who have speculated on their relationship that the Duchess, a complex and fascinating creature, was ardently given to obeying that curious contemporary urge to *s'encanailler* – that half-mystical (it has been judged) need, more Slav than European, of self-humiliation and expiation which drove so many of the wealthy high-born of eighteenth-century Europe to cultivate the company and share the relaxation of the lower classes. Inevitably in this connection one recalls Marie Antoinette playing at milkmaids at Trianon and the Prince Regent and his cronies applauding the bruisers at Hockley-in-the-Hole, cheek by jowl with the roughest riffraff of St Giles's. But such experiments were merely for the titillation of jaded nerves, and neither royalty carried demophilic freakishness to the extent of leaving a great deal of a huge fortune to their servants.

Bred in girlhood on Rousseau and the *philosophes*, Maria Cayetana lavished love and generosity on far less likely protégés than a plebeian portent like Goya; on a small Negro child of unknown origin, for example, and on another child, a servant's; on a poor old bumbling frowsy lay-brother; on one Benito, a total B-minus idiot. 'Here only Fray Basilio and I are good!' In some moods she might have stepped straight out of the pages of Dostoievsky. Excluding her husband Villafranca, whose chief interest in life was music, the Duchess's ruling passion might be epitomized as love of the unloved.

Lo que realmente se sabe . . . The essence of Maria Cayetana's relations with Goya, to sum up, remains matter for conjecture. It may well be that the archives of the Alba family still contain evidence capable of settling the question one way or the other, to the great relief of all true lovers of art. Though Goya was no great letter-writer, except to Zapater, there may be a single misspelt scrawl which would end much anxiety and theorizing on this score. Meanwhile it would seem to most neutral observers sufficiently underlined by the master's own pencil and brush. Plainly he suffered from her abominably, and, suffering being notoriously good for the artist, may thereby have owed to his wayward Duchess the brilliance of half a lifetime.

[1] *La Duquesa de Alba y Goya*. Madrid 1928; new edition 1959.

2 A phoenix takes off

SOME twenty miles south of Saragossa, and for some distance along a by-road which may have seemed in the eighteenth century – and even later – last mended in the reign of Sultan Abdulmalek Ibn-Hud, lies Fuendetodos, a village of no great interest save for its unlikelihood as a fount of genius. The house in which Goya was born on 30th March, 1746, stands intact, a national monument, with its memorial-tablet, in a lane called the Calle de Alhóndiga. It is a small two-storeyed building of rugged stone. In the stone-paved, low-beamed, white-washed kitchen-living-room the open hearth is flanked on either side by a long stone bench serving well enough, spread with pelts and gay striped blankets, for repose. Here on a winter night, when the logs were blazing and the northeaster howling over the plain, must have reigned a smoky comfort favourable to boyish dreaming.

Christened Francisco de Paula Joseph, the future prodigy was one of four children born to Joseph and Engracia Goya, natives of Saragossa and Fuen-detodos respectively. Of the child's brothers, Tomás was to become a rather more successful master-gilder than his father and Camillo, entering the priesthood, was to profit sufficiently by Francisco's future friendship with Godoy, Carlos IV's minister of state, to be awarded the desirable benefice of See p. 92 Chinchón, near Madrid. Their sister Rita died unmarried in her thirties. Their father, son of a Saragossan scrivener, had at this period temporarily abandoned his trade to farm, with little success, a piece of land at Fuende-todos which had been his wife's dowry. Doña Engracia, born Lucientes, was of bluer blood than her husband, being one of a considerable contemporary population of poor gentry – '*hidalgo*' deriving from *hijo de algo*, 'son of somebody' – existing frequently in great want but ever mindful of their caste. In later years Goya was to attach the patrician 'de' to his surname without self-consciousness. What artistic gifts, if any, he derived from his father are not discernible. Perhaps the elder Goya may have shown the child which end of the brush to hold.

In 1749 Joseph Goya, tired of playing at farming, moved his family back to Saragossa and returned to his gilding, taking a house in the Calle de la Morería Cerrada, in the old Moorish quarter; but it would seem that the boy Francisco returned to Fuendetodos at intervals, doubtless during holidays from school.

Heredity and environment alike seem to have relatively little to offer in explanation of the phenomenon Goya. There exists no record of his earliest years, and experts in child-psychology may peer around in vain for some clue to the fantasies of his maturity. The sparse remaining forests of Spain were not the playground of goblins, trolls, demons, and kobolds infesting the forests of the twilit North; nor, there being no Spanish nursery equivalent of the fairy tales of Grimm, would the child Francisco have been conditioned in infancy to the atmosphere of nightmare and violence prevailing in the *Caprichos*. If, like villages everywhere, Fuendetodos harboured some old half-crazy quean reputed to be in league with the devil, she would evoke teasing rather than terror. The scepticism of so many Spanish theologians from the seventeenth century, when the witch trials in the Basque country began, onward was not invariably reserved to the learned, nor is the Aragonese a gullible type. Attempts to probe Goya's early background for some explanation of his later *diableries* would seem a waste of time.

See pp. 217–28

'Restless and turbulent' was the sum of local reminiscence of young Goya collected by his friend Martin Zapater – also of Fuendetodos – in later years. One may lawfully picture a stocky, aggressive boy, soon expert at the stone-throwing said to be the agelong sport of Aragonese boyhood, co-ordinating hand and eye more successfully than the other village yobbos; a figure to the forefront likewise in rough-and-tumble fights and nocturnal raids on barns and hen roosts; a bane to farmers, carters, old wives, village elders, sacristans, and authority in general; given, as he grew older, to sketching caricatures on blank walls with a burnt stick, rude and vivid. He was always, old inhabitants recalled, 'scrawling' (*borroneaba*).

Early life may perhaps, after all, have bequeathed to the boy a few traumas discernible to a psychiatric eye and confirming the Freudian dictum that the artist as a type is an introvert 'elaborating his daydreams', with not very far to go to become a neurotic. Hence the apparition among The Black Paintings of Saturn devouring his offspring might be traceable to the boxing of ears by an irritable father. Memories of a mother's whacks when pestered at her cooking, again, may have emerged forty years later to inspire Capricho 19, in which a couple of witches are plucking a live human-headed fowl, hovered over by apparitions and deaf to the implorations of an old woman kneeling in the foreground. Actually his parents and the circumambient natives of Fuendetodos seem to have left Goya with no festering memories. If his typical hobbledehoys are not the graceful Arcadian swains of the poet Gaspar Gil Polo in the sixteenth century, they are – whether dancing, drinking, fighting, or walking in procession – not the type of homicidal thug, practising the seven deadly sins, who infests the plains of Castile for the sombre poet Antonio Machado in the nineteenth.

See PLATE XXX p. 163

See p. 38

Fuendetodos in due course had to endure young Francisco Goya only at intervals. At the age of eleven he was sent to school at the Saragossa establishment of the Píarist Order known as the *Escuelas Pías*, founded in the sixteenth century by St Joseph Calasanz for the free primary education of children

They will all fall (No. 19 of The Caprices), 1797–99
etching and burnished aquatint
$8\frac{1}{2} \times 5\frac{3}{4}$ in. (215 × 145 cm.)
The British Museum, London

of the working classes. Here, sharing a bench with a boy named Martin Zapater, henceforth to be his bosom friend, confidant and regular correspondent for many years, young Goya was to remain, holidays apart, till the age of fourteen; by which time his capabilities had apparently so impressed the parish priest of Fuendetodos that he allowed the boy to try his hand at decorating a side-altar in the village church. The heavily baroque painted curtains to be viewed – down to the late civil war – enfolding an altarpiece in the church at Fuendetodos might however attach to his later apprenticeship with Luzán. Fifty years on, according to Zapater, Goya remarked on seeing this work again: 'I don't believe I ever painted that.' Possibly a hasty alibi.

The classic fairy-godfather in due course materialized. Visiting Fuende-todos one day (the story goes) the Conde de Fuentes, overlord of that country-side, was informed by the priest of a prodigy, and on inspection agreed with him. However he was *detérré*, young Goya could certainly have chosen no better patron than Joaquín Piñatelli de Aragón y Moncayo, Conde de Fuentes; a potentate in Saragossa and a power at Court, a diplomat of distinc-tion, head of the wealthy art-loving Piñatelli clan, originally of Naples, a relative of the Albas and half the high nobility, and an ardent Aragonese.[1]

The first-fruits of Fuentes' interest was Goya's apprenticeship at the age of fourteen to another of the Conde's protégés, José Luzán y Martínez, a one-time painter to the Court, now a respected figure in Saragossa, wielding a brush of near-Italian lusciousness. In Luzán's studio the boy was to stay for the next three years; graduating fairly soon, one may believe, from mixing colours, washing brushes, and running errands, to the copying of casts and prints; in due course entrusted with minor touches or retouches to portraits in hand. His first independent piece of work may well have been the altar-piece-decoration at Fuendetodos already mentioned. A minor commission or two would probably follow. In Luzán's studio also he made contact, sooner or later, with the eminent Francisco Bayeu and his associates in the decoration
See p. 51
See PLATE VI pp. 54–55
of the Basilica of the Pilar. To Bayeu he was before long to owe a great deal, their ensuing relationship as brothers-in-law notwithstanding. Their future collaboration on the frescoes of the Pilar Chapel might be called Goya's artistic debut. His leisure at this early period is said to have been taken with music, which is difficult to believe, and fencing, in that age a sensible hobby.

At this point we enter for a brief space the *tercio*, in bull ring terms, of the picaresque, not untinged with legend. Eighteenth-century Saragossan youth was, it seems, addicted to outbreaks of gang-warfare, parish against parish, with fists, clubs, and even knives. The winds so often roaring through this windiest of Spanish cities tend no doubt to exacerbate adolescent Aragonese nerves. According to a gossip named Matheron young Goya's native bellico-sity involved him inevitably before long in a *motín* of this kind – the Pilar parish, his own, against San Luis, an enjoyable affray ending in wholesale arrests. Since the battle involved rival religious processions – possibly even rival Madonnas – during a fiesta, the matter fell under the scope of the local inquisitor of the Holy Office. Goya (the story tells) escaped a term in the cells only by headlong flight, with assistance from his father, to Madrid.

This story, one of several accepted and embroidered at some length by the eminent Eugenio d'Ors, is brushed aside by the more prosaic *afición*. The truth seems to be that by 1763 Luzán had nothing more to teach the young genius, and Goya turned to wider fields. With an Academy travelling-bursary

---

[1]Another candidate for the discovery of his talent is a Carthusian prior at Saragossa, Don Felice Salzedo. A very likely one, again, is Padre Piñatelli, brother of the Conde.

– he had failed with an application in 1763 – he would have no urgent need to dun a none-too-prosperous father. From the rewards of apprenticeship he had apparently saved enough over six years to maintain himself in Madrid for a time in a frugal way. A *douceur* from the generous Fuentes might well have assisted. The metropolis was beckoning; still more dazzling the light on Rome, a goal irresistible to so many artists of the age, and within the reach of any deserving Academy pupil.

Late in 1763 we find Goya in Madrid, where another picturesque undocumented story discovers him one morning soon after arrival lying at dawn in an alley near the Puerta del Sol with a knife-wound in his back. The story is not improbable. Together with attendance at the Royal Academy of San Fernando in the Calle de Alcalá, where competition for pupillage and bursaries was imperative, the prelude to the alleged stabbing-episode might well epitomize the primal interests of a twenty-year-old Aragonese of ebullient temperament visiting the capital for the first time.

The impact of the tempo and tumult of Madrid on the youth from Aragon would be, one may conjecture, dizzying. The unending stream of coaches, cabriolets, briskas, and other vehicles up and down the spacious Calle de Alcalá; the open barouches, drawn by gaily-caparisoned, daintily-stepping, bell-hung mules, conveying cargoes of pallid haughty beauty in high mantillas to the Prado, the Retiro, or the Alameda, with attendant cavaliers on horseback; the tall buildings, the parks, the fountains, the statuary; the crowded narrow pavements, the beaux pacing in brocades and satins, the cloaks and sombreros of the commonalty, the swarm of friars, habited in brown, grey, or black, the intelligentsia, sporting the owlish hornrimmed spectacles still *de rigueur* at this period; the notable dignity of the beggars, the bawling of the ballad-singers, the street-cries, the noisy taverns and chocolate-houses, the rumble and clatter of wheels, the whole metropolitan uproar drowned thrice daily by the clangour of the Angelus from the bells of Madrid's fifty or more churches, convents, and monasteries; the flashes of colour from passing cavalry, or some fashionable matador and his suite proceeding to the bull ring; the violent multicoloured thrills of the metropolitan *corrida* itself; the Plaza Mayor and the Plaza de Oriente under the moon – even Aragonese self-assurance could be shaken by all this.

The spacious gardens, enclosed by tall railings, of the nobility's town houses would turn faëry on a summer night when a myriad twinkling lights and the distant sound of fiddles announced a *bal champêtre*. The populace had its own frequent fiestas; among them the Ash Wednesday carnival and the riotous end-of-Lent rollick known as 'The Burial of the Sardine', years hence to produce one of Goya's most vital canvases. You hear the noise, you smell the smells. Neither contemporary Paris, nor London, nor any other European capital could supply Madrid's combined assault on eye and ear.

It may well be assumed that the turbulent proletarian quarters – especially

Ash Wednesday (or The Burial of the Sardine), about 1794
oil on panel
$32\frac{5}{8} \times 24\frac{3}{8}$ in. (83 × 62 cm.)
Real Academia de Bellas Artes de San Fernando, Madrid

a maze of narrow cobbled streets, courts, and alleys round the Plaza Mayor, then as now the finest square in Europe, and the Puerta del Sol – fascinated young Goya most. Recalling the story of the knife in the back, one may guess that he lodged in some alley where food, drink, and the Juliets of a night were well within his means.

His pencil would be busy. Here was the stamping-ground of the *majo*, a species of swaggering teddy-boy, and his mate, the *maja*. The *chispero*, a type of redoubtable husky from the blacksmiths' quarter of Maravillas, and the *manolo*, a smoother product from the largely-Semitic quarter of Lavapiés, with his opposite number the *manola* – these fauna also one may see young Goya furtively sketching at sight. They were to furnish him with as lavish material as the East End of London offered to Phil May in the 1890s.

Most decorative of the proletarian populace, the *majo* and his soulmate spelt irresistible fascination for the contemporary younger smart set. The *petimetre – petit-maître*, a beau on the Parisian model – had been for some time a feature of Madrilene society; Goya was later to portray a typical specimen making eyes at the Duchess of Alba. A more dashing model for youthful patrician bloods on the spree was the *majo*, whose costume they often adopted for frolicking occasions. The austere poet-statesman Jovellanos details it in a chilly satire. Inclusive of some three inches on either side of 'sideboard' whisker framing lean insolent features, ritually unwashed, it embraced a short tight jacket, wide black trousers with a broad crimson waistband, flat Córdoban hat, and an ample cloak, hooded like a burnous, with filigree buttons. Essential accessories other than the clasp-knife, *navaja*, the proletarian weapon, worn in the waistband, might be a guitar or a mandolin.

The costume of the *maja*, in which not a few great ladies, Goya's Duchess included, might choose to sit for a portrait, was simply a bodice, an ample skirt, and a mantilla, all of demure and becoming black; as in Nature, the brighter plumage was the appanage of the male. Contemporary poets, satirists, and writers of vaudeville gave both types lavish publicity, the *maja* especially. Thus Ramón de la Cruz in *La Maja Majada*, addressing women of his own world:

> *Una maja idolatro*
> *porque las majas*
> *corresponden con todas*
> *sus circunstancias,*
> *   y en las Usías*
> *son las correspondías*
> *falsas o tibias . . .*

    A *maja* I adore, for she gives all she has, while your ladyships' reactions are feigned or lukewarm . . .

Like every other metropolis, eighteenth-century Madrid harboured a bustling criminal underworld, speaking its own jargon, the *germanía*, and boasting

PLATE III. The Young Majas, about 1817
oil on canvas
$71\frac{1}{4} \times 48\frac{3}{8}$ in. (181 × 123 cm.)
Palais des Beaux-Arts, Lille

See p. 222 (27)

ATE IV. Carlos III, 1786
on canvas
$\frac{5}{8}$ × 50 in. (210 × 126 cm.)
useo del Prado, Madrid

See p. 46

among others – such as the gypsy – that historic crook-type the *pícaro*, immortalized long since by Cervantes, Quevedo, Mateo Alemán, Espinel, and lesser masters of the Golden Age: a slim, jaunty personage with a thousand tricks, Panurge with a dash of Brighella, able to slip through the cat-hole in a barred outer gate. Add then, to all these attractions, the vibrant vitality, yesterday as today, of the whole Madrilene scene, and one may well see the young *baturro* from Aragon looking a trifle dazed.

He had arrived at the right time. With surprising speed and efficiency the much-decried Spanish Bourbons – Carlos III especially – had turned what a native pessimist of the preceding century had compared to an African village into a comely European capital. The Bourbons could not, unfortunately, change the weather. 'Nine months winter, three months hell', says an old Madrilene jingle. Thanks to the implacable Sierra de Guadarrama dominating the skyline, any incautious citizen out of doors will continue to the world's end to risk heat-stroke in summer and pneumonia in winter. As some tavern-poet or other had sung in a past age:

> *El aire de Madrid es tan sutil*
> *que mata a un hombre y no apaga a su candil.*

So subtle is the air of Madrid that it kills a man without extinguishing his candle.

That native vitality already mentioned continues to defy a trying climate, and the revisiting ghosts of the Emperor Carlos V and his son Felipe II must have perceived long since that the unpromising site so arbitrarily selected for the hub of Empire exercises, under its luminous Velázquez skies, a spell of its own and continues to hold the enduring love of its citizens.

> *Lejos de mi Madrid, la villa y corte,*
> *ni de ella falto yo porque esté lejos,*
> *ni hay una piedra allí que no me importe . . .*

Far from my Madrid, the City and the Capital, I do not fail her, distant as she is; nor is there a single stone of her which does not matter to me.
– Eulogio Florentino Sanz, *Epístola a Pedro*

Like what warfare has left of Vienna, Madrid continues to exhale some of the grace and aroma of the past; nor, on moonlit nights, have all the ghosts of the Golden Age deserted her.

Since Goya never in his life kept a diary, it is not clear whether he was in Madrid early enough in 1766 to witness – even to take part in – an enjoyable hullaballoo known as the *motín de Esquilache*. In March of this year Carlos III's minister Geronimo, Marchese di Squillache, a native of the Kingdom of Naples, conceived the issuing of a decree abolishing the traditional long cloak and sombrero of the Spanish populace in favour of the more progressive jacket and cocked hat of the rest of Europe. As if this singular inspiration were

45

Majas on a Balcony, about 1795
oil on canvas
$76\frac{3}{4} \times 49\frac{1}{2}$ in.
(193.1 × 125.7 cm.)
The Metropolitan Museum of
Art, New York
Bequest of Mrs H. O. Havemeyer, 1929
The H. O. Havemeyer collection

not insult enough from a foreigner, the decree conveyed simultaneous orders for regular street-cleaning and the immediate provision of street-lamps in all the thoroughfares of Madrid.

The mob rose in fury. Squillache's town mansion was sacked, his new street-lamps smashed, his Walloon guards routed in vigorous fighting. It was very nearly a revolution. After two or three days and nights of uproar the King, who had, not without foresight, retired on the eve of the decree to the summer palace of Aranjuez, annulled it and dismissed his minister, who decidedly lacked the expertise of Peter the Great in abolishing the boyards' beards, or that of George II of England in proscribing, after the Jacobite rising of 1745, the immemorial predecessor of the short Highland kilt called the *féiladh-mór*, or equally that of Mustafa Kemal in widowing the Turk of his immemorial fez. Squillache's successor Aranda at length found a subtler way. Having been decreed the official costume thenceforth of the public executioner, cloak and sombrero by degrees vanished from the scene.

Had Goya taken part in the rioting, had he been merely a spectator, it is hardly conceivable that one of his sketchbooks would not have retained some record of a historic occasion, to be boasted of in later years among his fellow-expatriates in Bordeaux. But no such sketch is known.

Meanwhile, whatever his relaxations, he was doggedly pursuing a career. Examination at the Academy was essential to applicants for a travel-bursary. Goya had already entered for the preliminary examination, it seems, without achieving even a mention. This time it had to be. The Academy's rules were a trifle complicated, involving two separate competitions. In 1766 the qualifying set-piece for the first of these was an inspiring subject enough: 'Marta, Empress of Constantinople, pleading with Alfonso the Wise at Burgos for one-third of the sum fixed by the Sultan of Egypt for the ransom of her husband, the Emperor Baldwin.' Having passed this test and qualified for competition proper, Goya was required with eight other candidates to produce publicly and within two hours a canvas on a theme almost equally inspiring: 'Juan de Urbino and Diego de Parades deciding, within sight of the Spanish army in Italy, which of them should be given the arms of the Marquis of Pescara.'

Though Francisco Bayeu, brought by now from Saragossa to the Academy by the eminent Mengs, was one of the jury, Goya's name did not appear among the first three. It might be, and has been, suggested that his rustic manners or lack of them had not impressed the Academicians. It might well be that the kind of painting the Academy required, formal, rhetorical, polite, was beyond him. His failure at any rate aroused in young Goya, probably with a few homely oaths, the old Aragonese spirit. *Tudios! Redios!* If the Academy did not want him, damn its eyes, he would get to Italy without it.

We catch up with him, a few months later, in Rome. How he got there is not known. There is extant a picturesque story which in old age he received, according to the poet Moratín, or perhaps Yriarte, with an inscrutable smile, to the effect that he travelled part of the road from Madrid with one of those youthful bands of would-be bullfighters who possibly still exploit remote Spanish countrysides. Blasco Ibáñez sketches a typical company of the 1900s in *Sangre y Arena*; a ragged, merry, impudent gang, living from hand to mouth, always on the move, perpetually rolled in the dust and stamped on by angry cows and vivacious young bulls, not infrequently stunned or even gored, receiving kicks, curses, and rural hospitality equally, since any one of these ragamuffins might one day be the idol of Spain. Goya's lifelong passion for the corrida needs no underlining. In this agreeable fashion he could well have made his way, one may assume, to the nearest big seaport, Barcelona, Valencia, or Cartagena, whence he could easily work a passage to, say, Civitavecchia. Actually, since a vague reference to 'a stay in France' by Cean Bermúdez seems authentic, Goya elected to tramp it, as a sturdy young Aragonese should. Since he left no memoir, and since no Cervantes tramped with him, we may have lost some invigorating glimpses of the French high-road in the last decade of Louis the Well-Beloved and of a stocky belligerent figure lingering at rustic merrymakings, thumbing lifts in wagons, sleeping in barns, dashing off an occasional sketch, perhaps, in exchange for supper in some village tavern, indulging possibly in an occasional brawl, coming at last to that stirring first far-off vision of the City from the rise of the Cassian Way.

Of one or two dubious stories attaching to his stay in Rome one in particular is so steeped in improbability that it is faintly surprising to find it accepted and even embellished by any critic of standing. It concerns an alleged attempt by Goya to break by night, in pursuit of an attractive novice, into a convent of enclosed nuns; his capture by the police while scaling the outer walls; his escaping the death-penalty then attached to such an act of sacrilege only by the joint efforts of the Spanish and Russian ambassadors – the latter being already among his admirers – and his subsequent expulsion from the Papal States.

Such a foolhardy attempt might well be made at the period, in drink or bravado, by a native of some innocent Nordic country, or by some French playboy nourished from the cradle on Diderot and Voltaire. A Spaniard would know, or assume, some of the difficulties as well as the sanctions attached; for example, the existence within outer walls of massive locked doors and strongly-barred windows, not to mention that of a night-porteress with the alarm bell at hand. The hardiest film-producer might baulk at subjecting the most dashing of heroes to such hazards.

Another legendary frolic attaching to his stay in Rome is more credible. If he really climbed the exterior curve of the dome of St Peter's from the gallery to the cross, fifty feet up, this dangerous feat, long since reserved to the hereditary workmen on the fabric known as the *Sanpietrini*, was not unknown, and was as yet unprohibited. Among contemporary sportsmen achieving it in youth was that fine old English squire Charles Waterton of Stonyhurst. It required considerable nerve and athletic stamina. If authentic, this exploit remains unique in Goya's career.

One may plausibly conjecture that young Goya gave the remains of the Rome of the Caesars what the excellent phrase of a later day would style a quick once-over. We cannot imagine him seated, like plump young Mr Gibbon five years earlier, on the ruins of the Capitol, brooding over the Decline and Fall. Happy in the possession of a mind unlittered by classical or literary tags, Goya would – one feels – gaze dry-eyed on the sparse ruins of the Forum, a site as yet unexcavated, the haunt of goats, touts, and botanists. The Colosseum would undoubtedly strike him as a first-class bull ring wasted.

He would inevitably be fascinated, on the other hand, by the bustling pageant of the streets, with all the figures from Goldoni's comedies and the Commedia dell' Arte passing before his eyes. He could well have brushed shoulders more than once with a tallish hawkeyed young man in the cassock of minor Orders required to qualify as one of Cardinal Acquaviva's secretaries, and known accordingly as the Abbé Casanova. He might even have been jostled at a corner of the Piazza Navona by the superb charlatan Giuseppe Balsamo, known later to half Europe as Count Alessandre Cagliostro, wielder of ineffable secrets, Prince of Trebizond, Grand Cophta of Europe and Asia, Grand Master of the Cabbala, two thousand years old. Goya would, beyond doubt, linger to approve such a beautiful vista as that of the Tiber bridge, the river, and the castle of Sant'Angelo as Claude Vernet painted them round about this time. But chiefly we may see him applying himself vigorously to daily study, sketchbook ever ready, haunting churches, museums and galleries. He missed by two years, unfortunately, an ideal physiognomy for a future *Capricho* in the mephistophelian features of the celebrated Mr John Wilkes, who was in Rome with Boswell in 1765. Their merriment on issuing from the English Coffee-House on the Piazza di Spagna, incomprehensible to a Goya, might have inspired a future *Diabluras inglesas* of historic interest. A great deal of the painting and statuary Goya must have studied by day is detailed in the diary of that conscientious young connoisseur Lord Herbert of Pembroke, who was in Rome shortly after him. By night, undoubtedly, Goya relaxed with his fellow *rapins* in the traditional manner. Among them was quite likely the eminent David, a student of his own age, a liberal and a neo-classicist afterwards.

From some budding sculptor in their favourite tavern Goya must have learned interesting things about the flourishing contemporary racket in fake-antiques; the proper salting, in a later professional phrase, of the 'dig' in ruined villa-garden or abandoned vineyard; the way to tell a too-knowledge-able 'prospect' from a normal Grand Tour gull in three minutes. Another Roman, or rather international, industry of the period was the collection of fragments of broken torsos to be deftly assembled, provided with heads and limbs, stained thoroughly with tobacco-water, and sold to critical art-loving milords for a cosy sum. There was likewise a brisk contraband traffic in hollow 'bustos' packed with valuable lace. Painters were lamentably deprived of such opportunities, and Goya may at times have envied addicts to a sister-art.

It is curious that nothing reminiscent of the Rome of his twenties is visible in his huge mass of later work in four or five media, though he may have sketched more than one interesting nocturnal brawl; possibly a robbery or two, even an assassination. The proletarian Trastevere quarter across the river was rich in turbulence; the finger-flashing gambling game called the *Morra*, at which the Trasteverini were and – especially since it has been banned by law – are so adept, often ended in a gang-battle. Elsewhere in Rome at this period some of the streets were sufficiently dangerous after dark to warrant the hiring, by visitors who could afford it, of an armed guard. Himself an aggressive type, a product of an age of quick tempers and, at least down to the 1750s, swiftly drawn swords, Goya seems never to have assaulted even the most arrogant art-critic. Given his prehensile memory, however, it might be that recollection of these days was to contribute a little in later years to the violence of the 'Disasters of War' plates.

See pp. 229-39

Goya stayed in Rome at least four years. The economic query scarcely presents itself. When he came to the end of his original money there were several ways of making more, such as the copying of selected works for himself or others, bargaining with dealers and middlemen, taking commission on sales for friends. Above all there was the exploitation of the never-ceasing pilgrim and tourist-traffic of the City, the unfailing standby of so many. For this market Goya is presumed – evidence is missing – to have dashed off a quantity of unsigned colour sketches rich in cardinals, contadinas, beggars, pifferari, brigands, and other picturesque local fauna.

Subjects for saleable sketches on the spot were plentiful. On any afternoon in the Vatican quarter Pope Clement XIV, Lorenzo Ganganelli, in his shovel hat might ride slowly by with his attendants; hunched up in billowing vesture on a white palfrey in the peculiar manner depicted in several prints of the period; musing perhaps on the charm of the English, for whom he had an odd affection; brooding, more likely, on the increasing virulence of anti-Jesuit freemasonry at three Bourbon courts.

Issuing from the modest Palazzo Muti – today turned into business offices – in the Piazza degli Santi Apostoli, or taking a drive in the Pincio gardens, his comely, melancholy, slightly dissipated features still, in his hard-up fifties, retaining an air of gallantry and grace, could any day be seen Prince Charles Edward Stuart, *de jure* Charles III of England, with or without his brother the Cardinal Duke of York. Among other headline-notables from all over Europe to be viewed in the streets of Rome during Goya's stay would be the wayward Duchess of Kingston, formerly Miss Elizabeth Chudleigh. This celebrated charmer, ere long to be convicted of bigamy by her scandalized

Sketch for the Assumption which
forms part of the decoration in
the church of the Pilar,
Saragossa, 1780–81
oil on canvas
26¾ × 58⅝ in. 67 × 148 cm.)
Museo Discesano, Saragossa

fellow-peers in tribunal, had recently entertained London society by appearing at a midnight masquerade in what the discreet compilers of *The Newgate Calendar* describe as 'almost the unadorned simplicity of primitive Nature'. In her progress – fully clothed – in an open carriage down the Corso towards her yacht on the river the Duchess was liable to be escorted by an huzzaying mob. It seems impossible that a sardonic Spanish pencil could have resisted such a subject.

Where Goya lodged at this period is indiscoverable. His most likely quarter, one may surmise, would be the Trastevere, where an impecunious international art-colony prefiguring Mürger's Bohemians seems to have existed at the time. The atmosphere of Trastevere was and is stimulating. Its maze of alleys, its noisy vitality at work and play, the swagger of its denizens, who boast themselves the only Romans of the old original rock, have remained unchanged down the ages. More touchy, more voluble, more excitable than the Aragonese, the Trasteverino shares his self-sufficiency and clannishness. Traditionally quick with the knife, he can be, when he chooses, serviceable and friendly to the interloper. If, moreover, in Goya's time, you craved no more luxurious lodging than a garret in Trastevere, living in Rome could be exquisitely cheap. That miserly eccentric the Flemish-born sculptor Joseph Nollekens, R.A., purloiner of nutmegs from British Royal Academy dinners and clipper of George III's sacred nose with his callipers, used to boast that during a two years' residence in the 1760s his Roman dinner regularly cost him no more than threepence in English money.[1] A sturdy Aragonese of much the same age would probably have little use for Nollekens' nightly plate of 'cuttings' from a neighbouring butcher, but the existence of such amenities should not be overlooked by anyone craning at the length of Goya's stay.

[1] *Nollekens and His Times*, by John Thomas Smith, 1829; edited by Wilfred Whitten, 1920.

51

He left Rome in 1771, in which year we find him competing for a prize offered by the provincial Academy of Fine Arts at Parma, then a Spanish duchy. The theme was to be 'Hannibal gazing over the Plains of Italy from the Alps.' Although the Court painter and principal judge, a Frenchman named Péchaux, had been a fellow-student of Bayeu under the great Mengs, Goya achieved only a mention, the first prize going to a Signor Borroni. A fortunately-preserved notice in the *Mercure de France* reveals the judges' mention of 'Monsieur Goya, pupil of Monsieur Vajeu (*sic*), painter to the King of Spain', to have been both kindly and encouraging:

> In the second canvas the Academy observed with pleasure the excellent handling of the brush, the warmth of expression in the eyes of Hannibal, and an air of greatness in that general's attitude. Had Monsieur Goya departed a little less in his composition from the subject of the painting, and had he injected a little more truth into his colour, he would have shared the votes for the first prize.

At which, possibly, like Palamon in the old poem, Goya, already aware of his powers, 'bleynte and cridë "A"!' A rasping '*Tudios!*' would probably be the equivalent to startle his Parma landlady. The pensive Hannibal was scarcely a subject Goya would have chosen himself. Perhaps he was as short of money again as of academic recognition. The rejected canvas in question has not survived, and is doubtless no great loss. European art at this period was curiously ridden by what Freud calls, in a different context, 'skoptophilia', or the gazing-impulse: 'Brutus gazing on the Body of Caesar'; 'Marius gazing on the Ruins of Carthage'; 'Cromwell gazing on the Head of Charles the First' – academic rhetoric on the largest and dreariest scale. Even so early the temptation to inject a little rude life into Hannibal's Alpine musings with a circumambient covey of devils may have presented itself to young Goya.

In January 1772 Goya returned, at the summons of Francisco Bayeu, to Saragossa, where his first commission awaited him. Designs submitted by him for the decoration of the Chapel of the Pilar in that huge ornate seventeenth-century basilica had been accepted, thanks to Bayeu and to Don Matías Allué. These frescoes were to occupy Goya about five months.

See p. 51, PLATE VI pp. 54–55

They remain as he finished them, looming high up in the vault in a poor light; which may be an advantage, since by general critical consent the ensemble is not very striking.[1] Seated on their billowy clouds, these attitudinizing groups of buxom saints, angels, and cherubs might be gods, goddesses, and Cupids sprawling over the ceiling of a rococo South German opera-house. Lack of spiritual emotion is their most obvious characteristic; for their pose and gesticulation the label 'banal' would seem not excessive. Plainly the painter's heart was not in his work. It was a job to be done; even the conscientious Baedeker passes over his effort without comment. A Holy Family painted by Goya at this time is charming, but likewise entirely of this earth; the Virgin Mother is said to have been inspired by Bayeu's sister

PLATE V. The Crockery Vendor – tapestry cartoon, 1778 oil on canvas 102 × 86⅝ in. (259 × 220 cm.) Museo del Prado, Madrid

PLATE VI. (overleaf) Sketch for *Regina Martyrum* which forms part of the decoration in the church of the Pilar, Saragossa, 1780–81 oil on canvas 26¾ × 58⅝ in. (67 × 148 cm.) Museo Discesano, Saragossa

---

[1] The lighting has quite lately been modernized.

See PLATE I p. 33, p. 58

Josefa. On the other hand a Crucifixion of 1780 displays, one may venture to suggest, the agony of the divine features and their distinction with more intensity than Rafael Mengs' more famous study.

The Pilar work over, Goya turned to decorations for the Charterhouse of Aula Dei; eleven extremely large murals of statuesque figure-studies, of which a few survived the Peninsular War – a work occupying some two years. In March 1773 he married Bayeu's sister Josefa. Not long afterwards the Goya *ménage* moved to Madrid and settled in the Carrera de San Gerónimo in the fashionable quarter, a sufficient indication of increasing prosperity, ambition, and assurance. We hear relatively nothing henceforth, save in a letter or two to Zapater, of the faithful Josefa – 'Pepa' to her husband. For the next thirty-eight years she remains a dim immovable figure in her dynamic *See* p. 31 husband's existence: the housewife, the stand-by, the genius of the hearth, making a home for a roving and difficult genius, enduring no doubt plenty of 'temperament'. Of their children only two seem to be known – Javier, who outlived his father, and 'Paco' (Francisco), mentioned in a letter to Zapater and apparently dying young, possibly with three or four more. Eugenio d'Ors' assertion as a 'well-known fact' that Goya produced a family of twenty would seem more poetry than truth; a tribute to virility, so to speak, unsupported by any surviving parish register.

That Josefa and her husband loved each other is undoubted. The delicacy with which his portrait of her renders the pensive features with the superb black eyes, the suggestion of weary but devoted resignation in the set of the lips, is eloquent of an affection on both sides which no amount of roving could lessen. From Goya's determination to provide his family with the luxury which (as he remarked to Zapater) he liked himself may be deduced that 'la Pepa's' married life had many compensations.

Josefa herself was to have her moment of glory. Against the lovely autumnal background of the tapestry-cartoon called the *Vendimia* ('The Grape-Harvest') a few years hence Josefa stands, idealized, as gracious and comely as the Duchess of Alba, her hostess, and the idealized Goya, her husband, composing with one of their children that charming little group. The year is 1786; the scene, the gardens at Piedrahita, near Avila, in Castile, one of the Albas' several country-houses, where the Goyas with one of their children were the Duchess's guests. Graciously maternal, her figure itself suggesting imminent fruition, Josefa stands with a vintage-basket poised on her head and piled high with luscious black grapes. Her benign and beautiful hostess, the great lady seated in front of her, reaches out to accept a cluster from the elegant male figure seated on the right, swinging one shapely silkstockinged leg over the other; beaming, graceful, utterly content, slightly fatuous. Between them a boy-child reaches up clamouring for his share.

Such an idyll might almost have been subtitled, after Titian, 'Sacred and Profane Love'. Though the three principal figures are carefully disguised, their identities have been plausibly assumed. What Doña Josefa Goya, when

PLATE VII. *La Vendimia* (The Grape-Harvest) – tapestry cartoon, 1786 Oil on canvas 108¼ × 74¾ in. 275 × 190 cm.) Museo del Prado, Madrid

57

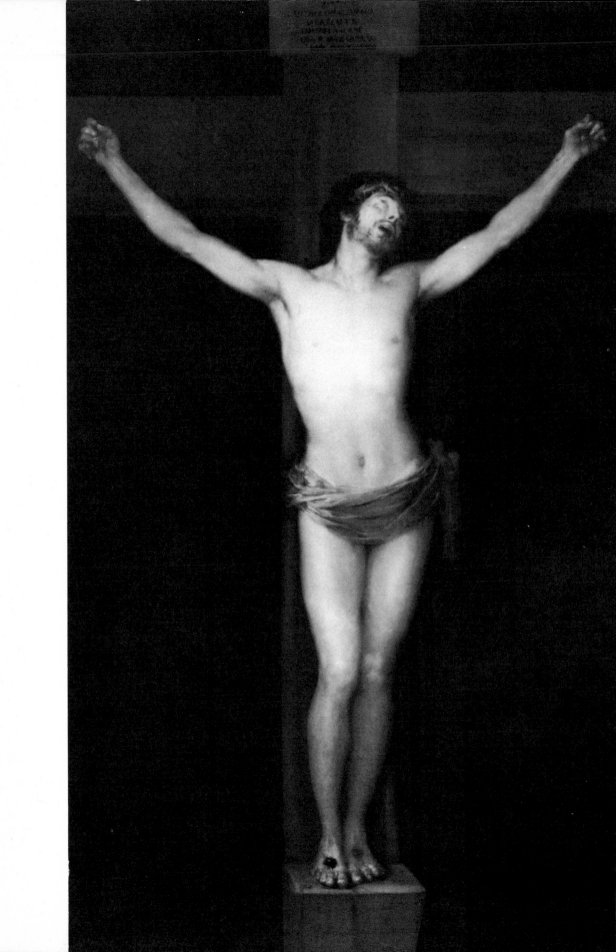

Christ Crucified, 1780
on canvas
10⅜ × 60¼ in. (255 × 153 cm.)
Museo del Prado, Madrid

free herself of the Duchess's spell, thought of the *Vendimia* – she is said to have possessed, when necessary, a tongue at home – would perhaps fail to harmonize with its delightful atmosphere. Even so she may have sympathized with her bitter Francisco when the end arrived.

Apparently Goya was reasonably faithful to her, apart from whatever his relations with the Duchess of Alba may have been. A celebrated remark made many years later by an old manservant that his late master had only two pastimes, 'the bulls and Eve's daughters', probably refers only to Goya's years of widowhood. Although the practice of the plastic arts is commonly assumed to demand sexual experiment as an essential routine, it is quite certain that Goya was never a professional Bohemian on the pattern publicized by Mürger and developed, with occasionally unfortunate effects on the Anglo-Saxon, by George du Maurier. Goya's ruling passion being his work, he would undoubtedly regard many current denizens of Montparnasse, Chelsea, or Greenwich Village with their alcoholic parties, their carefully cultivated squalor, and their festoons of mopsies, as trivial buffoons. He abhorred dirt and disorder, he was probably never drunk in his life, and he had the Latin cultus of the *familia*, cherishing his offspring and striving, as he told Zapater, to give them everything money could buy. Till the day of her death his wife Josefa remains a dim but solidly permanent feature in his background.

See PLATE IV p. 44

We return to 1776, in which year there came to Goya, thanks to Bayeu, with whom he was still on good terms, and to Mengs, an important commission. Carlos III had decided radically to reorganize the production of the Royal tapestry-manufactory established by Felipe V (1726) by the Santa Bárbara gate in Madrid and directed at this time by Mengs. New artists were being recruited, and Bayeu had put forward the name of his highly promising ex-collaborator and brother-in-law.

To say that the young man burst into this establishment like a whirlwind and gave it a new existence is not excessive. Compared with the splendid work of the past with which cathedrals, abbeys and famous churches all over Europe still decked their walls on major festivals, or with the ancestral hangings preserved in many noblemen's houses, the current production of the *Real Fábrica de Tapices* lacked the inspiration of the work of Houasse and Tiepolo; lacking the stiff hieratic grace of old tapestries based on Scriptural subjects and legends of the saints, the vim of medieval battle-scenes or incidents from *Don Quixote*, and the languid, mannered charm of scenes derived from, say, the *Roman de la Rose*. The Flemings had supplied a little contemporary vigour in the shape of rustic merrymakings.[1]

Goya's radiant cartoons, infused with the essence of the fullblooded Spanish life of his day, were to make a few contemporary confections look

[1]Some critics of standing assert that this vigour was traditional in native tapestry-art produced in the Spanish Netherlands until about 1720.

like a wooden puppet-show. Between 1776 and 1792 he was to produce well over sixty cartoons pulsating with life, colour, and high spirits, drawn from the contemporary scene: fiestas and dances; riverside luncheon-parties; tosspots, gamblers, stilt-walkers, children at play, a picturesque brawl or two; that vivid memento of a vanishing century called 'The Crockery Vendor', with the seated figures on the ground and the fine lady's coach rolling by, a couple of flunkeys in cocked hats hanging on behind. Before long would appear the incomparable *Vendimia*, conveying in its grouping so much to the initiate. *See* PLATE V p. 53 *See* PLATE VII p. 56

There came a day when the craftsmen of the *Fábrica*, sweating to express unwonted richness and complication in terms of silk and wool, came near to a strike, complaining to Mengs of Goya's lust for detail and his too-lavish demands for colour. At length one of his cartoons, depicting a group of Madrilene loafers listening to a blind guitarist, was returned to him for simplification; it may be that others had been toned down at the loom. Goya's retort, doubtless inclusive of an Aragonese expletive or two, was to send them a half-finished sketch titled 'The Fair at Madrid' to do what they pleased with. Before long the operatives gave in and accepted even the delicate and deliberate detail of 'The Swing' without a murmur. A subsequent directive from the King ordering the *Fábrica's* artists henceforth to include carpets in their output Goya seems to have ignored. *See* p. 63 *See* p. 62 *See* PLATE XIII p. 87

He had by now begun to make contact with the polite world and to lay the foundations of a metropolitan clientele. The existence of an Aragonese clique in high Madrid society has already been mentioned. In the absence of the Conde de Fuentes abroad, the fashionable playwright Ramón de la Cruz took Goya under his wing, introducing him to the leading salons and acting as what contemporary St James's would call his 'bear-leader'. One may lawfully visualize a short, square, well-dressed figure – Goya will be all his life something of a fop – musing stolidly amid acres of shining floor under elaborate crystal chandeliers, surrounded by every costly decorative caprice of the baroque, while round him swirls and chatters the smart crowd. Outwardly impassive as a Red Indian, Goya might well dismiss a flicker or two of trepidation with the realization that these people were not on the whole so godlike as they appeared to think themselves. The women . . . the artist's implacable eye would recognize, as he was borne away by his mentor to be presented to yet another figure in society, that beauty is relative, that hags are not exclusive to the backwoods, and that one or two great ladies present might, on quitting the assembly, more suitably summon their broomsticks than their coaches. On the other hand, as he would have to admit when he came to paint some of their portraits, there were more dazzling visions to be viewed at a Madrid reception in one night than you could find in his native province in a twelvemonth.

The Straw Dummy – tapestry cartoon, 1791–92
oil on canvas
105⅛ × 63 in. (267 × 160 cm.)
Museo del Prado, Madrid

A great day, or night, at length arrived. He was presented to the Duchess of Osuna, one of the two reigning queens of Madrid society; doubtless at her *See* p. 63

(above) Playing Soldiers –
tapestry cartoon, 1791–92
on canvas
$57\frac{1}{2}$ × 37 in. (146 × 94 cm.)
Museo del Prado, Madrid

(right) Men on Stilts – tapestry
cartoon, 1791–92
on canvas
$105\frac{1}{2}$ × 126 in. (268 × 320 cm.)
Museo del Prado, Madrid

(below right) The Picnic –
tapestry cartoon, 1791–92
on canvas
$107\frac{1}{8}$ × $116\frac{1}{8}$ in. (272 × 295 cm.)
Museo del Prado, Madrid

(above) Playing Giants – tapestry
cartoon, 1791–92
on canvas
$53\frac{7}{8}$ × 41 in. (137 × 104 cm.)
Museo del Prado, Madrid

bove) The Kite – tapestry
rtoon, 1791–92
on canvas
5⅞ × 112¼ in. (269 × 285 cm.)
useo del Prado, Madrid

low) The Blind Guitar Player
apestry cartoon, 1791–92
on canvas
2⅜ × 122½ in. (260 × 311 cm.)
useo del Prado, Madrid

posite above) The Wedding –
estry cartoon, 1791–92
on canvas
5¼ × 115⅜ in. (267 × 293 cm.)
useo del Prado, Madrid

posite below left)
ung Boys Picking Fruit
apestry cartoon, 1791–92
on canvas
⅞ × 48 in. (119 × 122 cm.)
useo del Prado, Madrid

posite below right)
e Fair at Madrid
apestry cartoon, 1791–92
on canvas
⅝ × 85⅞ in. (258 × 218 cm.)
useo del Prado, Madrid

ove right)
e Duke and Duchess of Osuna
d their children
on canvas
× 68½ in. (225 × 174 cm.)
useo del Prado, Madrid

palace of the Alameda. Her more fascinating rival, destined to bulk so largely
in Goya's existence, seems to have been away at the time on one of the Alba
estates. The two great ladies hated each other, as might be expected, almost
as cordially as a couple of goddesses of the stage. Snatching each other's
latest protégés – poets, toreros, actors, singers – was a routine pastime; Goya
himself will before long be a pawn in the game. In the matter of wilfulness
her Grace of Osuna may perhaps be said to have enjoyed a trifling lead, her
dearest hobby being hard and solitary cross-country riding; in 1780 moreover she followed her husband to the blockade of Minorca, disguised as a
sailor. On the other hand it was her Grace of Alba who conceived the delightful notion, according to one version of the story, of dressing her waiting-
women in exact replicas of her rival's latest-arrived gowns from Paris (the

authentic version makes her butt the Queen, her Enemy No. 1). She would shortly capture Goya with no trouble at all. He was at this moment sore from a brief and infuriating visit to Saragossa, where a new fresco designed by him for the Pilar had been rejected, owing – as Goya clearly saw – entirely to his brother-in-law Bayeu's withholding of approbation. A feud was impending. Being taken up by a duchess or two would be a timely lenitive.

No more accomplished cicerone than Ramón de la Cruz could have been found to steer a Goya into the great world. Well born, a man-about-town, an immensely prolific and successful man of the theatre, producing at least three hundred of those light satiric verse-sketches of contemporary society, peculiar to the Spanish stage, called *sainetes*, he was welcome in high circles everywhere. Not a few of his sketches were played at the town-houses of the nobility; hostesses, including her Grace of Alba, would now and again delight to play a small part. De la Cruz' adaptations of Italian and French comedy are notably graceful. Except that he lacked the corrosive wit of the creator of Figaro, he might be called the Beaumarchais of the contemporary Spanish stage; alternatively, and more obviously, the Goya of comedy. His sketches of the passing Madrilene scene are full of verve and amusing situations; his backgrounds range from the Prado via the Plaza Mayor to the proletarian Rastro; his satire is high-spirited, his eye for absurdity unerring. He was an especial friend of the current Duke of Alba, to whom he had lately dedicated one of his vaudevilles, *El Buen Marido* ('The Good Husband').

Whether he presented Goya to the Duchess at this time is not discernible. He would almost certainly have introduced his protégé before long to a select club of the intelligentsia meeting at a tavern in the Plaza del Angel called the Fonda de San Sebastián, with the poet Nicolás Fernández de Moratín in the chair. Perhaps this is the assembly which inspires a playful swipe in a sketch by Ramón de la Cruz called *Los Dos Libritos* ('The Two Little Books'). Doña Laura speaking:

> *Todos los hombres que siguen*
> *las literarias carreras*
> *deben ser menospreciados*
> *de las muchachas discretas . . .*
>
> Discreet young ladies should
> disdain all men who follow a
> literary career . . .

For literary types, she explains, are notoriously moody, jealous, apprehensive, and vicious.

The assembly at the Fonda was not such a distinguished company as Madrid could boast in either of the two centuries preceding. Barring Moratín, none of its members – Clavijo, Montiano, Yriarte, Cadalso, Luzán, and others – managed to achieve any fame to speak of. The romantic poet José Cadalso is notable chiefly for a long elegy, *Noches Lugubres*, based on the *Night Thoughts* of Dr Edward Young, which had such a cosmopolitan vogue.

Don Meléndez Valdés, 1797
oil on canvas
$28\frac{3}{4} \times 2\frac{1}{4}$ in. (73 × 54 cm.)
The Bowes Museum,
Barnard Castle, co. Durham

The architect Don Juan de
Villanueva, 1805
oil on panel
$37\frac{7}{8} \times 26\frac{3}{8}$ in. (90 × 67 cm.)
Real Academia de Bellas Artes
de San Fernando, Madrid

Don Sebastian Martinez, 1792
oil on canvas
$36\frac{5}{8} \times 26\frac{5}{8}$ in. (93 × 67.4 cm.)
The Metropolitan Museum
of Art, New York
Rogers Fund, 1906

PLATE VIII. Fernando VII
oil on canvas
$112\frac{1}{4} \times 80\frac{3}{4}$ in. (285 × 205 cm.
Real Academia de Bellas Artes
de San Fernando, Madrid

Don José Munarriz, 1815
oil on canvas
33½ × 25¼ in. (85 × 64 cm.)
Real Academia de Bellas Artes
de San Fernando, Madrid

The comedies of Tomás Yriarte are negligible, though the charm of his *Fábulas* in verse inspired to emulation Florian, that minor La Fontaine, in France. Montiano, critic and dramatist, is chiefly celebrated for his ruling that Part II of *Don Quixote* as conceived by Cervantes' plagiarizing Avellaneda is superior to the master's own performance. Nevertheless the company at the Fonda were all men of intelligence and culture, and in addition ardent students of tauromachy. They doubtless welcomed Goya with all the sincerity with which literary men are wont to admire rising genius in another sphere. The poet Nicolás Fernández de Moratín became Goya's close friend, as did, some forty years later and in exile, his son Leandro, a poet of mark likewise.

Much of the talk over the wine at the Fonda de San Sebastián must have been well above Goya's head until it turned to the bulls. The works of Tasso, Ariosto, Boileau, and Voltaire, among other classic foreigners, were, it is recorded, familiar to all present and freely discussed. At regular intervals members read aloud new work of their own for appreciation and criticism. There were accordingly perhaps a few quarrels; possibly a standing feud or two; even, at times, an unseemly uproar. A print of St Sebastian, the third-century military martyr, his body stuck full of Roman arrows, would normally decorate any Spanish tavern under his patronage. It would not seem out of place in any literary club in the world.

How differences of opinion between literary gentlemen were settled in eighteenth-century Madrid is not clear. According to the learned Menéndez y Pelayo the Council of Trent's ban on the duel, public or private, was permanently enforced in Spain, the last formal Spanish duel being fought by two noblemen at Valladolid in 1522.[1] Long after this, since for two centuries more every gentleman wore a rapier, the ban seems to have been ignored so far as informal affairs were concerned. An historic case is on record for March, 1611, when the poet Quevedo, seeing a lady struck by a testy gallant in the church of San Martín, dragged the fellow outside and, swords being swiftly drawn, ran him through after a few brisk passes and killed him. Only flight to Sicily saved Quevedo from the hand of justice. Though such an affray would hardly rank as a duel in proper form, the sanctions would be the same. One might conjecture that for any eighteenth-century Spaniard with honour to preserve the ban was merely a technical and avoidable nuisance.

Meanwhile Goya must have learned a great deal more about the bulls.

At this time a social problem of moment was certainly engaging him. High Madrid society at this period was an intricate maze of connections by birth, affinity, and intermarriage. Fuentes, to take a single instance, was a Piñatelli married to a Solferino, one of the Villafranca clan, themselves linked by marriage with the Albas, whose own connections were plentiful. Each and all bore a string of titles formally displayed in every legal document. Thus

PLATE IX. Francisco Bayeu, 1795
oil on canvas
44⅛ × 33⅛ in. (112 × 84 cm.)
Museo del Prado, Madrid

[1] *Cultura Literaria de Cervantes*: lecture delivered at the Universidad Central, 1905.

'Doña Maria Teresa Cayetana de Silva Alvarez de Toledo, Duquesa de Huéscar, Condesa de Oropesa, Alcaudete, Belbis, Deleitosa de Morente y de Fuentes, Marquesa de la Ciudad de Coria, de las villas de Héliche y Tarazona y de Jarandilla, Flechilla, y Villarramiel' designates the Duchess of Alba's mother in a second marriage certificate, while for practical purposes she was styled Duchess of Huéscar. The Duchess her daughter was similarly styled, before marriage, Marquesa de Coria and Condesa de Oropesa. It was plainly essential to any painter of Goya's ambition to know his way through this jungle. He set himself therefore doggedly to the task, assisted, it appears, by a notebook supplied by his mother, whose hobby seems, not too surprisingly, to have been genealogy; one may recall that Doña Engracia Goya had a claim to gentility and, undoubtedly, some education. With her help her son seems to have grappled more or less successfully with what must have become a headachy business. What high society made of the new prodigy may be feasibly conjectured. This provincial was apparently a portent, and any perceptible lack of polish in accent or manners would not – in a Spanish milieu, wherein today as then a duke and a shoeblack, equals in the sight of God, may converse without condescension on the one hand or servility on the other – invite either amusement or snobbery. Added to which, of course, was the eighteenth-century need to *s'encanailler*.

We find Goya very hard at work, and climbing.

His engagement at the *Real Fábrica*, which will continue in more or less desultory fashion till 1792, already occupied relatively little of his time. He had begun to interest himself in a new medium, which in 1778 produced a series of etchings after Velázquez paintings in the Royal Collection. A hurraying letter to Zapater in due course announces that his painting has been approved by the King, the Infante Don Luis, and the Infanta, whose hands he has kissed. Two years later he was admitted a member of the Royal Academy. In the same year, 1780, occurred the feud with his brother-in-law, already mentioned. A friendly monk having smoothed this crisis over, Goya dashed off a couple of new works with the minimum of exertion and returned to Madrid, still in a rage. The feuds of artists are little less tedious to contemplate than the feuds of the literary. A posthumous portrait of Bayeu painted by Goya in 1795 was to give his brother-in-law's slightly cantankerous features full value.

It is in 1781, the year after his disagreement with the Council of Works of the Pilar, that Goya, now permanently established in Madrid and an Academician, begins to assert himself. His cartoons for the *Real Fábrica* have already created him a reputation. More sketches from life, as yet undeveloped, must fill a few portfolios. He has not yet begun to excel as a portraitist – the first works of this kind attributable to him date from two years later – and a penchant for brownish backgrounds in *tierra de España*, fated to turn dark, has yet to be conquered. He is sufficiently certain enough

The Dwarf Sebastian de Morra
after a painting by Velázquez
etching
8 × 6 in. (20.5 × 15.5 cm.)
The Museum of Fine Arts, Boston
Collection Harvey D. Parker

Philip IV after a painting by
Velázquez
etching
14⅝ × 12¼ in. (37 × 31 cm.)
The Museum of Fine Arts, Boston

See PLATE XXXVIII pp. 186–87

See PLATE IX p. 66

The Village Bullfight
oil on panel
17¾ × 28⅜ in. (45 × 72 cm.)
Real Academia de Bellas Artes
de San Fernando, Madrid

see PLATE XXXVIII pp. 186–87

of himself, however, to enter a national competition for the decoration of the baroque church of San Francisco el Grande, the newest and largest in Madrid, for which he painted an altarpiece. In this year also he was taken up by the Infante Don Luis, for painting whose 'family of angels' (he wrote exultantly to Zapater) he earned *aplauso inesperado* and a thousand *duros*.[1] Moreover, he added, during his visit to Don Luis' estate at Arenas de San Pedro he enjoyed some good rough shooting with an agreeable host, and was presented, on leaving, with a gown for his wife; 'all over silver and gold' he informs Zapater, and worth – so he was assured by the Mistress of the Wardrobe – thirty thousand *reales*.

He was now making valuable social and other contacts outside working hours. How many evenings a week he spent with the cultured company at the tavern of San Sebastián, already referred to, is not ascertainable. If the literary talk bored him, as may be conjectured, he would enjoy the bull ring debates which equally engaged those ardent *aficionados* – had not Moratín himself produced that *Fiesta de Toros en Madrid* of which the seventy-five vibrant stanzas are inseparable from any anthology of Spanish verse? In this swinging sequence of balladry, set in the Madrid – 'Majerit' – of the Moorish kings, the excitement of the corrida, the valour of the Castilian hidalgo Don Rodrigo de Vivar, the ferocity of the fighting bulls he engages on horseback:

> *No en las vegas de Jarama*
> *pacieron la verde grama*
> *nunca animales tan fieros . . .*

> No more formidable brutes ever
> grazed the greensward of the
> plains of Jarama . . .

[1]It would be tedious to attempt to render late eighteenth-century Spanish money in modern British terms. The monetary and economic chaos of the previous century, whereby wages rose faster than prices, with an accompanying depreciation of copper vexatious to the labouring classes, had given place to a sound economy and increasing expansion in maritime and colonial trade, as in Spanish industry itself.

A Picador on Horseback, 1797–9
oil on canvas
22 × 18½ in. (56 × 47 cm.)
Museo del Prado, Madrid

– the beauty of the fair Zaida, beloved of the Alcalde Aliatar, the tumult of silver trumpets and drums, and the shouting of the crowd combine to make a piece of romantic pastiche as full of verve as a rhymed romance of Scott, though lacking that perceptible struggle with which the Scots master strives to animate his olde-tyme puppets.

Moratín and his circle were no dilettantes where the national fiesta was concerned. They knew their *tauromaquia*. At this period the selective breeding of the high-caste fighting bull, whose fearlessness Hemingway accurately styled 'almost unearthly', was not yet a serious technique, with the *nobleza* of the Andalucian breed recognized as pre-eminent.[1] To the critics at the San Sebastián tavern Goya must have listened with respect, and from them he undoubtedly learned not a little of value to his own art.

[1] Some modern authorities disagree.

See pp. 243–45

It may well have been Moratín who introduced him to the front-rank toreros of the day – Pedro Romero, Delgado, 'Pepehillo', Costillares – in due course to be immortalized by him in paint or etching. Goya's own passion for the bull ring was of course nothing abnormal. The corrida, as Felipe III had assured Pope Clement VII nearly two centuries earlier, imploring the Holy Father successfully to raise Sixtus V's ban of excommunication on bull-fighters and spectators alike, is in every Spaniard's blood. It was certainly in the blood of Don Francisco Goya. This greatest of illustrators of tauromachy was moreover fortunate in his period.

★   ★   ★

What had been in the Cid Campeador's time a sport for gentlemen on horseback armed with the lance, *rejón*, had developed into a complex, colourful ensemble demonstrating an art appreciated and criticized as knowledgeably by Demos as by his betters. The present-day *rejoneador* carrying on the tradition with amateur status has a notable seventeenth-century precursor in the person of the dashing, gifted, and scandalous Juan de Tassis, Conde de Villamediana; poet, courtier, duellist, immoralist, master of bulls and women, almost undoubtedly the prototype of the Don Juan of drama and legend.[1] The brilliant performances in the 1940s of the Peruvian *rejoneadora* Señorita Conchita Cintrón are still remembered, virtuosas in this field being rare.

In Goya's time the espada Pedro Romero was setting a standard of valour, grace, and the severe classicism of the school of Ronda never since surpassed. The master's forthcoming portrait of Romero was to radiate something of the calm hierarchic power of a Beethoven, with whom adepts of tauromachy have in his sphere compared him; not too grotesquely, both being masters of form, the one towering above composers of his and succeeding ages as the other does above all the *espadas* in history. Compared with the flamboyance of the rival school of Seville, by all accounts, Romero's performance in the bull ring was a perfect sonata in the classic mode. Even if he and his two colleagues *See* p. 30 were not recognizable in it, the furious caricature labelled *Volaverunt* would of itself breed scepticism concerning Ezquerra del Bayo's theory of the artist's 'friendship' with the lady. However, this vengeance was not due for some time. Goya's career was beginning and he was preparing to conquer Madrid.

One may pause a moment to reflect that the *ambiance* of the capital was with, not against, a newcomer of genius. A tendency, Whiggish in essence, to picture eighteenth-century Spain as wrapped, so to speak, in a tattered cloak and brooding in indolence, apathy, and squalor over the conquests and glories of the Golden Age is not in accordance with the facts, though it deceived

[1] There is a fascinating study of this personage in Gregorio Marañón's *Don Juan*, published in the 1930s and frequently reprinted.

WILLIAM HOGARTH Midnight
Conversation
etching
The British Museum, London

Napoleon for one. Between 1700 and 1800 the population nearly doubled. In the eighteenth century, to quote the *Cambridge Modern History*, the outlying areas of the Peninsula 'asserted themselves against the backwardness of Castile so as to share in the new standard of living which was spreading in Europe'. A modern French economist-historian, Pierre Vilar, has remarked an expansion during the same period in commerce and overseas trade, a *renaissance démographique*, a *refonte du pacte colonial*, and the beginnings of an industrial revolution.

Social or economic issues will not need, fortunately, to be touched on in these pages except where they inspire Goya's verve. Such a social phenomenon as, for example, a national plague of lawyers and, still more, the overcrowding of the religious orders – due in each case, as Godoy observes in his memoirs, to the determination of the Spanish middle-class mother to pitchfork at least one of her numerous offspring into the Law or the Church, with or without a vocation – will receive due treatment in the *Caprichos* and elsewhere. Goya's bulky friars (possibly laybrothers) lounging in taverns invite the satiric lash as naturally as do clerical types in contemporary England represented by the parson presiding over the punchbowl in Hogarth's 'Midnight Conversation', said to feature the Reverend Cornelius Ford, a well-known toper before the Lord, not unique of his kind; the difference being, perhaps, that the Spaniard has never been able to find intoxication very funny. Flicks at an outmoded Inquisition, the natural *bête-noire* of all liberals and Voltaireans of Goya's race and time, may be noted in their place.

It has been remarked already that Goya's approach is less Voltairean than Molièresque.

So (to resume) young Goya found himself in a bracing and welcoming world from the beginning, with plenty of patrons at hand from royalty down. The Infante Don Luis, as we have seen, was among the first of his admirers. 'Slow rises worth, by poverty depressed' – nothing even remotely resembling so many historic early struggles will delay Goya's progress up the ladder. Before the mid-1780s Don Luis, a connoisseur and, like Goya, a good shot, had presented him in Palace circles, and Carlos III had approved a portrait. It was, it is, a significant first performance in the *genre*. Against a background of rolling country backed by a distant sierra his Majesty – another good shot – stands in cocked hat and high gaiters, holding his gun. A favourite hound is curled up beside him. He wears no indication of rank but the inevitable sash under a loose, full coat. His Majesty's saturnine features, wearing a quizzical grin, are anything but flattered. A new era in Court portraiture has evidently set in, to flower a few years hence in the portrait group of Carlos' stout genial successor, Carlos IV, and his family at Aranjuez; a satire on nonentity, or commonly thus received, such as no other Court painter has ever dared before or since.

See PLATE IV p. 44

ee PLATE XXXVIII pp. 186–87

The portrait of Carlos III brought Goya in the summer of 1786 the appointment of Painter to the King, with a payment of 15,000 *reales* annually. Meanwhile other commissions were coming in; an authoritative post at the *Real Fábrica*; four figures of saints for the College of Calatrava at Salamanca, at 400 *doblones*; the successful entry in open competition for the decorations at San Francisco el Grande, shared with the painters Ferro and Castillo and yielding, after maddening bureaucratic delays, 4,000 *reales de vellón*. In May of this same year a jubilant letter ('Secret!') to Martin Zapater announces that the Academy has just appointed his friend assistant director, with the annual honorarium of 25 *doblones*. It is not yet Golconda by any means, but 'with no more than ten or thirteen thousand *reales* a year I am as content as the most prosperous'. If a portrait of him at this period by another hand lacks the Cyranoesque truculence of the earliest one, the aggressiveness in eyes and jaw remains eloquent enough. 'I am Goya', the *baturro* at the easel seems to be saying to the world at large. 'Who the devil are you?'

Zapater's praiseworthy preservation of Goya's side of an extensive correspondence yields us practically every stage of the master's debut. His letters, often long, often hasty, often involved, do not make smooth reading. The pen was never a handy tool to Goya save for sketching. He cares little for syntax and not a rap for clarity or elegance. Spelling is a trifle shaky, and he has a kind of shorthand – '. . . *y muchas gras. a Dios de lo poco qe. el peor librado fui yo y no es mas qe. estar desde el dia de Sn. Tiago qe . . .*'; scrawling as it were at top speed, with ever and anon a glance over his shoulder in quest of eavesdroppers. A bellicose figure emerges from a large part of this

Don Luis de Borbon
Oil on canvas
29¼ × 23⅝ in. (74 × 60 cm.)
Museo del Prado, Madrid

correspondence; an egoist, a hedgehog of a man, one might almost sum up; prickles ever at the ready; a type in some degree resembling his contemporary Hogarth, by all accounts a tolerably truculent character.

It is not on record – save in the dubious story of his flight from Saragossa in youth – that Goya ever resorted to violence like Torregiano, who broke Michelangelo's nose with one punch. He would doubtless have acquitted himself with fist or knife, if necessary, like a doughty son of Aragon. The thought protrudes itself that a general lack of social graces might even be the secret of some of his glamour in the eyes of the Duchess Maria Cayetana. She would not be the first, or last, great lady in the world to find piquancy in the acquisition of a rough diamond of genius; in Goya's case not quite so un-polished, perhaps, as one is tempted to assume.

Continuing Court contacts – in May 1788 he tells Zapater that he has just designed the decorations for the bedchambers of *las serenísimas Infantas* – must have had some effect on deportment; he had by now, it seems, likewise acquired by the efforts of a professor, and his own, sufficient French to be able to make a very passable show in a letter to his only confidant. Any mental picture, therefore, when he enters the Duchess's orbit – as he will shortly do – of patrician condescension on the one hand and tongue-tied uncouthness on the other may be summarily discarded. There was no class-consciousness about the dazzling Maria Cayetana, and Goya was well aware of his own worth. Both being Spaniards, human dignity was never in jeopardy.

When they first met – undoubtedly in Madrid – is not known, but the year of the *Vendimia*, 1786, has been held at least a *terminus a quo*. With his wife and one of his children, a small boy, Goya is staying at Piedrahita, the Albas' estate near Avila in Castile. The shimmery autumnal tints of this conver-sation-piece convey a singular blend of happiness, domestic and perhaps infatuate. The wife is as well graced as her hostess. It is clear that the painter's enchantment has begun.

See PLATE VII p. 56

PLATE X. Doña Isabel Cobos de Porcel, 1806
oil on canvas
$32\frac{1}{4} \times 21\frac{1}{2}$ in. (82 × 54.6 cm.)
The National Gallery, London

PLATE XI. (overleaf) The Parasol
– a tapestry cartoon, 1777
oil on canvas
$41 \times 59\frac{7}{8}$ in. (104 × 152 cm.)
Museo del Prado, Madrid

3 The Duchess

How much of the thirteenth Duchess of Alba's celebrated and certified spell was due to physical beauty remains still, curiously enough, a matter for discussion. Goya affords us little assistance. The wasp-waisted doll-like figure of the portrait of 1795, for example, with one arm awkwardly extended – apart from the magnificent eyes, features of a classic oval, and a superb casque of lustrous hair, how would this vision rank side by side with (say) Romney's Emma Hamilton, not to mention some of Goya's own subjects like Doña Isabel Cobos de Porcel or the 'Lady with a Yellow Scarf', or, even more, the delicious young *maja* reading the letter in the canvas at Lille? Other studies of the Duchess by Goya are far from helpful to a conclusion. An ink-sketch in which she is putting up – or even tearing – her hair makes her features almost commonplace, which might be said likewise for another to which a tiny round hat lends disconcerting effect. Contrariwise, another ink-sketch by Goya in which she is nursing a negress child, one of her protégées, lends her distinct physical attraction. This may be equally said for that curious drawing – possibly a private joke – in the Prado in which a figure closely resembling the Duchess is seated on the ground at the feet of an enormous prostrate soldier in a cocked hat.[1] The full-length of 1797, again, in which two rings inscribed respectively 'Alba' and 'Goya' are clearly visible on adjacent fingers, invests Maria Cayetana with a statuesque grace, but the features are cold – indeed almost stony, as in a drawing of 1795 by Sepúlveda in which the cascade of curls is crowned by a turban-like head-dress. A marble bust of the same period, sculptor unnamed, lends her, again, a haughty comeliness.

To form a judgement from these varying impressions is not easy. Undoubtedly the spell of breeding and personality, warmhearted generosity, entire freedom from snobbery of any kind, and vitality and zest for life created a magic aura. Describable perhaps in the pregnant French phrase *pire que jolie*, features which could be cold in boredom or weariness could be suddenly lit up and transfigured, radiant and compelling.

The Duchess' figure, or at least that displayed so liberally by the nude *Maja*, has not escaped criticism by modern specialists. A Spanish surgical authority not long ago observed that if the lady rose from bed and walked

See PLATE X p. 75

See PLATE XXVI p. 144

See PLATE III p. 43

See p. 80

See p. 131

See p. 35

GEORGE ROMNEY Lady Hamilton as Circe, 1782
oil on canvas
21 × 19½ in. (53.5 × 49.5 cm.)
The National Gallery, London

See PLATE XXIV pp. 139–40

PLATE XII. The Duchess of Alba, 1797
oil on canvas
The Hispanic Society of America, New York

[1]The drawing is entitled *La Maja y el militar*; alternatively *La Duquesa de Alba*, etc.

she would remarkably resemble a frog. This is plainly Goya's responsibility. The autopsy of 1945, to which we shall come in due course, testifies to a slim elegance of figure – Maria Cayetana was slightly under five feet in height – and a classic and patrician perfection of the bones. The bosom was admittedly faultless. Altogether, one might say, the Duchess merited most of the adulation she received from high and low, an adulation which was expressed in such musical tributes as a *tonadilla* for tenor voice, violin, bass-viol, oboe, and horn by Blas de Laserna:

> *. . . y a vista de Ustedes*
> *me ocupa un temor*
> *que me priva toda*
> *la respiración.*
>
> . . . and at the sight of You
> a tremor seizes me
> which completely stops
> my breath.

At least one notable foreign connoisseur – and he a Frenchman – was to confirm such dithyrambs. In his *Voyage de Figaro en Espagne* (1784) Jean-Marie-Jérôme, Marquis de Langle, makes a prose-poem of it:

The Duchess of Alba has not a single hair on her head which does not awaken desire. No woman in the world is as beautiful as she; it would be impossible to create a finer one . . . when she passes by the whole world rushes to its windows. Even children stop their play to gaze at her.

(above left) A Woman with Hand Raised, probably the Duchess of Alba
brush and grey and black wash
6¾ × 4 in. (17.1 × 10.2 cm.)
Biblioteca Nacional, Madrid
(No. 1271)

(above right) Couple Seated (detail), after 1800
sepia wash
8⅛ × 5⅝ in. (20.6 × 14.2 cm.)
Museo del Prado, Madrid
(Prado No. 249)

ETANO MERCHI Goya, about
95
onze
ght 18½ in. (47 cm.)
al Academia de Bellas Artes
San Fernando, Madrid

And again:

> Adorned with every grace, completely beautiful, the Duchess is a nonpareil. On the Prado, in the Retiro, at church, wherever she may be they run after her, they see nothing else.

The marquis was certainly smitten. The seasoned campaigner might almost have echoed the hapless Tisbea, one of the victims of Tirso de Molina's Don Juan:

> *Fuego, fuego, zagales! Agua, agua!*
> *Amor, clemencia, que se abrasa el alma!*

> Fire, shepherds! Fire! Water, water,
>   for love and pity's sake; my soul is
> aflame! – *El Burlador de Sevilla*,
>   ACT I SC. V.

It might well be, as Ezquerra del Bayo observes sardonically, that the perfumes of a Madrilene summer night had gone to the Frenchman's head. Nevertheless there can be no doubt of the Duchess' spell, physical and other. There is ample testimony that she retained till death, with outstanding graces of heart and mind, something of magic and youth which a grandee's birth and immense riches failed to spoil. There is a story that at the beginning of the French Revolution her servants discovered the second of two unsuccessful attempts to burn down one of her mansions. That night she entered her drawing-room with a lighted wax torch. 'At least I may be allowed to set fire to my own house', she said to her guests, and did so. She could of course afford such pleasantries; but her bequest of much of an enormous fortune to friends and an army of servants was no whimsical freak.

Her attitude towards the proletariat as a class is illustrated in a characteristic remark, quoted in Somoza's memoirs, to her husband after violently scolding a handful of her lower menials for making game of her especial See p. 35 protégé, poor old half-witted Fray Basilio. 'We shouldn't have such servants,' said the Duchess hotly, '*Canaille!* – they're capable of persuading us we're better than they are!'[1] Truly the Slavonic note. A few hundred miles north one may glimpse testy Admiral Lyesovsky, of Rimsky-Korsakov's memoirs, flinging himself weeping at the feet of a serf whose nose he has just bitten off in a fit of rage, and begging his forgiveness in Christ's name. Simultaneously may one glimpse wellbred eyebrows going up at Versailles, and the Duchess of Buckingham pausing aghast at her writing-table in St James's during the penning of her famous rebuke to the Countess of Huntingdon for turning Methodist. 'It is monstrous to be told that you have a heart as sinful as the common wretches that crawl on the earth. . . .' To most of European high society the wayward Spanish duchess would have seemed at times certifiable.

Maria Teresa – to adopt for once her own fixed choice from the thirty-one

---

[1] *Canalla! que es capaz de persuadirnos que somos mejores que ellos!*

saints' names bestowed on her in baptism[1] – had the advantage of a liberal education, as her age in its decline conceived it. Born at Madrid in June, 1762, of a subsequently widowed mother, Maria Teresa de Silva y Silva, Duchess of Huéscar, in a barrack of a palace on the borders of the proletarian quarters of Lavapiés and the Rastro, she was brought up from the age of eight on a regime of the *philosophes* of France by a distinguished grandfather, Fernando de Silva y Alvarez de Toledo, twelfth Duke of Alba; a soldier-grandee of considerable culture, Captain-General of the Army from 1770, a friend and correspondent of Rousseau and Fontenelle.

On Alba's library-shelves the works of these masters, with those of Bayle and Montesquieu, stood cheek by jowl with the spiritual writings of St Augustine, St Teresa, Fray Luis de Granada, and Maestro Juan de Avila, the plays of Calderón, Racine, and Molière, and serried tomes of military science. As a member of the Council of State the Duke had collaborated with the minister Aranda and his freemason allies, Pombal in Portugal and Choiseul in France, in the temporary expulsion of the Jesuits and the destruction of their ideal state in Paraguay. Whether or not Alba was a freemason likewise, he apparently retained some of his religion. An admirer of Rousseau's *Emile*, he had the child Maria Cayetana educated more or less in accordance with the theories therein displayed. Fortunately none of Rousseau's more idiotic fantasies seems to have beguiled him. One may doubt whether the child was allowed to smash windows when she felt like it, to be rude on principle to servants, and in a word, to behave generally like a yahoo. One may doubt also if any soldier could bring himself to forbid all punishment, as Alba's great mentor rules. Does anyone read *Emile* today? It is a work of advanced lunacy with which the smartest modern pedagogue has yet to catch up.

Her education did the girl Maria Teresa Cayetana no great harm, it seems. It certainly failed to spoil her personality. Rousseau's dominant theme that woman exists to make life comfortable for man may have provoked her in her 'teens to silvery laughter. *Qué tontería*! Doubtless her elegant and cultivated mother, whose hobby of translating French drama earned her in 1766 honorary membership of the Academy of San Fernando, was able to offset the babble of the Genevese without much difficulty. Her love of music and art Doña Maria Teresa certainly passed on to Maria Cayetana. Among the many fine paintings in the Madrid palace and in the Albas' country house at Piedrahita were Raphael's 'Holy Family', known also as 'The Virgin of Alba', and the Venuses of Correggio and Velázquez.

To find the ideal *parti* for a girl of high birth so dowered with intelligence, vitality, looks, and magnetism was doubtless not easy. Her mother and grandfather married her, in January 1775, at the age of thirteen, to José Maria Alvárez de Toledo Gonzaga, Marquis of Villafranca, who took his wife's title

RAPHAEL The Virgin of the R[o] about 1518
oil on canvas
$40\frac{1}{2} \times 33\frac{1}{8}$ in. (103 × 84 cm.)
Museo del Prado, Madrid

(opposite left) VELAZQUEZ The Toilet of Venus ('The Rokeby Venus'), about 1651
oil on canvas
$48\frac{1}{4} \times 69\frac{3}{4}$ in. (122.5 × 177 cm[)]
The National Gallery, London

(opposite right) CORREGGIO Mercury Instructing Cupid before Venus
oil on canvas
$61\frac{1}{4} \times 36$ in. (155 × 91.5 cm.)
The National Gallery, London

[1] These were (11th June 1762) María del Pilar, Teresa, Cayetana, Manuela, Margarita, Leonor, Sebastiana, Bárbara, Ana, Joaquina, Francisca de Paula, Francisca de Asís, Francisca de Sales, Javiera, Andrea, Abelina, Sinforosa, Benita, Bernarda, Petronila de Alcántara, Dominga, Micaela, Rafaela, Gabriela, Venancia, Antonia, Fernanda, Bibiana, Vicenta, Catalina.

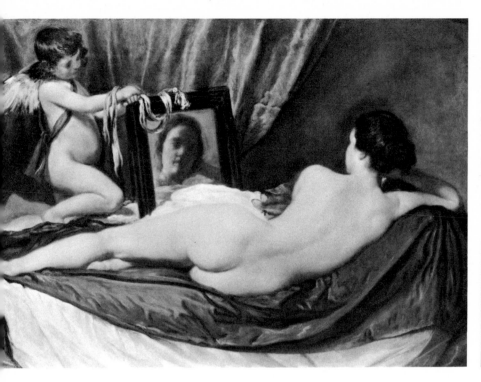

by a marriage-contract which likewise assured her a sufficient independent income, her husband's patrimony being relatively modest.

Since they thenceforth went their own ways without conflict, the marriage might be called successful. The pair had no interests in common but bulls and music, Villafranca's (henceforth Alba's) obsession, and a scholarly one. *See* p. 35 In the Goya portrait now in the Prado he leans with one elbow on a harpsichord; a tall, dark, spare, youngish, melancholy-looking aristocrat, long-nosed, bilious of complexion, modishly dressed, fingering a slim volume of printed music. The legibility of its title-page ascription to Haydn completes a character-study; here is no amateur of saccharine tinklings but a finished musician and, as all smart Madrid knew, a friend and patron of the Viennese master. The lemony tint of the new Duke's complexion seems to have been due to ill-health, and he found much solace in the company of a music-loving Court set. Goya's study demonstrates considerable strides in personality-fixing since his arrival in Madrid.

Though it remains seemingly impossible, as already remarked, to find even an approximate year for Goya's introduction to the Duchess, it is evident that *See* PLATE VII p. 56 they must have met before 1786, the year of the *Vendimia*. Goya was then forty, the Duchess twenty-four; in full exercise of charm and imperiousness, *See* p. 63 dividing the rule of Madrilene society with her rival, the Duchess of Osuna; each collecting such protégés in the public eye as actresses, bullfighters, poets, artists and the like. Having by now been taken up by royalty and the Osunas, Goya would automatically stand high on Maria Cayetana's list for appropriation. Her spell from girlhood is indicated by a contemporary gossip, Don José Somoza, a guest in his youth at Piedrahita, quoting an aged lady who knew the Alba family well and did not much care for the old Duke:

> The granddaughter, the little Duchess, is another matter. What she does for her people! What a kind-hearted girl! How vivacious, how happy! And what a head of hair – without exaggeration it can cover her to her feet.

The vitality and enjoyment with which the girl Maria Cayetana took part in proletarian relaxations on and around the Piedrahita estates – fiestas, dances, weddings, baptisms, processions, pilgrimages – was a byword. At a village ball she rarely failed to open the proceedings, commandeering the nearest hobbledehoy for her partner. On horseback or afoot she explored miles of the countryside, escorted or otherwise. The chief steward at Piedrahita is quoted by Somoza as remarking 'a thousand times' that if one of the Duke's rustic dependants had any petition or complaint to make it was necessary to remind 'the little Duchess' that he need not be given a yoke of oxen to go on with. All through life impulsive kindness, boundless charity, and an entire lack of affectation were to be her prevailing gifts. Her myriad servants adored her. She was haughty only, when necessary, with her equals; it is a timeless Spanish trait.

Another pleasing one in Maria Cayetana was her love of fine music, seemingly – the corrida apart – the only thing, as already remarked, she had in common with her husband. Haydn was the favourite composer of both of them, as he was in fact of most contemporary Spanish music-lovers; partly for the beauty of his works, partly on account of Spanish links with Austria, partly because Haydn was known to be a devout Catholic, turning for inspiration, when stuck with some temporarily-insoluble problem in composition, to his rosary. Amid a frivolous social round recitals in great houses of the music of Haydn and other contemporary masters was a regularly-recurring pleasure.

The wayward Duchess was, on many counts, a most attractive human creature. Goya has recorded some of her moods; teasing a well-loved old servant, hugging an infant negress on her knee, forlornly mourning the loss of a favourite dog. It is not impossible that allowing herself – features excepted – to be painted by Goya in the nude was merely another impulse of an unspoiled girlish nature, though this freak is admittedly more difficult to accept.

The *salon* of the chief rival, the Osuna, challenged any in contemporary Paris, extending a highly-cultivated luxury embracing concerts, balls, routs, theatrical performances, alfresco parties, day or night, in the Alameda ('the Mall'), a recently-acquired estate, then at the gates of Madrid, and, in short, every kind of entertainment wealth and culture can devise. Goya, a protégé and a frequent guest, recorded some of this gaiety – beauty swung in swings by wellborn *majos*, beauty in riverside parties, including one accident during an impromptu donkey race, and other frolics of an Arcadian kind – in paint

See p. 35

See PLATE XXIV pp. 139–40

See p. 63

See p. 61, PLATE XLI pp. 206–7,

PLATE XIII p. 87

The Greased Pole, 1787
oil on canvas
66½ × 35 in. (169 × 89 cm.)
Collection the Duke of
Montellano, Madrid

on the walls of the Osuna mansion in the park. Whether or not it was easy to detach him from this milieu, a couple of these paintings indicate that some time before 1786 Goya had met the Duchess Maria Cayetana, whose entertainments in the Calle Real del Barquillo, off the Calle del Alcalá, were as brilliant as her rival's. Quite possibly it was at one of the Osuna's al fresco parties that he received the *coup de foudre*. In *El Columpio* ('The Swing') the lady of quality swung between two trees by a pair of fashionable *majos* bears a visible likeness to the Duchess of Alba; in *La Caída* ('The Fall'), featuring the donkey-accident already mentioned, the Alba is in graceful tears at her hostess's fortunately harmless spill. It cannot have been long before Goya transferred allegiance from one great lady to another with a more potent magic, and Maria Cayetana might congratulate herself on a notable capture. Fuentes' prodigy, already taken up by royalty and besieged by clients of the great world, would undoubtedly fascinate her by his lack of the social graces, his infinite self-assurance, and a virility which was exuded at every pore. An ironic footnote to Goya's soaring fame is incidentally supplied by one of Horace Walpole's letters dated a little later. At a London party Walpole met the Hon. Anne Seymour Damer, that highly-gifted amateur sculptress, who had just returned from a stay in Madrid, had there become 'a proselyte to painting', and could talk of nothing but – Rubens.

One passion the Duchess and the artist certainly shared was the corrida, and especially that of the school of Seville, for which the Duke of Medina-Sidonia maintained a famous breeding-estate.[1] Here during the fiestas of San Juan and San Pedro in 1778 the young Duchess contributed a string of *novillos* – bulls over three years old and under six – wearing her own favours of white and yellow; a gift, it is supposed, from the Duke, her husband, who accompanied her. From a graceful cartoon of Goya's for the *Real Fábrica* tapestries entitled 'The Walk in Andalucia' (*El Paseo en Andalucia*), it has been conjectured that he was one of the party, but the evidence is excessively flimsy: the scene actually concerns a jealousy of fashionable *majos*. Not yet are the three leading *espadas* of Spain among the Duchess' dearest protégés; it seems likely nevertheless that Goya will have cause for jealousy on this score some time hence. His own expertise in *lidia* will be demonstrated years hence in the *Tauromaquia* etchings. Had he lived to see Fernando VII closing with a fantastic decree of 1830 – operative till 1834 – the Spanish universities and opening the Royal School of Tauromachy, with 76-year-old Pedro Romero, dragged from retirement, as director, his reaction as a liberal and an *aficionado* simultaneously might have been interesting. But by 1830 Goya had been dead two years.

Meanwhile (to return), he has won some praise (1784) for his painting of

The Fall, 1787
oil on canvas
66½ × 35 in. (169 × 89 cm.)
Collection the Duke of Montellano, Madrid

See p. 35

See PLATE XIV p. 88

See pp. 240–45

---

[1]Of the two contemporary schools of bullfighting that of Seville, personified by José Delgado, admitted fantasy and elegant play-acting, such as crowning the bull with the torero's cap, or provoking him to a charge by kneeling. The school of Ronda, personified by Romero, practised severely classical form with the absolute minimum of exhibitionism.

PLATE XIII. The Swing, 1787
oil on canvas
66½ × 39¾ in. (169 × 101 cm.)
Collection the Duke of Montellano, Madrid

ATE XIV. The Walk in
ndalucia – tapestry cartoon,
91–92
on canvas
8¼ × 74¾ in. (275 × 190 cm.)
useo del Prado, Madrid

an altarpiece in San Francisco el Grande, though the officially-set theme, 'St Bernardino of Siena preaching before King Alfonso of Aragon', was hardly one to inspire him. In 1786 he was appointed Painter to the King at 15,000 *reales*. 'I have established an enviable way of life', he writes to Zapater. 'Whoever wants anything from me now has to come and find me.' His income is now a little over 28,000 *reales*; he asks no more, and his old friend (no joking) is welcome to draw on it.

★   ★   ★

See PLATE IV p. 44

At the end of 1788 Carlos III died, Carlos IV succeeded him, and the clouds began to gather over a Spain which, outside the capital and the bustling mercantile cities and seaports – Bilbao, Barcelona, Cadiz, Huelva, Seville – had not changed much in essence to the casual eye since Don Quixote's time. Every province retained its own costume and its language or dialect, its traditional and distinctive songs, dances, and, so far as the peasantry were concerned, a few ritual grievances against some of the landowning class ruling about eight thousand villages. As with the contemporary squires of England, the barons of Germany, and their species all over Europe, these overlords, some of them fairly impecunious, were not necessarily oppressive or their subjects spiritless. In the previous century the peasantry of Quevedo's village of Torre de Juan Abad in La Mancha, refusing to pay him their dues, had barricaded themselves in the parish church against the police till the matter was settled. They were not unique.

A striking social phenomenon peculiar to the Spanish scene was the existence, already mentioned in the case of Goya's mother, of some thousands of poverty-stricken *hidalgos*, in whose behalf Carlos III issued a decree in 1783 indicating the manual trades – shoemaking, tailoring, carpentry – which might be practised without loss of caste. Casanova mentions somewhere in his memoirs a Spanish gentleman-shoemaker who rightly drew the line at measuring his feet. In vivid contrast to such genteel indigence, as to that of the peasantry in general, was the enormous wealth of a group of nobles – Albas, Infantados, Osunas, Fuentes, Alburquerques, Villahermosas, Abrantes and their like – with their palatial houses in town and country, their estates and farmlands stretching to the horizon, their armies of servants, dependants, and tenants. Such an anomaly aroused no resentment in the masses. The ancestors of these grandees had delivered Spain from the Moorish yoke and had earned their rewards. The wealth of the Church, largely traceable to the same honourable source, was another matter; towards the end of the century See p. 92 Carlos IV's minister Godoy, with entire papal approval, was to reduce it to more apostolic dimensions. The middle classes of cities the size of Barcelona, Valencia, Cadiz, and their like were prosperous enough, with commerce and industry alike on the increase and overseas trade expanding. A French economist already quoted has called the eighteenth century in Spain *un très grand siècle colonial*.

All over the country at this period were communities closely resembling the little Andalucian cathedral-city in which Pedro de Alarcón situates his ever-delightful novel *El Sombrero de Tres Picos* ('The Three-Cornered Hat' – period about 1805) which inspired the combined genius of Manuel de Falla, Massine, Picasso, and Diaghilev to an unforgettable ballet of the 1920s. In communities of this kind, undisturbedly peaceful save for the intermittent bells, ruled by a paternal bishop and a possibly pompous *corregidor*, life could be pleasant enough; such places being happy, as Alarcón remarks, in that diversity of human nature and temperament in every social class which vanished from Europe after the French Revolution. In such Arcadian enclaves time moved so gently that it might have stood still; every day, fiestas apart, resembling the last, from the bell for the dawn Mass to the bell for the evening Angelus.

As elsewhere in Europe, the highroads of Spain were more or less passable and the byroads usually appalling. Muleteers, friars, gypsies, *pícaros*, *contrabandistas*, and a bandit or two were common objects of the wayside. Brigands flourished especially in the sierras. In Cervantes' day they had been efficiently kept in check by the Holy Brotherhood (*Santa Hermandad*), a national highway police, horse and foot, with powers of summary trial and execution, established by Fernando I of Aragon. From this body derives directly the Guardia Civil of today. In Goya's time brigandage was again fairly rife; according to the careful Baedeker it lingered in some regions as late as the 1900s. Even today there are stories that the Sierra Morena is a lair for a sprinkling of desperadoes and deserters left over from the last civil war, but this may be fantasy. In eighteenth and early nineteenth-century romances by foreigners the Spanish brigand is not accorded the status of his more familiar Italian brother-professional, whose reported piety aroused the provincial mirth of Macaulay. There is no reason to believe that the Spanish branch of the profession was less efficient or, off duty, less devout.

Rural Spanish inns at this period dispensed the absolute minimum of comfort, and their fare was not above suspicion. The time-honoured national jape about the rural innkeeper's talent for turning stray cat into stewed rabbit probably still had some foundation. According to a company of carefree Madrilene tavern-epicures who actually experimented in the previous century, there is little or no difference in the finished product.[1] Whether Goya took food seriously is not ascertainable. Among the regional dishes of Spain there seems to be no notable place for the cuisine of Aragon, although chicken *a la chilindrón* can be a dish to remember. It might be that for Don Francisco the master-chefs of duchesses, like those of the leading taverns of Madrid, exerted themselves in vain.

Over most of Spain at this time the peasantry continued, especially in Andalucia, that traditional self-expression in original poetry and song which

---

[1]'Something between rabbit and squirrel – delicious!' reported Henry Labouchère of roast cat during the siege of Paris, 1870. But he was a jester by profession.

has remained, as the poet Federico García Lorca rediscovered and proclaimed in the 1900s, a living folk-culture. Itinerant ballad singers were rife. All over the south the guitar, that subtle and difficult instrument, had adepts in every parish. Muleteers, farm-labourers, milkmaids, and ploughmen improvised and sang at their work.

Aquel caballero, madre,
que de mi se enamoró,
pena él y muero yo . . .

Mother, that gentleman
who fell in love with me –
he is in pain, and I am dying . . .

Ramón Menéndez Pidal's survey of Spanish lyrical verse includes a wealth of impromptu song from proletarian lips unknown. Another form of rural self-expression current in Goya's time was pulpit-oratory of the type guyed in the 1750s by Padre José Francisco de Isla of the Society of Jesus in *Fray Gerundio de Campazas*, that diverting satire. The lower Spanish clergy at this time cultivated a high-flown *culteranismo* – the art of playing with words – of the most preposterous kind. An ideal opening for a preacher addressing a convent of nuns would be 'Celestial swans! . . .'

One more prominent feature of the national scene must be mentioned, namely the existence of some thousands of beggars, notable not so much for their numbers – Europe was full of them – as for their dignity as God's envoys enabling their fellow-men to practise the exquisite virtue of alms-giving. Since poverty has always been deemed by the Spaniard unshameful and charity an obligation, they went unpunished. And if there would seem no point of contact between beggary and the great world of Goya's duchess, one may assume as quite certain that, accosted on the highway and finding herself without money, Maria Cayetana would be capable of parting with her ear-rings on the spot. Not thus are the impulses of the rich always so predictable.

★　　★　　★

Such, very lightly sketched, was the Spain of the late eighteenth century. No foreign travellers of note have left any very memorable impressions. Spain was not on the map at the time for the British upper class making the Grand Tour, and towards the 1830–40s the pontifical Ford and the untrustworthy Borrow surveyed a much different Spain, that of the Carlist upheavals and the *pronunciamentos*, displaying enough unrest, misery, and apathy to earn the just contempt of any visiting Whig. On the whole we have probably lost a few ritual diatribes on the theme of indolence and superstition, but little of value.

See PLATE XXIII p. 137

The new King was in many ways an estimable character, being an almost exact Spanish replica of his cousin Louis XVI; portly, dull, good-hearted, honest, simple, addicted to tinkering at manual crafts. Unlike Louis, he was

Don Manuel Godoy, 1801
oil on canvas
$70\frac{7}{8} \times 105\frac{1}{8}$ in. (180 × 267 cm.)
Real Academia de Bellas Artes
de San Fernando, Madrid

an excruciating performer on the violin. 'Today I've been to see the King our lord', reports Goya to Zapater in the spring of 1792. 'He was very jovial (*muy alegre*), and talked about my Paco's pockmarks, which you already know about.[1] I agreed with him and he took my hand, and began to play his fiddle.' Unlike Louis XVI, finally, Carlos wore, metaphorically speaking, the horns; a misfortune of which all Madrid, including every embassy, was aware.

See PLATE XXXVIII pp. 186–87

> *Ronca el Cornudo y sueña que es dichoso . . . (Mensaje a Arnesto.)*
>
> Dreaming of his good luck, the Cuckold snores . . .

Jovellanos' bitter line is perhaps unfair to a monarch who undoubtedly slept too soundly to have any dreams at all. Having married a Neapolitan princess described by a current French ambassador as 'concentrating more perfidy than any woman alive', Carlos IV accepted his fate from the first like a stout philosopher. Goya's portraits of Queen Maria Luisa, a collector of jewels, cats, and attractive young men, convey the essence of her Majesty's character. Dissolute, domineering, implacable, vicious, shrewish, what Mrs Quickly would recognize as a frampold quean, Maria Luisa owed something perhaps to early pupillage under the eminent philosopher Condillac, whose attribution of conduct to sensation enjoyed a vogue in its day. Her responsibility for Spanish misadventure during the reign is considerable.

See PLATE XVI p. 106

See p. 136

Her principal paramour was now Don Manuel Godoy, formerly a cadet in the Royal Bodyguard, an aristocratic corps known to the Madrilene populace

---

[1]The child Paco (diminutive of 'Francisco') is not otherwise on record.

as the Chocolate Boys, *Los Chocolateros*, one of whose routine duties, according to the gossips, was to provide recruits for the Queen's bedchamber. Due ere long to become Prince of the Peace and as virtual master of Spain to cross swords in policy with Napoleon Bonaparte, Godoy has inspired much attentive prose, mostly to his discredit. He possessed nevertheless a quality or two. Among the rare visiting English Lord Holland found in him something to admire. The plump blandness of the Goya portrait (1801) in the uniform of Generalissimo has an undoubted flavour of satire. Much of the rectitude exhaled by Godoy's apologia, published (1835) in penurious Parisian exile, towards the end of a long life, might be attributed no doubt to the fact that his principal enemies were deprived of retort, being dead. An elusive, somewhat enigmatic character, perhaps more of pasteboard than steel. Lord Holland, who knew Godoy fairly well, awards him high marks in *Foreign Reminiscences* (1850) for 'humanity and magnanimity'; the eminent Whig being under the impression, mistakenly, that the Prince of the Peace was of humble birth – a mistake due no doubt to the nickname of *El Choricero* ('The Pork-Butcher') with which the populace endowed him, due to his being a native of Estremadura, the province then as now of pig-breeders. Godoy's family were actually of the impoverished nobility. Two of his brothers had no difficulty in proving eight generations of blue blood for admission to one of the Military Orders.

Spanish opinion of his character and his statecraft remains divided. What seems one of the latest examens to date, that of the Academician-historian Fernández Almagro, dismisses him as an opportunist and a rhapsodist (*fantaseador*). To Goya, at all events, he was a friend and an admirer; fundamental good-nature would even lead him to take the trouble to acquire an established sign-language to converse with the artist when Goya became totally deaf.

See PLATES XXIV & XXV
pp. 139–42

As the Queen's favourite Godoy could hardly be anything but a confirmed enemy of the Duchess of Alba, whom her Majesty so detested. But though Maria Luisa and Godoy were to behave a trifle ungracefully after the Duchess's sudden death by having her fantastic will annulled and acquiring a few of her art-treasures, including Goya's 'Two Majas', allegations in some quarters that the pair had the Duchess poisoned were undoubtedly absurd. It seems almost unnecessary to add to all this that Carlos IV was devoted to 'our dear Manuel' and deemed him a fine fellow to the end. Mr Harris, then British Ambassador to Madrid, had judiciously summed up the King, then Infante, in a despatch some years earlier: 'a stout, healthy prince with a good heart and a clear head; but by a neglected education, and a continued suite of childish amusements, neither the one nor the other does him credit'. The same might be applied to one or two more princes in contemporary Europe, no doubt.

The new reign, then, opened for Goya with every prospect of continued success. To attempt to keep pace with his production would be irksome. A

93

self-portrait – yet another – of 1788 – shows a Goya in velvet with spectacles, sidewhiskers, and the old challenge in eye and mouth. 'So what?' might well be written underneath. No doubt aggressiveness was not now his habitual bearing. He cannot have lacked charm of some sort; a few rough Aragonese edges must by now have worn off in contact with patrician society; anything of the *bon bourru* remaining to him would be more piquant than otherwise to what used to be called the jaded votaries of high-life. Contemplating the *Vendimia* once more, it may well occur to the thoughtful that the idealized male figure of the artist on the right, so smartly attired, so graceful, gay, and insouciant in gesture, is not entirely a figment of imagination, or even aspiration. Under the Duchess's spell a somewhat new Goya might well have emerged by now, hardly recognizable by the hicks of Saragossa. The official Goya was to remain, standing no nonsense, for purposes of self-portraiture.

Within four months of the new accession the minister Floridablanca, who had posed for Goya's portrait of him a few years previously with some hauteur and paid for it ('All in good time, Goya, all in good time') with some reluctance, announced to all officialdom concerned that the King had been pleased to appoint Don Francisco Goya Painter to the Household (*Pintor de Cámara*), at 54,000 *reales*. Goya reported this new success to Zapater with a whoop. Not long beforehand he had been complaining to his friend of a rush of commissions and not having enough time to give to 'things I like' (*cosas de mi gusto*). The type of picture he was no doubt referring to was a portrait of Carlos III, of 1780, ordered by the Banco de San Carlos, now the Bank of Spain: a banal 'official' confection, good enough perhaps for a leading bank but, as a work signed by Goya, negligible. Perhaps official portraits bored him; perhaps he was not in the best of health at the moment. There are several unexplained illnesses in Goya's life, revealing that the stocky ex-rustic was not as rock-like as he looked. Whether the deafness due to become total and permanent was already afflicting him at intervals is not ascertainable, but seems likely. It would take complete charge of him before long, hastened it seems by the most romantic of travel-accidents. Another explanation may be considered in due course.

★   ★   ★

Goya may now be said to have arrived; the favourite and official painter of royalty; an intimate of the highest circles of a rich and frivolous society of which, privately, he cherished no great opinion – or such might be gathered from a few slightly disparaging and apologetic references to his environment which crop up here and there in confidence to Martin Zapater. That Goya never found himself beglamoured by success at any time seems a fair assumption, and that streak of rustic self-sufficiency enabling him to keep his head undoubtedly appealed to the Duchess Maria Cayetana, surrounded by fops and flatterers.

Self portrait, 1787–1800
oil on canvas
$19\frac{5}{8} \times 11\frac{3}{4}$ in. (50 × 30 cm.)
Musée Goya, Castres

See PLATE VII p. 56

See p. 28

94

His painting was certainly affected by environment. Critics have noted the silvery greys and greens and vermilions and other pastel-tints – a special blue above all – which begin to lighten his palette from this period and which flowered in 1788 in the delicate tints of the *Pradera de San Isidro*, co-existent with the vigorous colouring of his proletarian studies. A contemporary engraving of Madrid from the same western viewpoint as Goya's reveals the etherealizing power of the master's brush. Against the sky on high sloping ground stands the same distant frieze of domes and spires. On the left is the massive pile of the Palacio Real. Through a low foreground wanders the shallow Manzanares, its nearer bank covered with trees which Goya will largely abolish. A spectacular bridge invites all the satire it inspired. Another bridge, a small one, is of curiously Japanese aspect. The general effect is slightly arid; the prospect seems at first glance hardly a playground for Madrilene society, as it nevertheless was. Critics who deduce that Goya took his inspiration from Watteau may be incorrect. To Zapater he complained of his difficulties.

Musing over the *Pradera* today, one feels it difficult to resist reading into this apotheosis of aristocratic picnicking a deliberate irony; the gay, graceful crowd, the coloured silks and satins, the cocked hats and silk stockings, the flirtations and the laughter, the pearly shimmering atmosphere in which Madrid on the horizon takes an air of faëry; the distant unheard rumblings across the Pyrenees over all. . . . Three years later the tocsins of Paris were to announce the beginning of the end of this kind of privileged world; a king arrested in flight and imprisoned; Demos asserting fantastic rights; the

Pradera de San Isidro (Grassland of San Isidro), about 1788
oil on canvas
$17\frac{3}{8} \times 37$ in. (44 × 94 cm.)
Museo del Prado, Madrid

Isidro's Chapel on the
stival Day, about 1788
on canvas
× 17⅜ in. (42 × 44 cm.)
seo del Prado, Madrid

Church marked for extinction; society riven from top to bottom; the dying Mirabeau cursing the tempest he had unleashed. It may be that Goya had no more sombre intuition in the creation of this idyll than had Watteau with the *Voyage à Cythère*, and that any attempt to discern prophecy in it is what pedants call otiose. Certainly a streak of Jacobinism, encouraged perhaps by a few fashionable or literary contacts – the outbreak of the Revolution revealed, as might be expected, a clique of sympathizers in advanced Madrilene circles – will be more or less perceptible in him a few years hence. Quite obviously the Aragonese *baturro* was never mesmerized by the brilliant world his genius had conquered.

By the 1780s there was something dissolvent in the air of Europe. More than likely the news from Paris in 1791 did not greatly astonish or consternate Don Francisco Goya, named in 1799 First Painter to the King. One can even hear him grunting in select tavern-company that 'they' had long been asking for it. But with or without satiric intent the *Pradera* remains a thing of light, colour, beauty, and delicacy of handling unique so far in Goya's achievement.

He may now be visualized as working daily like a beaver, and in leisure hours thoroughly caught up by the social merry-go-round in the Duchess's train; routs, balls, picnics, theatricals, whether in Madrid or one of the Alba country houses; in the season, bullfights. . . . We may pause for a moment to essay a glimpse of the virtuoso at home.

★   ★   ★

La Tirana, 1792
oil on canvas
$81\frac{1}{8} \times 51\frac{1}{8}$ in. (206 × 130 cm.)
Real Academia de Bellas Artes
de San Fernando, Madrid

June 1790 or thereabouts. On a bright blue morning Don Francisco Goya, painter to the Household and to half the leading Spanish nobility, is entering the studio of his house in Madrid, Calle del Desengaño, No. 1, then a very good address.

Goya is now verging on his fifties; the same square imperious figure, rather foppishly dressed, with thick grizzling hair; somewhat deaf, and by no means in good health or, sometimes, temper. The studio – an inventory of the house survives – is an attractive airy apartment, as befits a fashionable painter who charges a great deal and knows the value of money. The stipend attached to his recent royal appointment is pocket-money compared with the rest of his present income. He has a handsome house, furnished in accordance; the drawing-room elegant with yellow damask and gilt; armchairs, a large mirror, splendid cabinets. In the studio, not described, we may imagine a half-finished portrait on the easel. The sparse but elegant furniture includes a chair or two, a cabinet, a small table, a model's throne. A sofa in yellow or red damask might possibly, if gifted with speech like a similar article of furniture in a cynically diverting novel of the 1730s by Crébillon *fils*, have a tale or two to tell. Another notable room in Goya's house is a library valued at 1,500 *reales*. It is perhaps no surprise that the inventory of this apartment is chiefly concerned with coffers in it containing 55,000 *reales*-worth of jewellery. Goya's taste in pictures is naturally interesting. On various walls are mentioned a Correggio, two Tiepolos, two Velázquez portraits – possibly copies – a series of prints by Rembrandt, Piranesi, and Wouvermans, and a number of works of his own, notably a portrait of the Alba in a black mantilla, hanging in the dining-room and hence before his eyes at least once a day.

See PLATE XII p. 78

At this moment Goya's studio awaits a sitter. Some pupil or assistant has everything ranged and ready for the master's entrance – paint, oils, brushes, mahlstick. The easel is uncovered. The model's throne is prepared. On a side-table, no doubt, stand refreshments on a silver tray; on another, perhaps, a fan, a decorative flask of smelling-salts, and any other feminine requirements in a crisis. As Goya casts a searching glance around, a manservant announces the arrival of his sitter, some woman of rank, one of such an extensive clientele nowadays that it is no wonder that one or two portraits of this period are not of the first class. During the morning session one or two of his fashionable friends may pay him a call. Rather curiously, and contrary to the general practice of the profession, at least nowadays. Goya seems to have had no objection on occasion to the presence of a third party while he was at the easel. It is true that visitors had to behave themselves. At the least interruption during work, it is recorded, Goya was liable to fly into a spectacular rage and even to turn the offender, if his rank permitted, out of the studio.[1] One can hardly see a third person being present when the Duchess was being painted.

See PLATE II p. 34

See p. 23

The 1790s were to produce outstanding work in portraiture: the earliest study of Maria Cayetana and her little white dog; self-posed beauties like the Marquesa de la Merced; the famous Madrilene actress known as La Tirana; his brother-in-law Bayeu, frowning characteristically. The al fresco full-length of the Duchess is a triumph of finesse. Standing against a background of faintest grey with rising ground behind, wearing a white muslin gown with a broad girdle of crimson encircling a slim waist, her celebrated cascade of black hair flowing well below the shoulder, she points with her right hand to the sandy ground at her feet, whereon is legibly traced the inscription 'A la Duquesa de Alba; Fco. de Goya 1795'. A little white dog of seemingly near-Pekingese breed stands on her left. The portrait was painted, think some experts, in the grounds of the Alba town house in the Real Calle del Barquillo. A fleeting resemblance to a wax doll may – who knows? – have been deliberate; a private jest between the pair, perhaps, directed at her intense animation and zest for life. The features are faultless, though whether the Duchess can be correctly described here as a flaming beauty depends no doubt on the observer's taste and experience. Disraeli's remark about 'features which in moments of despondency we are apt to describe as classic' recurs inevitably in this connection. The eyes are certainly magical; black, haughty, magnificent. The hands are what the French would call *quelconques* – Goya is curiously ineffective with hands. The mouth is hardly more than a slit. But he certainly exhibits a great lady more fascinatingly alive than any of Gainsborough's duchesses.

Contemplating this and other portraits, drawings, and etchings, some of them so intimate, one may ask oneself again what she found in Goya to attract her. Genius and proletarian virility and forthrightness counted for much, doubtless. They certainly shared a ruling passion also. At this period, one may recall again, the *fiesta nacional* had became an art and a science. For the first time in history the bull of caste, fearless and intelligent, the bull of *nobleza*, had by now become distinguishable by characteristics still recognized in breeds like the Jijona, the Vistahermosa, the Vásquez and the Cabrera, all named after the original breeds.[2] Goya's esteem of the fighting bull is

See pp. 240–45

evidence alike in his letters to Zapater and the *Tauromaquia* series. The

---

[1] An imaginary painting of the studio many years later by Francisco Domingo y Marqués, showing Goya's visitors dancing to the castanets, seems unlikely.

[2] Some modern authorities disagree.

Tomb design possibly for the
Duchess of Alba
sepia wash
Museo del Prado, Madrid
(Prado No. 407)

(opposite) *Commedia del' Arte*
oil on panel
16⅞ × 12⅝ in. (43 × 32 cm.)
Museo del Prado, Madrid

Duchess not only loved the *toro bravo* but, as we have seen, at one time bred him. It is a bond not to be overlooked in their relations, and the three-act drama on the sand, as magnetic a spectacle for Spaniards of every social class today as in Goya's time, need call in these pages for none of the ritual niff-naffery commonly evoked in (say) foxhunters.

Whatever, then – to sum up – drew the Duchess to Goya, it cannot have been any graces of mind or physique; he was no Apollo, and certainly no intellectual wizard with tongue or pen; moreover, he was increasingly deaf. On the other hand, artistic genius combined with intense virility are assets powerful enough to captivate, for a time, a wayward great lady. That the Duchess Maria Cayetana tired first is nothing remarkable.

> *Un soplo de inconstancia, de fastidio,*
> *O de capricho femeníl . . .*[1]

He was to let her off, an outburst or two apart, fairly lightly, and in his

[1] Jovellanos, *Epístola de Fabio a Anfriso.*

design for a now-vanished mural for her original tomb is nothing but mourn- See p. 101
ing and regrets.

In 1790 he took his wife, who was unwell, to Valencia for a change of air. Returning in the October of that same year he set about completing his most impressive series of designs for the *Real Fábrica*, which he delivered by the October of 1792. He had been almost compelled to do this since, on his return to Madrid in 1790, he had found that Ramón Bayeu, younger brother of Francisco, had been given an order for tapestry-cartoons by the Santa Bárbara manufactory, and at an increased fee. A furious exchange with Larena, the minister responsible, might have developed into something serious but for the intervention of Francisco Bayeu.

Towards the end of 1792 a mysterious illness struck him down and for some weeks he lay paralysed and delirious. When his superb constitution finally reasserted itself, in the early part of 1793, he found himself totally and permanently deaf for the rest of a long life. A possible source of the disaster may be discussed in due course. That it affected neither his outpouring of genius nor his ability to charm women – and above all, her Grace of Alba – is, however surprising, a fact to be abundantly illustrated henceforth. But it cannot have improved his temper.

If 1792 was a fateful year for Goya, it was an equally fateful one for twenty-four-year-old Don Manuel Godoy, now Duke of La Alcudia and chief See p. 92
minister of State, who may here intimate the same in a typically baroque excerpt from his memoirs:

> It was thus, as it were, in the midst of a convulsion of Nature, on the brink of a volcano whose dark smoke portended an immediate explosion, when terror was at our gates and agitated every mind, that I was unexpectedly summoned – O God! – to the helm of the State.

He owed this to the French Revolution, the progress of which was filling with foreboding more Spaniards than Carlos IV, who had found no more See PLATE XXIII p. 137
capable minister to cope with a possible spread of the conflagration south than the doddering Aranda, now dismissed. The men of the Terror had rejected with howls of contempt Carlos' proposal to spare the lives of the French royal family by handing them over to Spanish custody; and in Spain the forces of freedom and liberty had not a few sympathizers among the intelligentsia. It being no function of these pages to touch on the history of the period except insofar as it concerns the affairs of Goya, whom it apparently concerned very little down to the invasion of 1808, one may merely record that after a stoutly-resisted French military offensive in Catalonia in 1794 Godoy was able temporarily to conclude a passably advantageous peace treaty at Basle in the following year.

Goya's view of the opening scenes of the Revolution is not on record. The master's eye must have discerned in the Madrid newsprints not a few etchable incidents as the Terror developed. His eminent friend Leandro Fernández de Moratín the poet, lately returned from Paris, could have even described to him *de visu* the witchdance of Democracy past his hotel-window, bearing on pikes to the Temple, to amuse the royal prisoners, the severed head and the naked body of the innocent Princesse de Lamballe; a theme very adaptable for a *Capricho*. Unfortunately it was too late to expect Goya to listen much to anything. By 1793 he had become, as already remarked, permanently and totally deaf.

★   ★   ★

on Leandro Fernández de
Ioratín
l on canvas
$3\frac{3}{4} \times 22$ in. (73 × 56 cm.)
cal Academia de Bellas Artes
e San Fernando, Madrid

Two explanations of the cause of this visitation hold the field; the one romantic, the other the reverse. That his deafness might be traceable to adventure not unconnected with the story of the knife-wound in the Madrid alley at dawn, or even with student days in Rome, is apparently not impossible; the death under age of all but one of his children and his own periodic attacks of fainting and collapse might seem to point this way. That he lived into his eighties, beating another illustrious invalid of the century, that huge mass of disease Dr Johnson, by seven years, must be a tribute to a very tough constitution. How, to begin with, any invalid of the period survived thus long the sketchy sanitation – largely a matter, summer and winter, of open garbage-channels and cesspools – of London, Paris, Madrid, and every other European city seems at times miraculous. Even personal hygiene was not a fetish, at least in Nordic circles. For most of the century the use of strong perfume was a social duty not confined to exclusive Parisian salons, though men of rank and fashion like Topham Beauclerk, described by Horace Walpole as dirty, verminous, and a laudanum-addict, were doubtless rare.

Since no contemporary diagnosis of Goya's condition is available, a theory hinted at already may not be untenable. It is the theory that his deafness was directly due to syphilis, a major scourge of the eighteenth century, exploited by a myriad quacks. Modern medicine, it must be added, is not unanimous on this point. A French specialist, Dr Le Guen, rejected it in 1962, after careful study, on the grounds that Goya lived till eighty-two without showing any sign at any time of his life of mental deterioration. Recent application to Harley Street for an opinion on this matter elicited the following specialist comment:

> Goya's swoons, starting in early middle age and associated with progressive deafness, suggest episodes of acute vertigo resulting from degenerative or inflammatory lesions in the inner ear on one or both sides; to produce total deafness, of course, the inner ear on both sides would have to be affected. Beethoven became deaf from syphilis, and Goya could have done the same; but this is not very common in acquired syphilis even in the absence of effective modern treatment.
>
> There are other possible explanations, such as otosclerosis and the syndrome of Ménière (1860–1), which are not dependent on the patient's behaviour. Whatever the cause in Goya's case, it was obviously not a life-shortening disease, several possibilities being thus excluded.

There is no recorded echo in Goya's case of the despair suffered by Beethoven, to whom total deafness nevertheless brought harmonies of a sublimity till then unheard by mortal ears.[1] In Goya's case it probably thickened the mood of the future Black Paintings, but his disability seems not to have affected his relations with the world at large, apart from a penchant for equipping the Faculty in the *Caprichos* with asses' ears. This whimsy need not be taken too seriously. A portrait of himself prostrate in his doctor's arms, dated 1820, is inscribed 'Goya in gratitude to his friend Arrieta for the skill and care with which he saved his life in the acute and dangerous illness suffered at the end of the year 1819, at the age of 73.' And he was to live nine years more.

So much for one theory. An alternative reason for Goya's total deafness is decorative enough to defy all but the most hardshelled of sceptics. The authority (1860) is Yriarte, a serious writer, quoting a tradition apparently confirmed by the Duke of Osuna and by intimates like Zapater and Carderera. The story goes as follows:

In January 1793 Goya applied to the King for two months' sick-leave, which was granted. The Duchess Maria Cayetana, herself at the time not in normal health, bade him accompany her to Sanlúcar de Barrameda on the Guadalquivir, not far from Seville, where the Albas possessed yet another princely estate, to which, according to contemporary gossip, the Queen had just banished her.

For a Spanish lady of the Duchess's rank, wealth, and period, taking the road would normally imply a cavalcade of at least three or four coaches conveying guests, menservants, and waiting women, together with an armed escort on horseback. Studying that vibrant Goyaesque piece of action in paint called 'The Attack on the Coach' (1787), with its single commanding figure posed erect on the box, superb against the dawn, surveying, musket in hand, his comrades and the casualties lying below, any lover of the picturesque may regret that the crossing of the Sierra Morena, the mountain-barrier over which runs the highroad branching later to Granada and Seville, did not provide Goya with a real experience. In technique the Spanish brigand resembled the Red Indian; the noiseless stalk, the sudden rush. Unlike the highwayman of Great Britain he preferred, whenever possible, the knife to the pistol or the blunderbuss. A century or more earlier, it may be recalled, the horse and foot police known as the Santa Hermandad had cleared most of the Spanish highroads of these types. To clear out their mountain lairs was a different matter. One may agreeably devote a moment to musing on an affray which could have inspired a canvas more than matching the one above quoted.

'*Halt son li puis e li vals tenebros*' – the clang of the opening line of the

[1]'. . . aggravated by senseless physicians, cheated year after year in the hope of improvement, finally compelled to face the prospect of a *lasting malady* . . . but little more, and I would have put an end to my life.' (To his brothers Karl and Johann, 1802.)

PLATE XV. The Countess of Chinchon, 1800
oil on canvas
85 × 56¾ in. (216 × 144 cm.)
Collection the Duke of Sueca, Madrid

See p. 112

See PLATE XXXIX p. 188

See p. 63

The Attack on the Coach, 1787
oil on canvas
66¼ × 50 in. (168 × 127 cm.)
Collection the Duke of Montellano, Madrid

ATE XVI. Queen Maria Luisa
on canvas
¼ × 49¼ in. (209 × 125 cm.)
useo de Prado, Madrid

Chanson de Roland suits the Sierra Morena far more than the slightly disappointing Pyrenean slopes at Roncesvalles. As no Cervantes-addict will need reminding, the Sierra is part of the Quixote country; a desert of peaks, caves, and chasms, and the scene of a memorable all-night vigil. Crossing it, particularly from the south, is an impressive experience as the high-road achieves the thousand-feet climb to the Puerto de Despeñaperros, the Pass of the Throwing Down of the Moorish Dogs, traversed today by a series of tunnels through the rock. It would be here, at the summit, under the same angry night sky, with a bitter gale blowing, that the Duchess's cavalcade should have been abruptly halted by a fractured axle-tree. However, what is on record – according to the story – is sufficiently animated.

Amid the bawling and confusion following the accident on the Seville road Goya took charge, being doubtless not unwilling to afford an effete aristocracy a taste of plebeian quality. Ordering a roadside fire and calling for tools, he threw off his coat, tucked up his shirt-sleeves, performed the necessary repair, whatever it was, with efficient despatch, and, accepting congratulations with complacency, resumed his coat and his seat in the Duchess's coach, sweating profusely. Had any brigands materialized on this occasion to offer Don Francisco further scope for action such a diversion might conceivably have amused the Duchess, a woman of spirit capable of snatching up a pistol herself. As it was, Goya's reward for the night's performance was a fever which left him totally deaf for the remainder of his life.

Sceptics rejecting this ideal moral story for infant democrats rely chiefly on an alleged confusion of dates and – more important – the distance of Sanlúcar from Madrid, nearly five hundred miles, which would make the known return of Goya and the Duchess to Madrid within a month difficult, if not impossible. This does not seem a convincing rebuttal. The Duchess being a creature of impulse who invariably got her own way, the return journey for Goya's sake could well have begun long before the outward one was completed. It is permissible, noting such a temperament, to recall once more that a warm heart and a generosity lavished on high and low made the Duchess so generally loved that a long tribute from the poet Quintana lamenting her last illness in the cry of the populace at large:

> *Oh Dios! Si ella viviera,*
> *cesara nuestra mísera amargura,*
> *Lloráramos tal vez, y el llanto fuera*
> *de dulce gratitud y de ternura!*

> Ah God! If she is spared
> our bitter misery will vanish;
> perchance we may weep – but our cry
> will be one of sweet and tender gratitude!

– is devoid equally of exaggeration and sycophancy. Her vicious enemy Queen Maria Luisa, writing on one occasion to Godoy that 'the Alba was here last evening, crazy as in her early days', was actually paying her a compliment of the finest.

In the absence, therefore, of evidence making Yriarte's story impossible, the accident on the road to Sanlúcar, which could have inspired the master Granados to add a nocturne to the *Goyescas*, might be accepted as a supplementary factor in Goya's deafness for the next thirty-five years and the basis of most of his later misanthropy. For a man of his stubborn and irritable Aragonese temper it must have been for a time, whatever its source, a burden almost intolerable.

Work provided the unfailing anodyne. He flung himself into the completion of a series of satirical etching-plus-aquatints[1] later known as *Los Caprichos* *See* pp. 219–28 ('Caprices') on which he had been engaged for some six years. In 1799 eighty plates were published in one volume at 320 *reales* with the title of *Ydioma Universal* ('The Universal Tongue'). That this volume was within forty-eight hours delated to the Inquisition and duly ordered by the King to be withdrawn for revision is no great surprise. Goya had made the Holy Office a notable target.

Moribund and discredited as it had become by the 1790s, this State department was still to be reckoned with. Though the Age of Reason had now abolished corporeal sanctions even in Spain, opposition to the established religion was still – as in England, where a dogged minority continued to pay extra taxes and enjoy official ostracism – punishable.[2] Goya's printed declaration that his object was to castigate 'a number of prejudices, impostures, and hypocrisies consecrated by this age' covered, it seemed, several plates turning Holy Office judicial procedure into ridicule. No less his target were the overcrowded religious orders, concerning which a plate entitled *Ya es hora* ('Now it's time') appeared to advocate a clean sweep. Religious devotion in itself would seem to be guyed in the plate *Lo que puede un sastro* ('What a tailor can do') in which a crowd is seen kneeling before a tree displaying in its branches a crumpled monastic habit. Was the artist attacking superstition, for which no theologian could arraign him, or had he a broader target? Whatever the truth may have been, Goya took steps to avoid prosecution by the shrewdest of moves. Thus in a hasty letter to the King:

> Since foreigners are very desirous to acquire the original plates, for fear lest they fall into such hands after my death I wish to present them to the King, my master, for his collection of engravings.

The Inquisition was checkmated. Goya moreover accompanied his gift, in the ritual form, with a petition, requesting a modest annuity – not for himself but for his remaining child, the boy Javier, himself a promising painter *See* p. 31

---

[1] The aquatint, a French invention of the 1750s, is a glorified etching with stronger tonal effects, produced by the employment of resin on the plate.

[2] As late as 1782 two poor Catholic labouring families in Yorkshire were sold up for non-payment of the regulation fine for non-attendance at the Established Church.

Ya es hora.

Lo que puede un Sastre!

(above left) Now it's time (No. ⁙ of The Caprices), 1797–99 ⁙ching ⁙he British Museum, Madrid

(above right) What a tailor can ⁙o (No. 52 of The Caprices), ⁙797–99 ⁙ching ⁙he British Museum, London

(wrote his father), wishing to go abroad to study. The King complied immediately with an annuity of 12,000 *reales* – about £200, perhaps – and the *Caprichos* were duly reissued, unrevised, in 1803. The Madrid newspaper *El Diario*, dated the 19th February 1799, had already printed an advertisement on the artist's behalf:

Persuaded that the censure of human error and vices, which would appear to be the peculiar function of eloquence and poetry, can be likewise extended to art, the artist has selected from the innumerable extravagances and follies common to human society . . . those which seem to him most aptly to invite ridicule, at the same time indulging his fancy. Since the greater number of plates collected in this work represent figures of imagination, it may be assumed without temerity that their shortcomings will be easily excused by the intelligent . . .

Like poetry, painting selects from the universal what seems most apropos of its ends, uniting in a single figure of fantasy character and circumstance which Nature presents as shared among many. From this conviction, ingeniously interpreted, results pleasing travesty, whereby the skilful deviser earns the title not of servile copyist but of inventor.

Plate No. 1, the hirsute self-portrait with the wide sombrero cocked over militant eyes, well conveys the artist's invitation to critics clerical and lay, singly or in bulk. Like most caricatures these plates are a catharsis, recalling that offered by the classic fairground exercise whereby the cash-customer dispels his private fears and anxieties by hurling wooden balls at crockery or, better still, at a battered wedding-group or a Happy Family. Hence the *Caprichos* naturally throw much light on the satirist's subconscious. *See* p. 29

As a caricaturist-critic of the passing show Goya is less of a club-brandishing *farceur* than his contemporary Hogarth, wielding likewise a less sophisticated rapier than his successor Daumier. But under the brilliant lighting of the long glass cases in the Prado those rows of original studies, each on a sheet about 6 × 7 in., exhale a force almost hypnotic. In a minimum of strokes Goya can lend the human features a cunning, an imbecility, a malignancy which needs no footnote; his fantasy, moreover, is richer and more ruthless than that of either of his brethren in the trade above cited. As André Malraux has remarked, the *Caprichos* are not illustrations, they are a literature; the fruit of the dreams of a genius obsessed by his own creations.

When discussing the *Caprichos* it is of great interest to study a list of inscriptions or footnotes to the plates which appear in a nineteenth-century

posite left)
rlesque vision
ck ink
× 5½ in. (20 × 14 cm.)
useo del Prado, Madrid
rado No. 264)

posite centre) That is how
eful men end up, about 1810
ck ware ink
× 5½ in. (20 × 14 cm.)
useo del Prado, Madrid
rado No. 46)

posite right) Drawing often
ociated with The Caprices
awing in sepia pen and ink
× 5½ in. (20 × 14 cm.)
useo del Prado, Madrid
rado No. 32)

ght) May God forgive her! –
d it was her mother (No. 16 of
e Caprices), 1797–99
hing
e British Museum, London

Dios la perdone: Yera su madre

manuscript, although almost certainly not in Goya's hand. They can be as disconcertingly banal as one or two of the plates themselves. In No. 16, for example, an outstanding case, a well-dressed hussy is sweeping disdainfully past an old beggar-woman beseeching a dole. The plate is entitled 'May God forgive her! – and it was her mother', and the comment matches this inspiration:

(from left to right) Plates from
The Caprices: They say 'I will'
and give their hand to the first
that comes along (No. 2);
Hunting for teeth (No. 12); Is
the pupil any wiser? (No. 37);
The sleep of reason produces
Monsters (No. 43); Look out!
There it goes! (No. 66)
etching
The British Museum, London

She quitted her native soil very young, served her apprenticeship at Cadiz, came to Madrid, and won a lottery. There are daughters who can arrive at not knowing mothers forced to beg for their living.

Since Goya can hardly be said, judging by the price attached, to be aiming his work at the many-headed, such a pink-sugar offering seems quaint. But one lapse into unsophistication does not affect the range of a macabre imagination. The Goyaesque underworld of fantastic and richly-assorted *diablerie* is to reveal itself here for the first time. In Plate 12 ('Hunting for teeth') a woman veiling her face with a handkerchief is wrenching a tooth from the jaw of a hanged corpse. 'The teeth of the hanged', explains the footnote, 'are good for weaving spells. Of what is a lovesick woman not capable?' The witchcraft *motif* will repeat itself hence at regular intervals with Wagnerian effect, alleviated by satire of varying quality at the expense of fops, doctors, procuresses, charlatans, pedants, friars, inquisitors, and contemporary Spanish society at large.

It is plain that the artist takes particular pleasure in his phantasmagoria of goblins and gargoyles, witches and satyrs, phantasmal and hideous human shapes with bats' faces and birds' or asses' heads, grotesque monsters and nightmare visions of all kinds, and it is a deprivation to the later science of psycho-analysis that the apostle Freud, apparently unacquainted with the art of Goya, failed to examine this world of fantasy from the angle of dream-symbolism. Doubtless his fancies would have turned out fundamentally sexual, a judgement by no means self-evident to the uninformed.

Not a few of the *Caprichos* are the bluntest of satire, notable chiefly for the consummate skill of the etching-needle; for example No. 2 ('They say "I will" and give their hand to the first that comes along'), in which a young woman, shielding her face with an open fan and escorted by two repugnant duennas, extends a hand to the old crock of a bridegroom escorting her to the altar. This, we are told, is a shaft directed against 'blind' unions, such as are contracted by princesses and maids of honour. In No. 37 ('Is the pupil any wiser?') a four-footed ass in a pedagogue's gown, brandishing a ferule with

See p. 24

(from left to right) Plates from The Caprices: Tale-bearers (No. 48); The Chinchilla's (No. 50); First attempts (No. 60); good teacher! (No. 68); Wait till they've finished greasing you! (No. 67)

etching

The British Museum, London

one hoof, is teaching the ABC to six smaller asses. Anticlericalism of varying shade takes charge now and then, the mendicant Orders naturally receiving their ration of lash. In Plate 48 ('Tale-bearers') an enormous man-faced bat, mounted on a flying cat hovers over a group of slumbering friars, while fantastic figures murmur to right and left. According to the inscription this represents the sacrament of penance, which seems to have irked Goya at the moment to the pitch of blasphemy. Plate 50 ('The Chinchilla's), in which he returns to social satire, features a couple of mummified human forms, richly costumed and girt with the dress-rapiers of the aristocracy. Their mouths are wide open and padlocks close their enormous ears. One of them, reclining, holds a rosary; into the mouth of the other, standing, a man with asses' ears is pouring something with a spoon from a nearby cauldron. Despite an informative title – a chinchilla is the least useful type of rat – this plate remains a trifle obscure, even with the footnote to the effect that admired native stupidity is increased by spoonfed ignorance.

Goya's sense of humour may now be more or less defined. It is ruthless and sardonic, with at times a dash of sadism almost recalling the Tiberan devil-dance masks decorating Mr Lurgan's establishment in *Kim*; 'horned masks, scowling masks, masks of idiotic terror'. Such a plate as No. 65, entitled 'Where is Mummy going?' illustrates his fancy at its most playful. A monstrous naked female, elderly, bloated in every limb, is being borne along and aloft by three fantastic goblin-shapes, one mounted on a white owl; a furry cat flying above holds aloft a parasol. In the distance, below, lies a village in a valley. Underneath is the footnote: 'Mamma is hydropic and has been ordered to take the air. It is God's will that she could have some pleasure.' Here, so to speak, is Goyaesque fun and delight in ugliness for its own sake. Two or three plates immediately following convey to some extent a carry-over of this jovial mood. In 'Look out! There it goes!' a man and a woman fly through the air with bats' wings, clutching a broomstick and a serpent ridden by a cat. 'Here', explains the inscription, 'goes a woman riding on a crippled devil, which is sometimes useful.' In 'Wait till they've finished greasing you!'

an impatient he-goat with one human foot, striving to take off for flight, is restrained by a demon daubing one foot with a brush from an earthen pot; a squinting witch squats in the foreground. In the plate following ('A good teacher!') an attractive young naked witch shares a broomstick in flight with an ugly aged one, naked likewise, while an owl flies above.

A sufficiency of commentatory ink has been expended on Plate 43, entitled 'Sleep of reason produces monsters'. A male human figure lies on his side asleep, like Gulliver among the Lilliputians. On, around, and above him swoops and hovers a horde of tiny faëry grotesques – owls, bats, cats, 'apes and anticks'. Into this inspiration has been read a tribute to *La Raison* which any contemporary worshipper of that goddess north of the Pyrenees would applaud. As we would say today, Goya was playing up to the Left. There is no doubt that, though no deep philosopher, he was by temperament on the fringes of this school of thought all his life. The interpretation of No. 43 is non-committal enough:

See p. 112

> Abandoned by Reason, Fancy produces monsters; united with her, she is the mother of the Arts.

What the cloud of tricksy apparitions actually signified at the time is another matter. There have not been wanting commentators to perceive in this plate a shaft directed at established order, starting again with the Inquisition, a natural target, and, perhaps, including institutions far more venerable. Apart from such implications, if they were really in Goya's mind, the fantasy, brilliantly drawn, is unremarkable.

He returns to native Goyaesque form in Plate 60, entitled *Ensayos* ('First attempts'), which might ideally adorn the messroom of any Air Force training-squadron. A formidable squatting he-goat with amply curling horns dominates the murky scene. In front of him an elderly witch, stark naked like her plump young instructress, floats awkwardly horizontal a couple of feet up, held steady by the hair; the feet of the instructress herself barely skim the earth. In the foreground a couple of cats mount guard over a pot of magic unguent with a damaged human skull lying beside it. The expression of the seated cat, facing the spectator, is admirably sinister. On the ground a couple of distaffs lie ready for trial-flights. An indescribable air of routine overhangs the scene; it is the kind of performance, Goya seems to be saying, you might come across at any time in these parts during your evening walk. This is one of the most rollicking of the *Caprichos*, exhibiting a mockery of the Dark notably absent from The Black Paintings of years later, when he was a morose refugee *pro tem.* from humanity, and himself the prey of a whole covey of devils.

It is inevitable to quote Baudelaire:

See p. 113

> *Goya, cauchemar plein de choses inconnues,*
> *De foetus qu'on fait cuire au milieu des sabbats,*
> *De vieilles au miroir et d'enfants toutes nues*
> *Pour tenter des démons ajustant leurs bas . . .*

PLATE XVII. The Spell, about 1798
oil on canvas
$16\frac{1}{2} \times 11\frac{3}{4}$ in. (42 × 30 cm.)
Museo Lázaro Galdiano, Madrid

(overleaf) PLATE XVIII.
Inquisition Scene, about 1794
oil on panel
$17\frac{3}{4} \times 28\frac{3}{8}$ in. (45 × 72 cm.)
Real Academia de Bellas Artes de San Fernando, Madrid

Who is the more devoted?
(No. 27 of The Caprices),
1797–99
etching
The British Museum, London

Goya, nightmare full of things unknown –
of human embryos cooked in the midst of
witches' sabbaths, of hags at the mirror and
young naked girls adjusting their stockings
for the luring of demons . . . – *Les Phares*.

The poet is here, a precisian might suggest, drawing a trifle more on his own imagination than the artist's. The elegant culinary inspiration is not Goya's, nor is the luring of the demons; he would probably have been delighted to embellish the *Caprichos* with either idea. Nevertheless these lines continue to express the quintessence, so far, of the Goyaesque *gaieté noire*. To the student of English history they must irresistibly recall the reply of unfortunate Queen Elizabeth Tudor in her final years to courtiers urging her to bed. 'If you were in the habit of seeing such things in your bed as I do when in mine, you would not persuade me to go there.' A contemporary Goya could have illustrated the old woman's terrors to perfection, not excluding a covey of hanged-and-disembowelled-alive priests on the wing, gibbering horribly. In the *Caprichos* the sinister frequently has a tinge of the comic. The Black Paintings will be another matter.

Whether the *Caprichos* surprised his aristocratic clientele is not on record. What nobody in Madrilene society could possibly miss in them was a demonstration that the course of true love, insofar as this applies to his *See p. 30* relations with the Duchess, was not running invariably smooth. In Plate 61 (*Volaverunt*) an obvious representation of Maria Cayetana, with butterfly wings on her head and arms outflung, stands poised for flight on three figures resembling witches but identified, rightly or wrongly, as the three most famous bullfighters of the age. The inscription:

> The Duchess of Alba. Three toreros elevate her on their heads.

To deduce from this caricature a furious attack of jealousy requires no great penetration.[1] Every drawing-room in Madrid doubtless made the most of it. Goya himself may have known a qualm or two. The half-length portrait, painted about this time, of the incomparable Pedro Romero pays tribute, possibly reluctant, to the lean patrician features, the steadfast dark eyes, the firm lips, the long shapely right hand of the proletarian genius who made bullfighting a science and an art. Romero remains a nonpareil and a legend *See p. 103* for audacity, grace, and skill, as the poet Moratín's ode to him proclaims. Lecturing at the Madrid Athenaeum a few years ago on the art of the corrida, the eminent torero Domingo Ortega saluted him as a Titan. 'Can you imagine what it means to kill nearly six thousand bulls without once being lifted off your feet?' At the period of Goya's portrait the master had completed sixteen of his twenty-three years in the arena at a period when, according to Ortega, anarchy reigned on the ranches and the fighting bull was distinguished more for vicious cunning than for the *nobleza* which should be his

PLATE XIX. Giant figure wearing
cape and hood
drawing in sanguine wash
Museo del Prado, Madrid
(Prado No. 195)

PLATE XX. Procession of
flagellants, about 1794
on panel
⅛ × 28¾ in. (41 × 72 cm.)
Real Academia de Bellas Artes
San Fernando, Madrid

[1] A more violent plate may be reserved for discussion in its proper place.

hallmark. Caricaturing such a popular idol and fellow-genius as Romero might have afforded even a Goya a stab of ensuing regret.

Four – to return – of the *Caprichos* concern other headline personages with what might be styled a *double-entendre* approach. In No. 27 ('Who is the more devoted?') a gallant, hat in hand, is conversing with a disdainful lady over the footnote 'The Duchess of Alba and the artist'. Plate 5 ('Two of a kind') depicts another tête-à-tête; a lady of high rank, in black with a mantilla, a gentleman with cocked hat and rapier, and a couple of old women in the background sniggering at them – the footnote: 'Maria Luisa and Godoy'. The Favourite has two more personal *Caprichos* to his address. In No. 56 ('Rise and fall') a seated satyr raises, by the feet, a figure in a richly-embroidered coat, plastered with orders and decorations, the hair and hands emitting smoke and flame, while two other personages fall headlong from above. 'The Prince of the Peace', explains the note. 'Luxury lifts him by the feet. His head is filled with the smoke and flame he discharges on rivals.' Finally, in Plate 72 ('You won't get away') a beautiful smiling young girl is pursued by four winged monsters. Footnote: 'La Duten, pursued by Godoy, endures and weeps.' It is curious to find the Favourite, with all his short-comings never unamiable to Goya, thus pilloried. Doubtless the unaccount-able touchiness of the artistic temperament may be blamed; perhaps, again, the enmity towards the Duchess displayed by the Queen, Godoy's mistress; perhaps, also, Godoy's responsibility, in the eyes of the majority, for Spain's misfortunes at this later period. *See p.* 119

It may be agreed that some of the *Caprichos* are none too easy to probe for meaning, whereas one or two are simplicity itself. The witchcraft-obsession inspires, imaginatively and artistically speaking, the cream of the collection, the anticlerical *motif* producing – as might be expected – little more than the repetition of themes worn threadbare by satirists down the ages. The Inquisition, now doddering to its end, was a fair enough mark. To quote a modern Spanish theologian, it had been 'historically if not morally defensible'. In its time, as the liberal philosopher Salvador de Madariaga has agreed, there was a case for it. It preserved the 'idea' of Spain spiritually and cultur-ally intact; as a State department it saved the country from the lootings and destruction, the despairs and the chaos of the Reform, the crazy sects and the odious new plundering rich. By the late eighteenth century, however, the Inquisition had become an anachronism of which the intelligentsia were ashamed, due long for abolition. At this period its ex-officials could even include a mythologist like Llorente, whose destruction before dismissal, after composing a history of the establishment, of the documents pertaining was reasonable enough from his standpoint. The less vindictive Lea was to express his conviction a century later, in his own study of the Spanish Inquisition, that the number of its victims – actually unascertainable – must be considerably smaller than is generally imagined.

Outmoded and enfeebled by the end of the eighteenth century, with the

Two of a kind
(No. 5 of The Caprices),
1797–99 etching
The British Museum, London

Rise and fall
(No. 56 of The Caprices),
1797–99 etching
The British Museum, London

You won't get away
(No. 72 of The Caprices),
1797–99 etching
The British Museum, London

(right) Don Antonio Llorente,
about 1813
oil on canvas
74¾ × 44⅞ in. (189 × 112 cm.)
The Museum and Art Gallery,
São Paolo

French Revolution to deal it a final blow, it was the most obvious and popular of Aunt Sallies and a gift to the cynical. The *auto da fé* had gone out of fashion, doubtless to Goya's regret – he could have decorated that theme with some pretty fancies – but the tribunals dealing with offences against religion and morals remained, and their hooded acolytes Goya exploits with gusto. The gestures of one of these personages in the canvas entitled 'Inquisition Scene', are so dramatic that the genial smile of the gentleman in the armchair, one of the *familiares*, contemplating the prosecutor with silk-stockinged legs gracefully extended, seems positively Voltairean ('My *dear* sir! . . .'), and was doubtless so intended. Only two of the *Caprichos*, actually, are devoted to the tribunals of the Holy Office. In No. 23 ('As you sow') a woman wearing the *coroza*, the overall-badge of the guilty, is hearing her sentence read from a pulpit in a crowded hall. In No. 24 ('There was no remedy') a woman seated astride a donkey, hands tied, followed by two mounted alguacils, is sped by a jeering crowd on her way – according to the commentator – to execution, though the abolition of capital punishment by the Inquisition, one of Godoy's reforms, seems to make this unlikely.[1]

See PLATE XVIII p. 116–17

On a whole, indeed, Goya's satire at the Inquisition's expense is hardly

---

[1] Official records having been destroyed by the ex-inquisitor Llorente before dismissial, the date of the last execution by the Inquisition in Spain remains conjectural. From 1750 onwards its business steadily declined; the tribunal of Toledo (e.g.) dealt on an average with one offence a year. Godoy finally abolished the *auto-da-fe*, apparently long since inoperative.

more damaging than, say, a modern political cartoonist's onslaught on some outdated Government department. It amused the liberal, annoyed the conservative, and had no notable effect on the march of events. The Spanish Inquisition was suppressed, after fierce debate, by the Cortes in 1813, restored by Fernando VII a year later, a pallid ghost of its former self, and abolished for good in 1820. In its heyday it had exceeded the English or Elizabethan Inquisition in scope, being a State department of a vast empire, but fallen short of it in inventive savagery, having no genius like Master Richard Topcliffe to devise and direct the torture; nor were any of its victims disembowelled alive; nor, for that matter, were their heirs and descendants penalized by extra taxation for more than two hundred years. It seems only just to recall these differences in an age of more subtly scientific torture: the age of the Double-Think and the Conditioned Reflex, outlined by George Orwell in '1984'; the Abreaction and the Brainwash (or 'Thought-Reform').

Less explicable than the barbs directed at a moribund State department is Goya's obsession with witchcraft at a period when it was regarded by the majority of the European intelligent as a ridiculous old wives' tale. It may be noted that Spanish officials and clerics did as much to explode an agelong superstition as any infidel like Voltaire. As long ago as the 1600s the eminent inquisitor Antonio de Salazar had announced that the majority of admissions at witch-trials were hysterical nonsense, the fruit of imagination and terror; for asserting which at the famous trial of the Basque witches of Zugarramurdi he was freely ridiculed. Salazar's views were shared by an equally celebrated contemporary, the German Jesuit Friedrich von Spee, whose textbook *Cautio Criminalis* (1632) established that witchcraft trials involved continuous miscarriages of justice and bristled with serious abuses; for one single example, the employment of torture in examination by judges who could only justify themselves by discovering guilt. Only twenty years before the *Caprichos* the Spanish Benedictine theologian Feijóo had dealt with the whole tragic harlequinade afresh in *Cartas Eruditas y Curiosas*; exposing the stupidity of rustic evidence at witch-trials, the 'unworthy zeal' of judges to secure convictions, and the fact that the application – at times even the threat – of torture drove many of the unfortunate accused out of their minds, causing them to believe that they really were what they were alleged to be.

Goya's preoccupation with witchcraft at the end of the eighteenth century may seem therefore a trifle out of date. Artistic whimsy, native egotism and obstinacy, recollection of Aragonese old wives' tales, and a temperamental addiction to the fantastic-macabre may account for most of it. Why Freud ignored such an outstanding illustration of polymorphous perversity, maladjusted introversion, lack of automotor-control, unbalanced thyroid and pituitaries, and the rest of it, is curious. The fascination of the nightmare had not inspired such a master since the days of Bruegel and Bosch. It is, of course, perennial. One may imagine that Goya would have been delighted to listen, with an interpreter, to the old Sussex dame who described to Kipling

See PLATES VIII & XXXVII
p. 65 & p. 185

(opposite left) As you sow . . .
(No. 23 of The Caprices),
1797–99
etching
The British Museum, London

(opposite right) There was no remedy (No. 24 of The Caprices),
1797–99
etching
The British Museum, London

a village seance of the mid-Victorian era involving the sacrifice by a local 'wise woman' of a black cock at midnight. ('There was Something trying to get *in*, like.') And he might more swiftly than most have discerned in the late *magus* Aleister Crowley a charlatan.

That his witches are almost purely creatures of his own fancy seems obvious. The amount of practical witchcraft still existing in Spain in the late eighteenth century was negligible, even in the Basque country, in Old Castile, or outlying districts of his native Aragon, and was not taken seriously. 'By a strange paradox', remarks Julio Caro Baroja in a work already quoted, 'Spain was quicker than any other country to exchange judicial error for a more sane idea of the reality of witchcraft.' Being moreover no great student, Goya can hardly be visualized in the act of reading up the subject from standard medieval tomes, Latin or otherwise. His witches and sorcerers are nevertheless strenuously alive. One can hear their cries in flight – 'Garr! Garr! Garr! Right to left, left to right! Tatagran! Mazagran! Padul, Baalberith, Astaroth, help me!' – and imagine them at that midnight parody of the Mass which every major treatise describes. Some of the women are ancient hags of incredible ugliness; others beautiful and young. Goya plainly derives as much satisfaction out of depicting them all as Mrs Radcliffe and other novelists of the Gothic Bloodfreeze School did from the imaginary horrors of the cloister.

Hideous or comely, his witches are plainly what we style today 'dedicated'. Their features are alive with an ardour for – might one suggest? – conscientious and active non-welfare work which distinguishes them from, say, their professional sisters participating in the Walpurgis Night scenes of *Faust*. To suggest that Goethe's witches somewhat resemble in their chatter a coffee-party of lewd Weimar spinsters would probably be excessive, yet one may observe that Mephistopheles himself is a trifle critical. 'My dear', he says to a sorceress-witch exhibiting her stock-in-trade of bloodstained daggers, poisoned goblets, and so forth, 'you are behind the times. Try a few novelties.' There may exist likewise purists to complain that compared with those pictured in the vivid contemporary woodcuts illustrating the treatises of demonologists like Nicolas Rémy, Public Advocate of Lorraine, Bodin, Guazzo, and others, Goya's witches lack the sacred executive flame. We see them taking off for, or returning from, some rendezvous unknown. We do not see them actually exercising that essential spite against mankind – raising storms, blasting crops, abducting or murdering the new-born, spreading plague, and so forth – illustrated in the works above mentioned; being urged thereto by their inseparable familiars or Little Masters, whom Goya curiously excludes.

Still less – though we see them once or twice in conference – do we view Goya's witches at their public devotions, saluting the Great Goat with the Infamous Kiss or performing the ritual back-to-back dance, revived some years ago in London night clubs. Goya in fact seems chiefly interested in their

(left) HIERONYMUS BOSCH
The Seven Deadly Sins
Oil on panel
47¼ × 59 in. (120 × 150 cm.)
Museo del Prado, Madrid

(right) SIGNORELLI Antichrist
Fresco
The Cathedral, Orvieto

LICIEN ROPS
Satan Sowing the Tares
Drypoint
Bibliothèque Royale de
Belgique, Brussels

domesticity and hours of relaxation. That these could possess a Barriesque allure is perceptible from the fully-documented trial – after torture – of the North Berwick coven of the 1590s, whose admitted business was to destroy James VI and his recent bride Anne of Denmark by raising a storm during the royal return voyage. Their relaxation was, *inter alia*, a well-attended midnight conversazione and dance round North Berwick Church and churchyard – two hundred dancers, with Dr Fian as M.C. and the young organizing witch, Gellis Duncan, supplying the music with 'ane tromp' – which might have come out of *Auld Licht Idylls*. All work and no play makes Grimalkin a dull girl. It is reasonable likewise that the witch should have a home-life. Hence, perhaps Goya can hardly be arraigned for not concentrating chiefly on her duties. As well might Blake be blamed for not making the Angels of the Thirteen States in *America, a Prophecy*, wave a starred-and-striped flag apiece.

Doubtless Goya never lighted on the woodcuts illustrating Rémy and the others, which were not reprinted in his time. He may perhaps have browsed in the Royal Library, or some private collector's, on the work of earlier masters in the macabre-grotesque like Leonardo, Bruegel, Grünwald, and above all, Hieronymus Bosch. It is permissible to imagine him at his first sight of, say, Bosch's celebrated panorama of the Seven Deadly Sins, uttering a '*Tudios!*' half-ecstatic, half-envious. The dreadful mountain-island, like a flat-topped extinct volcano, with its caves and terraces rising from a grisly sea; its swarming, entangled, fantastic population of dog-headed, toad-headed demons and ghouls, with limbs like fair young girls, the hags with dangling breasts and the faces of evil babies embracing half-human shapes with long hairy spider-legs, the tables spread with loathsome fare, the

125

atmosphere of hopeless and eternal torment – all this would doubtless ravish and excite him. Though such peaks of orgiastic frenzy could never be attained by him – the Fleming was plainly mad – Bosch's phantasmagoria would obviously awaken a responsive chord. However, whether or not he happened on the work of the earlier masters, Goya's own rich dark imagination amply suffice him for plenty of zestful play on the macabre; a zest exacerbated, as has been reasonably conjectured, by the ordeal of deafness. We shall perceive when we come to the paintings in the Quinta del Sordo that the diablerie-obsession remains a constant.

PLATE XXI. The dome and apse of San Antonio de la Florida, 1798
fresco

In this connection it may or may not be significant, though it seems never to have been discussed, that amid the gambols of his witches and demons Goya introduces the figure of their Master very rarely; chiefly in The Black Paintings, and in the hierarchic and traditional guise of the Great Goat. *See* PLATE XXXIV p. 175 Goya could hardly be aware of course that rehabilitation of the Devil was just below the horizon. The process begun a little before his death by Byron, to be developed by Victor Hugo, exhibited no Master Aliboron of medieval nightmare but a Victim of divine injustice, noble, beautiful, wronged, and suffering. Dating from the 1820s–30s, it might, had it been publicised during his earlier career, conceivably have influenced Goya as to some extent it influenced that minor Goya of the mid-nineteenth century, the Flemish artist Félicien Rops. For the most part a specialist in frivolous *See* p. 125 diabolism for decadents, Rops proved capable of producing at least once a 'Satan Sowing the Tares' of sinister dignity, physically not far from the impressive Antichrist of Luca Signorelli at Orvieto. No doubt such musings *See* p. 125 are otiose, but no serious modern diabolist can afford to overlook these things.

4 Under two flags

See PLATE XXXVIII pp. 186–87

MEANWHILE Spain became involved in war for two violent years. In December, 1792, the Convention in Paris had rejected a proposal by Carlos IV through his ambassador that the French royal family should be handed over to Spanish safe-keeping. Lavish bribery of selected deputies had had no effect. On 7th March, 1793, the problem of unwanted royalty having been solved by the French the short way, the Republic declared war on the Spanish Bourbon, Louis XVI's cousin, with a list of seventeen grievances.

See p. 92

Carlos IV and Godoy, with the country behind them, accepted the challenge. The call for volunteers – Spain's standing army at the time was one of barely 36,000 – was ardently answered. From grandees down to smugglers and the blind ballad singers of Madrid the public's contributions to the war-chest poured in, with a profusion of cathedral and monastic plate, voluntarily surrendered by the clergy for melting. On 17th April a Spanish force under General Ricardos crossed the frontier, and by November it had driven the French back to Perpignan.

ATE XXII. Detail of the coration in San Antonio de la orida – this may be a portrait the Duchess of Alba, 1798 sco

A Spanish fleet sent to co-operate with the British off Toulon failed to do so, owing to reciprocated dislike. By 1795 the French had rallied and driven the Spanish forces in bitter fighting back into Catalonia. Spain's coadjutors had by now begun notably to lose their ardour. An incidental plot of Jacobin sympathizers in Madrid to assist further invasion was detected in time, and the ringleaders banished to the Indies. Since the French themselves seemed to lack further enthusiasm for conquest, a peace-treaty was signed at Basle in July 1795 with relief on either side; the French agreeing to hand over Madame Royale, to accept Carlos IV as mediator with the Holy See, and to restore all territory lately seized, the Spaniards relinquishing the island of Santo Domingo in return – a tactical blunder on Godoy's part which did not affect the number of honours heaped on him. Created Prince of the Peace and Captain-General, admitted to the Order of the Golden Fleece, and granted half a dozen rich new estates, he was now the second man in Spain, holding thronged levees on a quasi-royal pattern with an assured and easy suavity against which his many enemies were powerless.

See PLATE II p. 34
See PLATE IX p. 66

During all these alarms and excursions Goya continued to live only for his art, producing among others such celebrated portraits as that of the Duchess of Alba with her dog, already mentioned, that of Francisco Bayeu, lately deceased, and, now or a little later, that of Pedro Romero. A more complex commission occupied him in 1795. He was engaged at the royal command to suppy the decoration for the recently built Hermitage of San Antonio de la Florida, Madrid, near the Puente Verde on the banks of the Manzanares, that much-satirized river. The Manzanares was, and has been for centuries, a standing Madrilene joke as it trickles wanly for most of the year through its sandy bed, crossed by a long, pompous bridge, its banks fringed by vocal washerwomen. Góngora among the seventeenth-century poets airs an unseemly jape about increasing its flow. Lope and Quevedo and half a dozen more notables took their fling at it. Even a Bonaparte who jested with difficulty was heard to complain, on his entry into Madrid, about having to wade the Manzanares 'with sand in my mouth'. It must have been a more or less standard topic with Goya when engaged on the spot.

See PLATES XXI & XXII p. 127 & p. 128

The interior of San Antonio de la Florida, built in 1792 in the form of a Greek cross, with a central dome eighteen feet in diameter, affords an example of virtuosity on the grand scale somewhat bewildering to anyone fresh from contemplation of the 'Pradera', which jewel measures only three feet by one and a half. In the many-coloured crowd on the walls and dome of St Antonio de Florida watching (or not watching) St Antony of Padua restore a corpse to momentary life below is represented every kind of contemporary Madrilene type from Court ladies to beggars. The legend illustrated is itself spectacular, relating how St Antony's father, a native of Lisbon falsely accused of murder, was vindicated from the victim's own mouth by a miracle performed by the saint in public. The variety and vigour of the surrounding figures, their diversity of poses and gestures, the pulsating life of the whole huge composition is impressive; nor, as some critics have oddly judged, are these frescoes utterly devoid of spirituality. While they cannot compare with at least three works by Goya of unquestionable spiritual inspiration – two of them already mentioned, the third depicting a thanksgiving Mass after childbirth – they represent, in the opinion of a French critic, Jean-François Chabrun, humanity at large testifying to the Redemption and to the august mystery of the Mass celebrated at regular intervals at the altar below them. Even if one of Goya's angels resembles her Grace of Alba in feature, this does not affect the theme. The San Antonio decorations are essentially a religious work, and the artist has been rightly entombed under them.

See p. 96

See PLATE XXII p. 128

The work was carried out in a notably undevotional manner, fit to have shocked a Fra Angelico; Goya apparently being for the most part in a rage during the process, harrying his assistants and never satisfied. For his background of clouds and sky he used a novel process. The builders' men had left the walls of San Antonio covered with a neutral grey wash. To cover this Goya employed a large earthenware bowl of water to mix his colour, dashing it on the walls with a succession of sizeable sponges and the brio of a theatrical scene-painter, and, when this wash dripped, growling freely. The result endures, as a morose critic has remarked, while Da Vinci's master work in the refectory at Santa Maria delle Grazie moulders, thanks to a bad wall, to inevitable decay.

See PLATES XXIV & XXV pp. 139-42

Meanwhile Goya has produced the over-celebrated two *Majas*, in a very different key.

In the Prado, where they hang today, the *Majas* are rarely without their ring of visitors. All the world has heard of them; all the world wants to see them.

There seems little doubt (think experts) that they were painted in the Duchess's country-house of La Moncloa, to hang in her private apartments. A plausible theory exists that in accord with a custom of the time, popular with a certain school of art-lover, they could be superimposed by a simple mechanism, the relatively-clothed *Maja* covering the naked one at the touch of a spring. More than one 'curious' painting of the period was thus masked by a blameless landscape when required.

Over the question whether the Duchess actually sat (or rather, lay) for the *Majas*, and especially the nude, a whole covey of experts has clashed without issue. In the opinion of the three learned specialists who conducted the autopsy of 1945 final judgement is not possible. Goya once made a classic remark, about the only one of its kind in circulation: 'Any man calling himself an artist should be able to reproduce from memory, with pencil or brush, any scene or incident in its essential traits after seeing it once.' The word 'essential' opens up a wide field of conjecture.

The *Majas* emerged into notice in 1805, three years after the Duchess's death at the age of forty-three. In view of the authorities above-mentioned, the morphology of the nude *Maja* indicates a woman untouched by childbirth. This certainly applies to the Duchess, who, on the other hand, was just under five feet in height and elegantly slim, unlike the lush twin creations in the Prado. The least likely theory of all, put out by a grandson of Goya some years after his death, to the effect that the model for both *Majas* was a protégée of an aged friar in Madrid, was demolished without effort. That the relations between Goya and his hostess come more or less under the heading of what in divorce-court reports is styled 'intimacy' might seem deducible from the evidence of an album of drawings made during his stay at Sanlúcar de Barrameda. It contains a sketch showing the Duchess ending a siesta; reclining knees up, on the bed, while a nearby maidservant busies herself in removing a domestic utensil not usually illustrated in polite art. Here the features are to some extent substituted, or masked, without offering any serious puzzle. The same applies to the *Majas*. Their features are not especially attractive, the lightly-veiled charmer being, as has often been remarked, the lewder one. Their figures have been criticized by anatomists; their walk would be a waddle. Their pose is voluptuous but far from enticing, the leer of the veiled *Maja* being the only obvious obscenity in both.

A few modern art critics tend to be fairly severe on her naked sister. They especially point out the 'incompetence' of the arms, the 'curious' position of

he Duchess of Alba at nlúcar de Barrameda pia wash blioteca Nacional, Madrid o. 1270)

the breasts, the 'unconvincing' conjunction of head and neck; though what would convince a critic in this matter is not clear. In a word, a doll. Yet the naked *Maja* is less lewd, by a majority of votes, than her sister with the transparent vesture. The fastidious will appreciate her most recent reincarnation in the sphere of the domestico-decorative arts; namely her reproduction in painted glass as the top of an expensive cocktail-table lit from underneath, viewed recently in a Madrid shop-window.

Much ink has been expended on this unblest pair of sirens. That the Duchess was approaching middle age and that Goya had attained it does not necessarily establish platonic relations. Nor for that matter does the portrait of 1797, in which her right hand displays two rings, plainly inscribed 'Alba' and 'Goya' respectively, establish the contrary.[1] Again, whether the two *Majas* were painted at La Moncloa or – as some critics assert – at Sanlúcar de Barrameda, the Albas' place near Seville, they were certainly, as the lighting reveals, painted indoors and, so to speak, for private consumption; though if, by substituting other features for the Duchess's, Goya hoped to evade identification by the entire fashionable world he was certainly an optimist.

See PLATE XII p. 78

The Duke, Maria Cayetana's husband, had died in 1796, or it might have taken quite a number of Haydn quartets to restore his equanimity and indifference. *Cornudo*, one syllable longer than *cocu*, is no less handy a missile. Perhaps after several years of marriage to a portent nothing could surprise this melancholy nobleman. He would have had further reason for disquiet in 1800, when malicious tongues – naturally Queen Maria Luisa's for one – linked the Duchess's name with that of a dashing new Minister for War, Don Antonio Cornel, a soldier of deserved celebrity; *grave y correcto*, according to Ezquerra del Bayo, and merely a friend of the Duchess; according to her enemies, a lover – as for that matter were alleged to be Pedro Romero and the other toreros she patronized. As for the handsome young guardsman Piñatelli, son of Goya's earliest patron Fuentes, his tactless desertion of the Queen on falling in love with the Duchess was naturally provocative of war to the knife. Thus the world wags.

See p. 35

See PLATE XVI p. 106

But for the scandal attaching to their origin the *Majas* would hardly enjoy their enduring notoriety. If it is not possible to deduce with any certainty from these portraits a sexual liaison between the painter and his model, it may be accurately said that they must have been at any rate on unusually friendly terms. To deduce on this basis an impulse of vulgarity in the great lady may not be ungallant. Eighteenth-century society anywhere in Europe could supply plenty of illustrations of waywardness of this kind. Fielding's *Joseph Andrews* typifies many a handsome young footman of the period whose virtue was endangered by ladies of quality inflamed with the *besoin de s'encanailler*. Lady Arden, who refused to lower the handkerchief one

---

[1] On being cleaned a few years ago this canvas revealed an inscription on the ground: '*Solo Goya*' ('Goya only').

132

inch from her bosom when being modelled for a bust by Nollekens, was possibly not representative in her delicacy of the British female peerage at large.

To accept any platonic thesis it is necessary to account for at least two outbursts of vengeful rage on Goya's part, publicized by his own etching-needle; *See* p. 30 the one, as already noted, being *Capricho* No. 61, the other, far more obvious, being an extraordinary etching dated 1797 and never published, entitled *See* p. 30 *Sueño de La Mentira y la Inconstancia,* 'Dream of lies and inconstancy'. Only a single copy exists.

Difficult to explain, more difficult to explain away, the *Sueño* is a complex and bizarre performance, as a few attempts to elucidate it may testify. Ezquerra del Bayo is so far perhaps the most successful, however much his case is damaged thereby. Thus his judgement:

> This etching reveals a state of mental disorder and a more or less fundamental obsession, centred on the Duchess of Alba. . . . The Duchess, having two faces and butterflies' wings attached to her head, has Goya at her side, embracing one of her arms in a frenzy of love. Another feminine figure, likewise two-headed, reclining across the Duchess, grasps her free hand, which coincides – though not clearly – with the hand of a young man demanding silence with his left index-finger to his lips. In the foreground a fantastic head, supported by arms resembling bags, is gazing at a serpent in the act of hypnotizing a small toad.

Compare Beruete, an art critic of standing totally foiled by 'the witch, the old woman, the tortoise, etc.,' dismissing these as fantasies impossible to explain, but sound enough on the essential, namely 'the group formed by the reclining woman and the man grasping her arm':

> This woman with two heads and butterfly wings is indisputably the Duchess of Alba; presented yet again, and in almost identical terms, as a light woman – the butterfly-wings can convey nothing else – in this series of the *Caprichos.*

Beruete has no doubts concerning the male figure grasping her arm:

> It is the artist himself, Goya, faithfully portrayed; his typical physiognomy, with features so strongly marked, so personal, that any confusion is impossible.

One other expositor, Viñaza, quoted by Ramón Gómez de la Serna, is completely at sea:

> A young woman, half-nude, with two faces. A man holds, pressed to his breast, one of her hands. Another woman, also double-faced, holds the other hand of the former one. Below, with head erect and supported on arms with elbows resting on the ground, is a witch or a demon, sarcastically contemplating a serpent fascinating a sparrow (it looks to me like a tortoise), and about to swallow it. Behind, a woman standing with a finger to her lips as if demanding silence. In the distance, a fortress.

Ezquerra del Bayo attributes the *Sueño,* like the *Caprichos,* to Goya's breakdown between 1792 and 1794; but is it possible to regard such a feat of etching as the work of an invalid? However much it has baffled later generations, and however inexplicable the symbolism of the more fantastic shapes, perhaps connected with venomous tongues in Goya's and the Duchess's circle, it is obviously a cry of rage and wounded passion needing no footnotes.

How the Duchess Cayetana received it seems not to be known. Possibly it amused more than it annoyed her. Since in fact she and Goya remained on at least terms of friendship till the year of her death, 1802, it may well be that she chose to regard it – at any rate in public – as an act of homage; of a different kind, certainly, from the kind of adulation she was used to receiving in print from poets and playwrights, and for that very reason more piquant. In that age of flying lampoons, libels, and caricatures it was *de rigueur* for the great to receive such insults with a smile, and even to commend their literary or artistic quality, if any, from the standpoint of the connoisseur. Like Lord Chesterfield with Johnson's famous broadside ('This man has great powers') the Duchess may have kept the *Sueño* lying about, and even pointed out its beauties to guests after dinner. If she and Goya had indeed been lovers in the accepted sense she had doubtless become bored with his lack of the social graces, which, for a time, she had found fascinating.

Her other pets of humble origin were less trying and continued to retain her ardent affection; poor old halfwitted Basilio the laybrother, the negress child María de la Luz, little Luisito Berganza, son of one of her servants, an autograph-note to whom is preserved with veneration by his descendants. It is one of several:

> Dear beloved little Luis of my life,
>   I had much pleasure from your letter, and much more from knowing that you are steadily learning and making me happy by being a good boy. The little girls send greetings and I send you a hug right from my heart, my darling boy.
>   J. M. Teresa de Silva

The maternity denied her was a stronger passion with the Duchess, undoubtedly, than any other. Coming of a race which has always regarded liberal motherhood as the joyous and natural achievement and crown of a woman's life, and indeed her *raison d'être*, she may be pitied.

★   ★   ★

Between 1792 and 1794, we may recall, Goya was suffering from one of those illnesses of which, in the absence of any medical communiqués, nothing is known. That big violent dynamo of a head was plainly liable – assisted by the rigours of the Madrilene climate, winter and summer – to breakdowns. Overwork is an obvious factor. Cerebral haemorrhage has been credibly diagnosed from reports of sudden swoons at the easel and protracted unconsciousness. There are several intervals of inactive sickness in Goya's life, apart from the deafness which began in 1792. Towards the end of his life in 1824 Dr Arrieta was to order him by arrangement to the spa of Plombières in the Vosges for six months; a year later he was to be granted leave from

(opposite left) The Infanta Doña Maria Josefa
oil on canvas
$28\frac{1}{4} \times 23\frac{5}{8}$ in. (74 × 60 cm.)
Museo del Prado, Madrid

(opposite right) The Infante Don Francisco de Paula Antonio
oil on canvas
$28\frac{1}{4} \times 23\frac{5}{8}$ in. (74 × 60 cm.)
Museo del Prado, Madrid

The Infante Don Carlos Maria Isidro
oil on canvas
$29\frac{1}{8} \times 23\frac{5}{8}$ in. (74 × 60 cm.)
Museo del Prado, Madrid

The Infante Don Antonio Pascual
oil on canvas
$28\frac{1}{4} \times 23\frac{5}{8}$ in. (74 × 60 cm.)
Museo del Prado, Madrid

See PLATES VIII & XXXVII
p. 65 & p. 185

See PLATE II p. 34

See p. 98
See p. 23

See p. 41

See p. 92

See PLATE XXXVIII pp. 186–87

Fernando VII to do the same at Bagnères in the French Pyrenees. In neither instance is the illness concerned discernible or the spa visited.

In 1795 we find him restored again, and once more painting the Duchess Maria Cayetana. Among portraits of this period that of the eminent Madrilene actress Rosario Fernández, known, owing to her actor-husband's fondness of roles in Ercles' vein, as 'La Tirana', presents an impressive figure, every inch a leading lady. Equally regal stands the Marquesa de la Merced, fan in hand, against a rural background. The full-blooded riot of the proletarian post-Lenten carnival called 'The Burial of the Sardine', dated round about 1794, will demonstrate with what ease the painter could change his social key.

A masterpiece of effrontery – or accepted as such by most authorities – was now to engage him. Early in 1800 Carlos IV wrote to Godoy: 'Let Goya paint your wife's portrait, and when that is done let him come to the Residence' – the summer palace of Aranjuez, where the royal family were spending some weeks – 'and paint us all together.'

The ensuing group-portrait, now in the Prado, has been compared to a travelling circus-exhibit, with the trainer hovering discreetly in the shadows of the background.[1] The pursy benevolent stupidity of the King; the tight-lipped shrewish malevolence of the Queen, in whose features the audacious Goya has contrived to convey a hint of all the broomstick-cavalry of the *Caprichos*; the nullity of the rest of the royal family – though the children are, like every child painted by Goya, charming – these need no footnotes. One

[1]A cleaning-process in June 1967 revealed the presence on the wall behind the Royal group of a picture in the romantico-classical style, depicting a nude male figure caressing one of two female semi-nudes. His features are markedly those of a youthful Goya; the application, if any, remains obscure.

member of the group stands out as a major personality: that sardonic old hag the Infanta Maria Josefa, with the great luminous eyes of a screech-owl and the expression of surprise, as of one asking herself where the devil was Exhibit A, Her Majesty's fancy-man, is quite superb. Painted eight years before the regime vanished in smoke and flame, the group has naturally become invested with prophetic meaning as a parade awaiting inspection and dismissal by General Destiny. On a blazing summer afternoon in modern Aranjuez, with all blinds drawn in the baroque yellow palace which replaced Felipe II's original rural retreat, it is impossible not to imagine this same company still standing motionless in the great drawing-room among the bronzes and the china, the marbles and the tinkling clocks. . . . Eight years onward Godoy too will be present at Aranjuez, so celebrated for its roses, nightingales, and moonlight, barely escaping with his life from a howling mob.

So much for a portrait-group generally accepted as an audacious satire. With this judgement a leading modern authority on Goya vigorously disagrees. The royal family was actually far more homely in features than the painting suggests, comments Xavier de Salas. Goya's preliminary studies, many of which survive, demonstrate in fact that what he produced was practically an idealization:

> From all these comparisons emerges one and the same impression. If in these studies, made swiftly and with the certitude of genius, Goya captured the physiognomical essence, the colouring, the expressions of his models, then when he transferred these features to their corresponding place in the composition itself the result became slightly transformed. In each and in every case he made them more plump, more imposing, gave colour to the features and even to the silhouettes, and supplied a comely expression, in each case embellished. Evidently it was no problem of transcript which dictated this; such transformation was a matter of judgment.[1]

In a word, Goya has here flattered the features of royalty in the manner of any Court painter from Holbein down to, say Winterhalter, who turned pursy, pop-eyed young Victoria of England into the Queen of the Fairies. It was – it possibly still is – what Rabelais would call 'matter of breviary'; a consecrated formula deriving from the one-time dogma of the divine right of princes, and bestowing on the least attractive specimens of royalty a grace and dignity omitted by their Creator. This, many contemplators of Goya's production may feel, can itself become satire of the subtlest kind. Here, therefore, the connoisseur and the amateur may for once shake hands.

★   ★   ★

And now the skies were darkening visibly over Spain. It would be tedious to follow all the intricacies of Godoy's diplomatic manoeuvrings over the past few years. By signing a treaty with the French Directory in 1796 he plunged

Queen Maria Luisa on horseback
1799
oil on canvas
$131\frac{7}{8} \times 109\frac{7}{8}$ in. (335 × 279 cm)
Museo del Prado, Madrid

See p. 73, pp. 134–35

PLATE XXIII. Carlos IV on Horseback, 1799
oil on canvas
$120\frac{1}{8} \times 109\frac{7}{8}$ in. (305 × 279 cm)
Museo del Prado, Madrid

PLATE XXIV. (overleaf)
The Nude Maja, about 1805
oil on canvas
$37\frac{3}{8} \times 74\frac{3}{4}$ in. (97 × 190 cm.)
Museo del Prado, Madrid

PLATE XXV. (overleaf)
The Clothed Maja, about 1805
oil on canvas
$37\frac{3}{8} \times 74\frac{3}{4}$ in. (95 × 190 cm.)
Museo del Prado, Madrid

[1] *La Familia de Carlos IV*, 1959.

See PLATES VIII & XXXVII
p. 65 & p. 185

See p. 92

See PLATE X p. 75

See p. 200

See PLATE XII p. 78

See PLATE XVI p. 106, p. 136

LATE XXVI. Lady with a Yellow
carf – Señora Sabasa Garcia
l on canvas
8 × 23 in. (71 × 58 cm.)
he National Gallery of Art,
ashington, D.C.
ndrew Mellon Collection

Spain into a war with England which lost her Trinidad. Two years later his enemies, headed by Fernando, heir to the throne, brought about his temporary dismissal, but he remained active and powerful behind the scenes. In 1801 he afforded Goya another exercise in satire on being appointed Generalissimo in command of a force of 60,000 men despatched to prevent Portugal by force from imminent annexation by the French; an object achieved in a four-week walkover. The complacency of the plump military buck lounging on a sofa at G.H.Q. in Goya's canvas is given full value. It seems only fair to add that a professional critic, General Gómez de Arteche, has since awarded Godoy high marks for speed and efficiency in this exercise. His diplomacy was otherwise. 'I can use him,' said Napoleon to his brother Lucien, 'but I despise him.' Contempt was not entirely justified. In 1803, for example, Godoy, back in power, stood up to the First Consul – shortly to be Emperor – with firmness, refusing to drag Spain into war with England again after the breaking of the Peace of Amiens, though in 1804 he gave in, being thereby responsible for heavy Spanish losses at Trafalgar. Having an array of powerful enemies at home, headed by the volcanic Infante Fernando, his walking of a perpetual tightrope was not without dexterity.

Goya continued to paint, employing a new translucent blue. Several beautiful women – the Countess of Haro, Doña Isabel Cobos de Porcel, the Lady with a Yellow Scarf, Doña Antonia Zárate – are among his clients down to 1810. He once more painted the Duchess Maria Cayetana, now to all seeming involved at the age of forty in an affair with the handsome well-born ladykiller Lieutenant-General Don Antonio Cornel; such at any rate being the report spread by Maria Luisa and Godoy.

Whatever Goya's reaction to this, he had not long to rage. On 23rd July, 1802, the Duchess died quite suddenly – 'of a colic', according to the certificate of the Albas' chief family physician, Dr Jaime Bonell – at La Moncloa. Rumours that she had been poisoned by the Queen and Godoy were swift to fly round Madrid. Goya's reception of the news of her death leaves no room to doubt of his feelings towards her. For some days, it is reported from Dr Bonell, he wandered round the streets of Madrid in a kind of trance, agonized, haggard, dumb and unapproachable, unable to endure any kind of human contact, incapable of any kind of work. It may well be that he never wholly recovered.

Conjecture has since been rife. Gómez de la Serna, for example, suggests that the Duchess might have died of an epidemic, of the normal fevers of summer, of eating a fresh lettuce, of an ice compounded from the snow of the Guadarramas, or even of an *horchata*, the almond-based beverage which proved fatal in the following century to the ex-Empress Eugénie. The possibly lethal properties of the *horchata* have apparently since been neutralized, since it continues to be a highly-popular Spanish summer drink. One more theory concerning the Duchess's death was that she was poisoned by one of her 390 servants.

Of such legend and conjecture, constantly repeated, the late Duke of Alba, diplomat, connoisseur, and historian, was moved to dispose in 1945 once and for all by inviting three eminent medico-legal specialists to conduct an autopsy on the Duchess's remains in the cemetery of San Isidro, Madrid. Four years later Drs Blanco Soler, Piga Pascual, and Pérez Petinto published their findings in two hundred pages of erudition medical, psychological, and historical, not devoid of literary grace.[1] Their last word is as follows:

> To sum up, we believe ourselves to have shown clearly, after patient research, the absurdity of the rumour alleging the Duchess of Alba to have been poisoned. We have pursued our task with the conscientiousness and respect required by the confidence placed in us by the Royal Academy of History and by its President, the present Duke of Alba. We wish to thank those who have entrusted us with this medico-legal inquest for the satisfaction produced by complete investigation.

Among the illustrations in this volume is one of peculiar fascination – a photograph dated November 1945, and aptly titled 'Sic Transit', of the dazzling Duchess's remains; a vision fit to inspire elegiac verse, though so far none of the poets of Spain seems to have responded. She died, then, neither of poison nor – yet another theory, redolent of the romantic 1830s – of the consumption which carried off Mimi of *La Vie de Bohème* and Dumas' Lady of the Camelias, but of a meningo-encephalitis giving place to a pleuroneumonic lesion.

The tomb in the crypt of the church of the Jesuit noviciate was to suffer under the French occupation. The body was removed, when this fine building was demolished in the 1850s, to its present resting-place in the San Isidro cemetery. The Madrid gazettes of 1802 paid proper tribute to her rank, her beauty, her charm, and her boundless charity, 'succouring widows and the sick, founding schools for destitute children, providing careers for worthy orphans, ceaselessly lavishing large sums on her dependants, who loved her like a mother'. A mural designed by Goya over the original tomb depicted her being interred by three mystical figures, cloaked and hooded. The present tomb displays merely an undistinguished bust. With Maria Teresa Cayetana ended the direct Alba line, the title thence passing to the Berwick or Stuart branch, descended from James II of England.

What Goya, Painter to the King, thought of the murder-rumour involving the Queen and Don Manuel Godoy, Prince of the Peace and Generalissimo, is not ascertainable. His position as the late Duchess's intimate was complicated by his friendly relations with her enemy Godoy; in whose behalf, since his star is shortly to set, it may not be out of place to pause a moment at this juncture to give Don Manuel a trifle of his due, notwithstanding his diplomatic dithering and easy morals. *See* PLATE XVI p. 106, p. 136, p. 92

Over and above the improvement of highroads, the foundation of medical

---

[1] *La Duquesa de Alba y Su Tiempo.* Madrid, 1949.

and veterinary colleges, relaxation of the Press-censorship, the curbing of the Inquisition, the encouragement of arts, letters, and sciences generally, and taxation of the rich – including the trimming, with Pius VI's approval, of the higher clergy of some of their agelong bequests – Godoy may be awarded a sizeable mark for the re-establishment of the Foundling Hospital at Madrid on a sound basis and the alleviation of the misery of the deaf-and-dumb. With all his faults he was, in fact, a generous and kindly person, as Goya would doubtless be the first to admit, for the Prince of the Peace, who admired him enormously, took, as already mentioned, the trouble to acquire a sign-language to converse with him when his total deafness arrived.

See PLATE IV p. 44

It affords a pleasant mental picture of a winter day: the Minister's apartments in the huge granite pile of the Palacio Real, rebuilt by Carlos III fifty years before, like its predecessor, on the site of the original Alcázar, the fortress of the Moors; the spacious windows overlooking the Manzanares and the snowclad line of the Sierra de Guadarrama; a *décor* of baroque and rococo in velvet, marble, and gilding; silver braziers burning crushed olive-stones; the plump silk-stockinged genial master of Spain, his hair dressed *à la Titus* – hairpowder had gone out long since – in the latest Paris fashion, gesticulating vividly with hands, lips, and eyebrows; the square, stocky genius in the armchair opposite striving to follow, sherry-glass in hand; a liveried royal lackey or two in discreet attendance.

PLATES II & XII p. 34 & p. 78

Godoy, who could, when he chose, radiate considerable charm – *teste* Lord Holland, among others – professed some taste in pictures, and was not devoid of a sense of humour rare in politicians. He had long since acquired the professional art of saying nothing in flattering confidence. It seems unlikely that Goya ever had much of interest to report to the Duchess Maria Cayetana on his return. On the other hand Godoy was able possibly to acquaint the Queen that evening with yet another folly of *La Alba*. The feud between the ladies must have amused him more than the continuous and wearisome fencing with Bonaparte, to which exercises direct Napoleonic action was shortly to put a violent end.

See p. 31

Whether the statesman and the artist were on such close terms at the end of July, 1802, seems doubtful. Even if the poison story was a fable, the behaviour of Queen Maria Luisa and Godoy immediately following the Duchess's death was of a kind, one would imagine, to stir Goya to a rumble of oaths. With Maria Cayetana's body still unburied, the Queen intimated to the legal authorities concerned that the Duchess's will – which incidentally included a bequest of 3,500 *reales* a year to Goya's son Javier – must obviously be set aside as fantastic and inoperable. Her Majesty's hard black eye was in fact on the Duchess's jewellery, and especially on two items in the inventory; a set of pearls valued at 384,000 *reales* and a diamond ornament valued at 300,000. These she intended to buy. Though the Spanish crown jewels included far more magnificent and historic gauds, the pleasure of flaunting a detested rival's jewels was invincible.

DIEGO VELAZQUEZ The Surrender of Breda (Las Lanzas), 1635 oil on canvas 120⅞ × 144½ in. (307 × 367 cm) Museo del Prado, Madrid

This moreover was only a beginning. Within a week Carlos IV addressed an urgent personal letter to Godoy, plainly at his wife's order and for publication. Beginning with an appreciation of his Minister's absolute integrity, the King continued that having had doubts of that of the late Duchess's physicians, he had ordered an investigation into her death. Natural causes (the King continued) being established, it was discovered that during the Duchess's last moments certain of her private papers had been abstracted by disloyal servants. These, since they affected the beneficiaries, must be retrieved and delivered to the law, or, if necessary, to the Crown. It was Godoy's business, the King ended, to see to this matter promptly and in a manner conformable with 'my peace and my honour'.

As many authorities have surmised, this was an order to commandeer anything in the late Duchess's papers compromising the Queen and Godoy which their late fair enemy may have designed for future use. It incidentally enabled the Queen and Godoy to secure the pick of the Duchess's treasures when they duly came up for sale; alternatively, when seized. To Godoy fell the Velázquez ('Rokeby') Venus now in the National Gallery, London, Correggio's 'School of Love', a Virgin and Child by Raphael and – characteristically – Goya's Majas, which must have afforded him and the Queen some pleasant after-dinner discussion. After his fall and exile they were acquired by the Academy of San Fernando. Some years later they took the road to the Prado, where they continue to ravish art-lovers of all nationalities for whom Velázquez produced 'Las Lanzas' in vain.

See PLATE XXIII p. 137
See p. 92

See p. 83

See PLATES XXIV & XXV pp. 139–42

Rumblings of the coming storm were now becoming audible. To complete the Continental blockade necessary to bring England to her knees it was essential to Napoleon – now Emperor – to subjugate England's ally Portugal. A treaty signed at Fontainebleau by Godoy's ambassador accorded French troops passage through Spain for this purpose, Godoy reserving to himself the kingdom of Algarves in payment – or, in Napoleon's later words, 'as an asylum'. What is known as the Escorial Plot of October 1807 is too involved to be detailed here. Its main feature was the discovery of a letter from the

See PLATES VIII & XXXVII p. 65 & p. 185

Infante Fernando to Napoleon begging him to rescue the Spanish crown from 'perfidious egotists', and accepting an offer of marriage with one of the Empress Josephine's nieces. Other documents were discovered in the same key. Fernando grovelled and was forgiven. Following a subsequent pro-

See PLATE XXIII p. 137

clamation by Carlos IV beginning 'The voice of Nature disarms vengeance' came the announcement to a cheering crowd of his abdication in Fernando's favour. A modern Spanish historian, Angel Salcedo Ruíz, dismisses the imbroglio, rather curiously, as quite possibly a vindictive comedy planned by Godoy and the Queen – who hated her eldest son equally – to destroy Fernando's chance of succession. Whatever the truth, real trouble was brewing, and the populace in due course supplied it.

Had the considerable mob which poured up the main avenue of the summer palace of Aranjuez on the evening of 17th March 1808 to cheer its idol Fernando and to lynch Don Manuel Godoy discovered the latter's garret hiding-place, his fate would not greatly have perturbed Napoleon, who had no further use for him. The Emperor's plans had begun smoothly unfolding five months previously. On 18th October 1807, General Junot crossed the frontier with a force of 25,000 enigmatically styled 'the Corps of Observation of the Gironde', a label curiously suggestive of a party of Nature-lovers out for a stroll. In November Junot's troops reached Lisbon, much the worse for wear, to find the Portuguese royal family and government away on the high seas, bound for Brazil with a British naval escort. Meanwhile a second Corps of Observation 24,000 strong had been followed into Spain by a third of 30,000 styled 'the Corps of Observation of the Ocean Coast'. As these came to a halt across the frontier a French force took possession, half by guile and as it were with a friendly wink, of the fortresses of Barcelona and Figueras at one end of the frontier and Pamplona and San Sebastian at the other. Thus was played the overture to a war which was to begin Napoleon's downfall. He had misjudged the Spanish character, as others have done, by mistaking steel for tin. Doubtless, also, his spies had over-estimated the number and influence of the *afrancesados*, those Spaniards of the intelligentsia who saw in him, as many of their kind all over the world were to see later in Lenin and Stalin, an apostle of liberty and progress. Among these, even after

See PLATE XXVIII p. 153

the glorious date of 2nd May 1808, was presumably Don Francisco Goya, Painter to the King.

Poor old bewildered Carlos IV, Maria Luisa, and Godoy, summoned to

Bayonne for consultation, were shortly to be joined at Napoleon's order by Fernando, who, as Spain's new king, had been received in Madrid on 24th March with acclamations, two days after 40,000 French cavalry and infantry, Spain's deliverers, entered the capital. At their head rode Joachim, Marshal Murat, cherishing the impression – to echo the acid Bourrienne – that he was conquering Spain for himself. *See* PLATES VIII & XXXVII p. & p. 185

It was a colourful entry. With Murat at the head of his troops rode Berthier, his chief of staff, both splendidly bedizened. Murat's travelling wardrobe is a diverting singularity in the make-up of this fearless bad-tempered swaggering Gascon, the innkeeper's son of La Bastide, one of the finest soldiers in history. At Spitz a year previously he and Berthier had so bedazed the Austrian gunners by their audacity and their finery – Murat in a richly-bestarred tunic of red and gold, cocked hat with ostrich feathers, and red morocco boots, with a diamond-hilted sword, Berthier almost as superb – that they held their fire and allowed the two horsemen to take the bridge together by a trick of sheer daring. For the ceremonial entry into Madrid Berthier is said to have almost outshone his chief in a Hungarian pelisse of astrakhan with a gold-braided, fur-trimmed dolman, a black-and-gold sash, and a crimson shako with a white heron-plume aigrette.

The Madrilene populace remained glowering and unmoved by this parade. It must have seemed to even the *afrancesados* vulgar; to some thousands more, insulting. These atheist French seemed to assume themselves to be impressing a nation of savages. Such a circus was emphatically the wrong kind of psychological approach. Heartily as the Madrilenes had acclaimed the downfall of Godoy, they were Spaniards with a long, proud history. A few ritual acclamations died swiftly. Within six weeks arrived the inevitable. On 2nd May 1808, a date forever splendid, a conflict outside the royal palace touched off a national explosion. *See* p. 92

See PLATE XXVIII p. 153

★   ★   ★

The spark arrived quite suddenly.

On the morning of 2nd May, the tramp and jingle of French infantry and cavalry up the Calle de Alcalá in the direction of the Plaza de Oriente quickly drew a crowd to that spacious square. They found a travelling-coach drawn up in front of the main palace entrance, ready to move off and guarded by a strong cordon. Comprehension soon dawned. The last remaining member in Madrid of the heirs to the Spanish throne, the boy Infante Francisco de Paula – in Goya's group he stands between the King and Queen – was to be spirited to Bayonne to join Napoleon's other guests. This was not to be borne. With cries of 'They shan't have him!' the crowd surged forward and a struggle began. Within a few moments the French officer in command gave the order to fire, and the first combatants of a five-year war died for Spain. *See* p. 135

The news swiftly spread. Within a short time the main streets of the quarter were thronged with a mob brandishing any weapons it could lay hands on. It took Murat four hours to quell the rising, during which occurred that hand-to-hand combat in the Puerta del Sol, immortalized by Goya's brush, between citizens and a detachment of Mamelukes; turbanned cavalry from Egypt armed with curved sabres, mounted on small wiry horses and sufficiently recalling the Moor of the Reconquista, the historic enemy. In Goya's canvas the savagery of this clash – the whirling sabres, the leaping citizens, knives in hand, the fury of the combatants, the terror in the eyes of the horses, the yelling mouths, the confusion – the effect is nearly as audible as it is visual.

Was he an eyewitness?

The final answer seems to have been supplied quite recently by Santiago Arbos Balleste in a Madrid illustrated weekly.[1] In a contemporary engraving which adds grenadiers to the Mameluke detachment, the attack on the latter takes place almost directly under the windows of a spacious four-storeyed eighteenth-century house on the corner of the Puerta del Sol and the Calle del Arenal. This house, since vanished, was almost certainly, it appears, the one in which Goya in 1808 occupied the whole first floor, with four large windows and a balcony fronting the Puerta del Sol and one round the corner. He might therefore be assumed to have enjoyed a ringside view; hence no doubt what has been justly called the cinematographic quality of the resulting masterpiece. Other aspects of the ferocities of 2nd May – the battle for the artillery-park of Monteleón, for example, and the affray at the Ayuntamiento – have been recorded by painters like Alenza and Sorolla with remarkable brio, but some way after the style of the master.

His gunners having gained control of the situation by the same efficacious 'whiff of grapeshot' employed by Murat against the Paris mob in 1795, he then, in the neat phrase of some historian or other 'shot a hundred men, pardoned the rest, and sat down to dinner in high good humour, satisfied that Spain was conquered'. On arrival of the news at Bayonne a raving Napoleon ordered the whole dynasty to abdicate. His brother Joseph, King of Naples, was shortly afterwards proclaimed King of Spain. Within a month the country was aflame. The natives of the bleak Asturias in the north-west were the first to declare war on the invader. Aragon, Galicia, and Estremadura followed, and the revolt spread swiftly south, east, and west to envelop the smallest villages.

Goya's reactions to all this are not recorded. For all his Aragonese blood he was not, it is disappointing but essential to realize, a fighting man, nor, it soon turned out, any fanatic for patriotism. His energies during the coming conflict would in fact be centred chiefly on the practice of his art and the welfare of Don Francisco Goya. He was nevertheless sufficiently moved by Murat's reprisals to record the fusillade of a group of patriots on the Montaña

See PLATE XXVII p. 153

[1] *El Dos de Mayo; Blanco y Negro*, 30th April, 1966.

del Príncipe Pío, outside the city, where, apparently, an eyewitness took him over the ground a few nights later. The canvas now in the Prado is a justly-acclaimed piece of dramatic reportage: the little group of the condemned lit up by a lantern under a grim night-sky, stoic, haggard, defiant, recoiling; the white-clad central figure shouting defiance with blazing eyes and outflung arms; the friar by his side, bent down with hands clasped in prayer; the body in the foreground near the open grave; the line of levelled muskets, bayonets fixed, and the file of bearskins behind them.

That a very great artist was, like many of us, no hero – not even a pacifist enduring persecution for his ideals, which may demand as much courage as the battlefield – must be reluctantly conceded. Through all the bitter conflict of the Peninsular War that minority of Spaniards already noted continued to admire Napoleon. Amid a nation in arms this required courage in display. If no such display is reported of Goya, to whom the unpleasant word 'collaborator' has certainly been applied, it might be that with him, as with any artist of his absorption, a liberalism possibly instinctive was no more than skin-deep; a whimsy for off-moments, not allowed to interfere with the sacred pursuit and worship of Art. Though he did not share his contemporary Blake's tremors over the 'dark horrors' of the French Revolution –

> My Angels have told me that seeing such
> visions I could not subsist on the Earth
> But by my conjunction with Flaxman, who
> knows how to forgive Nervous Fear . . .

– it is difficult to believe that Goya spent much time in cheering the Jacobins on.

> Tout passe – L'Art robuste
> Seul a l'éternité;
>   Le buste
> Survit à la cité . . .

He would certainly have agreed with Gautier.

★   ★   ★

Soon most of Spain had become a battlefield.

It is no function of these pages to trace the progress of the bitterest conflict in European history. The war was barely two months old before Napoleon nearly succumbed to apoplexy at the news that Dupont had surrendered his army of 20,000 at Bailén to a small force under Castaños assisted largely by fifty thousand Andalucian hayseeds armed with flails, scythes, and pitch-forks. Though this shame would before long be wiped out, the impact of the Bailén surrender on an astonished Europe can hardly be exaggerated. The legend of French invincibility was being rudely shaken. Following the evacuation of Junot's corps of 25,000 from Portugal by sea after a rough

PLATE XXVII. (above) Madrid, 3rd May, 1808: Executions at t[he] Mountain of Prince Pius, 1813 oil on canvas
$104\frac{3}{4} \times 135\frac{7}{8}$ in. (266 × 345 cm[)] Museo del Prado, Madrid

PLATE XXVIII. (below) Madrid, 2nd May, 1808: Battle with the Mamelukes, 1813 oil on canvas
$104\frac{3}{4} \times 135\frac{7}{8}$ in. (266 × 345 cm[)] Museo del Prado, Madrid

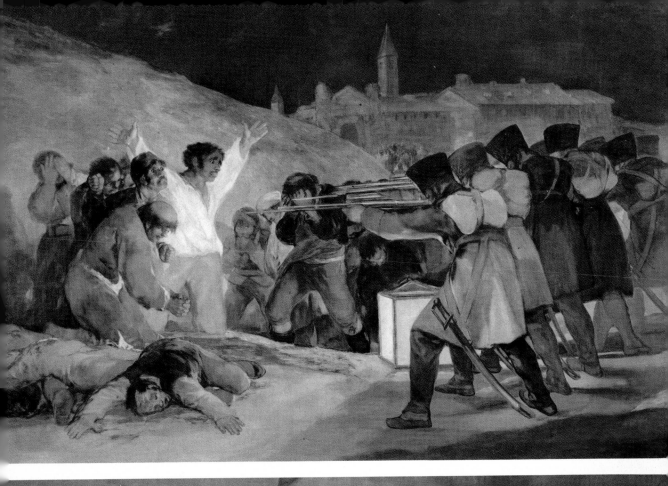

TE XXIX. The Duke of
llington
on panel
× 20¼ in. (60.3 × 51.5 cm.)
e National Gallery, London

handling by a recently-landed British expeditionary force, and following
King Joseph's hasty bolt – the first of three – from Madrid, the conquering
eagles of Austerlitz, Jena, Eylau, and Friedland had taken a woundy knock.
And as if Bailén were not enough, the civilians of Saragossa were withstanding
continuous waves of bloody assault by Lannes and Mortier and the half-
tumbledown fortress of Gerona held out likewise, against all reason.

There were now three French army corps in Spain, some 130,000 strong.
In August 1808 the arrival of Marshal Ney, a legend for brilliance and
audacity, revived their offensive spirit, and the steam-roller continued to
advance.

> *Entendez-vous dans la campagne*
> *Mugir ces féroces soldats*
> *Qui viennent jusque dans vos bras*
> *Egorger vos fils et vos compagnes?*
> *Aux armes, citoyens!* . . .

The howl of the 'Marseillaise' down the wind was to be blent before long with
a sardonic flavour to which the Spanish temperament is traditionally responsive. Loot, rape, torture, hangings, the sacking and burning of churches and
convents ('All human conflict', said Cardinal Manning in a lapidary phrase
of the 1890s, 'is ultimately theological'), and the summary execution of rural
clergy inspiring or leading revolt swiftly became a routine with the invader.
Two of many militant *curas*, Merino and Tapia, are gratefully remembered
in Spanish history-books, together with guerrilleros of the standing of 'El
Empecinado' – 'The Pitchy One', so called because he was a cobbler's son –
Mina, Sarasa, and half a dozen more.

See p. 196

Surrounding towns and villages with cordons which no enemy despatch
rider could get through alive, specializing in surprise, ambush, night-attack,
and tireless reprisal, the guerrilleros and their peasantry kept French nerves
constantly on the stretch. Sentries were leaped on silently and strangled.
Pickets or stragglers were stabbed in the back, shot from behind walls,
garrotted in wayside taverns. Retaliation by burning more villages or hanging
a few more ringleaders and parish priests was answered by nightly assassina-
tions ever more daring and ingenious.

For the French soldier it soon became hardly safe to close an eye. Any
attempt at fraternization, not to mention *la vieille galanterie gauloise*, was the
most lethal kind of folly. The female of the species proved often deadlier
than the male; to accept a mug of wine from some kindly old beldame might
be to sign a death-warrant. It was soon seen to be impossible for the invader,
flushed from all the victories of the Republic and the Consulate, to intimidate
this stubborn race. Retaliation became a crusade, inflamed all the more by
the anti-religious fanaticism of the French. The formidable Requetes of
Navarre in the 1930s, with their rosaries as handy as their bayonets, were
pre-figured in the 1800s on a national scale.

La heroica España, en tanto que al Bandido
Que a fuego y sangre, de insolencia ciego,
Brindó felicidad, a sangre y fuego
Le retribuye el don . . .

Heroic Spain, returning with interest to the
insolence-blinded Bandit his gift of fire
and blood, will know in her piety what
solemn and noble monument to raise to them.
(the heroes of May the Second) – Juan Nicasio
Gallego, *El Dos de Mayo*.

(far left) El General Urrutia
oil on canvas
78¾ × 53⅛ in. (200 × 135 cm.)
Museo del Prado, Madrid

(mid-left) The Marquis of Sant
Cruz, 1805
oil on canvas
Collection the Marquis of Santa
Cruz, Madrid

(above) Ferdinand Guillemarde
1798
oil on canvas
72⅞ × 45¼ in. (185 × 115 cm.)
Musée du Louvre, Paris

The long siege of Saragossa, with its heaps of rotting civilian corpses, Soult's
excessively savage sacking of Alcántara and his enormous loot, Augereau's
fancy for decking the trees along the highroads of Catalonia with swinging
patriot corpses – all had as little effect on the national spirit as Suchet's
attempt to placate Aragon by suppressing plunder and admitting a few local
collaborators to his temporary government of the province.

The arrival of a British expeditionary force of 14,000 in Portugal in August
1808, as already noted, to put Junot's corps out of action with the assistance
of some 1,600 Portuguese levies, was a notable tonic, but not till 1813 were
Wellington and his auxiliaries in a position to deliver vital blows at Badajoz,
Salamanca, and Vitoria, where in June of that year the main French force
was put to flight and King Joseph fled. Napoleon himself had paid a flying
visit to the Spanish front in December 1808, directing in person the crossing
of the Sierra de Guadarrama by the pass called the Puerto de Somosierra, the

See PLATE XXIX p. 154

n Miguel y Lardizabal
on canvas
e National Gallery, Prague

n Ignacio Omulryan y
urera
on canvas
× 25½ in. (78.7 × 64.7 cm.)
e William Rockhill Nelson
llery of Art – Atkins Museum
Fone Arts, Kansas City

way to Madrid, though not in time to prevent unfortunate Sir John Moore and his troops from escaping later to the sea at Coruña.

From a balcony of the inn overlooking the opening of the Somosierra Pass today it is not difficult to summon up the scene of that vital winter afternoon with its howling blizzard, charged with hail and snow and fierce enough to blow horse and man together off the precipices; the increasing drifts; the long halted train of cavalry, infantry, guns, commissariat; the Imperial Guard at the head of the column, arms and accoutrement in parade condition, stamping freezing feet; beyond them at some little distance, standing on a rock with a ring of officers below, a short plump figure in greatcoat and sable travelling-cap shouting to the engineers and pioneers toiling for dear life with gunpowder, pick, and shovel – the Emperor, clearing the road, restoring the order of the advance, calling Nature's bluff, as it were, with a more steely will of his own. That same night Napoleon crossed the Guadarrama on foot with his Guards, to be recalled to Paris a few days later by a messenger with news of intrigue behind his back by Talleyrand and Fouché, and leaving his commanders in the field to their quarrels. He did not return to Spain.

$$\star \qquad \star \qquad \star$$

'War is a chancy business (*une chose aléatoire*)', remarked the enigmatic General Boulanger, who failed to upset the French Republican regime in the 1880s, enunciating one of the great military truths of all time. Historians sweating in the wake of Oman and Fortescue to compress the five years of the Peninsular campaign into less than 250 pages must command the deepest respect of anyone who served in either of two recent world wars. Brilliance, stupidity, inspiration, desperation, fatigue, lunacy, good luck, bad luck, arm-chancing, and other ritual concomitants of high professional strategy in the field seem on the whole less tedious to endure than to describe.

The campaign of Spain was fought by twenty Marshals of France commanding nine strong if not wholly first-class armies, three of them curiously named – the Corps of Observation of the Gironde, the Corps of Observation of the Pyrenees, the Corps of Observation of the Ocean Coast, the Army of the North, the Army of Aragon, the Army of Portugal, the Armies of Andalucia, Catalonia, and Valencia; in all some 200,000 troops. The best of the Marshals was the dashing Ney, the contemporary god of battles; the worst, perhaps, the aged fumbling Jourdan, who however had the misfortune to be saddled with that great strategist King Joseph Bonaparte.

On the other side the allies – Wellington with a strengthened force,[1] a small but tough regular Spanish army under leaders of the calibre of Castaños, *See* p. 18 Alvarez de Castro, Palafox, and Blake, with his oddly un-Iberian surname, and a variable contingent of Portuguese, backed by some hundreds of

---

[1] By March 1809 the strength of the British expeditionary force had been increased to over 26,000.

formidable guerrilleros and an innumerable militant peasantry – enjoyed several advantages outweighing superiority in force, not the least being the jealousy rife among the French marshals, who quarrelled at intervals like chorus-girls. Unexpected aid for the allies was early provided when the Marqués de la Romana arrived at Santander from Denmark in October 1808, escorted by British warships, with 9,000 first-class Spanish troops which Godoy had lent Napoleon in the previous year. This slightly fantastic *See* p. 92 escapade, engineered in the first place by a Scottish monk from Ratisbon disguised as a commercial traveller in the chocolate-trade, bears all the marks of picaresque fiction except that it is strictly authentic.

The heroic civilian defence of Saragossa has already been mentioned. The long siege of the half-ruinous fortress of Gerona provided another vexatious surprise for the French. The holding down of overrun provinces by Soult and Ney in Galicia, Augereau and Saint-Cyr in Catalonia, and Suchet in Aragon soon became a problem insoluble either by brutality or diplomacy. The Junta of the Resistance kept up a flow of recruits for Wellington, whose *See* PLATE XXIX p. 154 victory at Talavera startled the French high command into an appeal to the Emperor for more troops. Andalucia, connected in the French mind, as in many others, with guitars and moonshine, provided a severe shock by routing the combined forces of Gobert, Dupont, and Vedel. National morale continued unshakable. In 1810 the Central Junta operating unperturbed from besieged Cadiz declared Spain a regency headed by General Castaños, the patriarchal Jovellanos – the Nestor and in satire, perhaps, the Juvenal of his age – Saavedra, Floridablanca, and other elder statesmen under the presi- *See* p. 28 dency of the Bishop of Orense.

There is no need to pursue the course of the war in detail. In 1811 Wellington routed Masséna at Fuentes de Onoro and Soult took a thrashing at Albuera from Castaños, Blake, and Beresford. In the next year came the siege at Ciudad Rodrigo which earned Wellington the Spanish dukedom and estates still in the family. Following came Marmont's defeat at Badajoz and a smashing half-hour victory at Salamanca which opened for Wellington the road to Madrid, whence King Joseph withdrew in haste to Valencia.

In 1813 the war took on a quicker tempo, Joseph having transferred his capital to Burgos with a train of three hundred baggage-waggons, and – a stroke of immense good fortune for the allies – having assumed command of the entire French forces. On 21st June 1813 at Vitoria the eminent royal strategist with Marshal Jourdan and 65,000 troops in a bad position faced Wellington and his coadjutors, 45,000 troops and auxiliaries, in a good one. The action ended with a whole French army streaming back pell mell across the mountains to Pamplona, leaving behind five years' accumulation of priceless loot. 'Well, gentlemen,' said old Jourdan to his staff as the rout began, 'you've had your battle.' Within a month, like one or two others, he was retired in disgrace, the hard-pressed Emperor now having Russia and half Europe on his hands. Thenceforth the French in Spain were fighting little but defensive and rearguard actions. On 7th October 1813, having retaken Pamplona and San Sebastian, the Allies attacked the line of the Bidassoa. In the evening of that day they were across the frontier and the war was over.

Thus, also an epoch. 'With these military and political happenings', remarks the historian Manuel Ballesteros Gaibrois, contemplating the subsequent return of Fernando VII to absolute rule as if nothing had happened since his departure, 'ended the second stage of the liquidation of the Old Régime.'

See PLATES VIII & XXXVII p. 65 & p. 185

> *O corona de Iberia, alza la frente!*
> *Tiende la vista ; en iris de bonanza*
> *Se torne al fin la tempestad sombría!*
>
> Crown of Iberia, raise high thy head!
> See! the grim tempest gives place at length
> to the tints of fine weather! (*Quintana,*
> *Al Armamento de las Provincias Españolas*
> *contra los Franceses.*)

The poets played up nobly to the fighting men. Not the least remarkable figures of the period for courage and imperturbability were the statesmen and lawyers composing the Central Junta to which Marquess Wellesley, Wellington's elder brother, acted as British ambassador in 1809. A Cortes operating from Cadiz was to merit the same respect. Cut off from all contact with the rest of the nation it continued to represent the *de jure* government of Spain, though its deliberations and decisions could have little or no effect.

The Peninsular War is sufficiently summed up from a modern French standpoint in *L'Inconnu*, Félix Olivier-Martin's penetrating examen of the Napoleonic legend. It marks the beginning, for the Empire, of 'that haemorrhage which will be the chief material factor in its collapse; involving the loss of 400,000 men, more than it will leave behind in Russia'. Napoleon himself, having simultaneously taken on the disastrous Russian gamble of 1812 – 'the ultimate madness', as it has well been styled – had curiously little to say about Spain to his faithful Bertrand at St Helena, apart from censuring the Infante Fernando for plotting behind his father's back with a foreign sovereign (himself), and from criticizing Godoy. 'He was far from being a clever man.

See p. 92

He should never have allowed a foreign army to cross the Pyrenees. A steel fist was required on the Pyrenees.'[1] To the quarrels between his marshals and to the blunders of his commander-in-chief – 'Soult did not quite understand

See p. 190

a field of battle,' said Wellington suavely – the ex-Emperor made no allusion.

So Fernando VII, backed by British bayonets, returned from imprisonment as Napoleon's guest – apparently a servile one – in the château of

See PLATE XXXVIII pp. 186–87

Valençay to regain his throne. Godoy, now a refugee in Rome with Carlos IV and the Queen, was shortly expelled at Fernando's demand and moved on

---

[1] *Memoirs of General Bertrand*, deciphered and annotated by Fleuriot de Langle, 1953.

for the rest of his life to Paris. After existing some time in relative penury he was granted a 6,000-franc pension by the frugal Louis-Philippe. Visiting him in 1838 in his shabby fourth-floor lodging, Lord Holland found him 'good-humoured, jovial, and hearty . . . speaking with less bitterness of Fernando, and with more of Don Carlos, than I had expected'. In 1847 the one-time master of Spain, known to children playing in the Tuileries gardens as 'Monsieur Manuel', had his titles and estates restored by a decree of Isabella II, but before the complicated legal business pertaining was completed Godoy was dead, at the age of eighty-five. After his fall, apparently, he had no further contact of any kind with his one-time admired friend and protégé Goya, who was in Paris for three months in 1824. Perhaps there were memories neither wished to revive.

See PLATES VIII & XXXVII p. 6 & p. 185

See p. 134

See p. 92

★   ★   ★

Don Francisco Goya, First Painter to the Spanish Crown, had had, in the cynical phrase of a later age, a pretty good war.

Portrait-commissions from both sides had continued satisfactorily. That of 'El Empecinado', glaring and whiskered, has survived that of King Joseph I, the belaurelled central figure in an allegory entitled 'The City of Madrid', due before long to be painted out to celebrate the historic date of the Second of May. It is not possible to guess at Goya's private reactions during the hostilities. They may have varied at intervals. Doubtless the most ardent idealist collaborating with his country's enemies must go through some bad moments with his conscience. The news from his heroic native Saragossa in particular may have shaken him; one or two French or francophil sitters might even have quailed at a sudden outburst evoked by some casual jape on the subject. One would not do Goya the injustice of assuming that he really wished to see his country a puppet-state under Napoleonic domination, and he would not, one feels, be the only Spaniard of his kind to be disappointed with the result of five years' war; perhaps not without reason.

See p. 196
See p. 28

A more glassy-eyed reactionary than Fernando VII never occupied a European throne, and liberalism at this period was a growing force in Spain – a liberalism, it is necessary to add, of a kind distinct from that flourishing elsewhere in Europe. However tinged with Voltaireanism it was normally hostile neither to the Catholic religion nor to national tradition, aiming for the most part merely to abolish the shoal of ancient privileges and anomalies, ecclesiastical, social, and political, still complicating Spanish existence. Nor had its adherents for the most part been deeply enamoured of French liberalism as recently expressed in terms of conquest and pillage. But even the aftermath of this might have been more endurable than the straight-jacket absolutism of a Fernando, and Goya must have resumed his official position – having been curtly reminded by his new master that he deserved a garrotting – with no great enthusiasm.

See PLATES VIII & XXXVII p. 65 & p. 185

e Knife Grinder, about 1812
on canvas
¼ × 19⅝ in. (68 × 50 cm.)
épmüvészeti Múzeum,
dapest

e Forge, about 1812
on canvas
½ × 49¼ in. (196.7 × 125 cm.)
e Frick Collection, New York

See pp. 229–39

Whether Goya could be called a patriot of any kind at this time seems a matter for debate, considering the impartiality of his brush. It is fair to add that he does not lack defenders. They argue that by many of the Spanish intelligentsia the French were regarded as liberators from feudal ignorance and absolutism. Goya himself (they add), being a progressive idealist, belonged to this group, which at one time included several of the nobility and a few of the higher clergy. Whether or not this theory explains away the idealist's gallop, with no loss of time, back to service under Fernando VII is questionable.

Since even genius may be harassed at intervals by a conscience, it is possible, as already remarked, that during five years' martyrdom of the Spanish people Don Francisco Goya passed some bad moments of solitude in his house in the Calle del Desengaño. The usurper was not personally difficult to endure. In Napoleon's fraternally-contemptuous references to Joseph at St Helena (Bertrand reporting), his younger brother appears a genial, likeable duffer, extremely fond of women and under an illusion or two concerning his intelligence and military qualifications. 'Joseph thinks he is a great general', Napoleon had said years previously to Belliard. 'He thinks he can lead an army as well as I.' As temporary King of Spain Joseph Bonaparte seems to have essayed everything possible to court popularity. If his nickname among a derisive populace – *Pepe Botellas*, 'Joe Bottles' – ever reached his ears he may have taken it for a mark of affection. That Goya could paint his portrait in laurelled glory doubtless strengthened such illusions. That Goya was hagridden likewise at intervals with despair, fury, remorse, and perhaps even shame, is clear from a series of eighty-five etchings on which he was engaged at this time. Finished around 1815, Waterloo year, they were not published till 1863.

The distinctive mark of 'Disasters of War', as the series is called, is that not a single plate is concerned with any kind of military operation. Barring one glimpse of two or three cavalrymen tumbling off their horses, Goya is absorbed totally by the sufferings of the civilian Spanish proletariat over the recent five years; a record of sadism, starvation, epidemic, torture, murder, every kind of brutality which might more simply have been labelled 'The Terror'. Hacked-off human heads and limbs dangle from trees. Women facing rape cower before leering and jeering soldiery, with dead or dying children clasped to them. Naked civilian corpses are heaved into the plague-carts for conveyance to the common pit. Monks escaping from sacked monasteries are pursued by whooping soldiers, sabres in hand. No kind of savagery seems to be omitted. The 'Disasters' might possibly be styled a self-inflicted penance for what has seemed to some to amount to collaboration as well as an indictment of the French, not to say of total war. Two of them bear the comment 'This I saw'; '. . . and this as well'.

A significant work of imagination occupied Goya at this period equally – a painting called 'The Cannibals Prepare the Body of the Archbishop of

he Water Girl, about 1812
on canvas
¾ × 19⅝ in. (68 × 50 cm.)
zépmüvészeti Múzeum,
udapest

Quebec', inspired apparently by the fate of two of the seventeenth-century Jesuit martyrs of Canada. In a stony waste a trio of Redskins is feasting on flesh torn from a naked corpse dangling from a rope above them.[1] The application seems obvious. Today, one gathers, this arresting canvas hangs in the municipal art-gallery at Besançon in the Jura, doubtless to the discouragement of cannibalism in that sedate little cathedral-city. Together with the 'Disasters' it may have cleansed Goya's bosom of much perilous stuff. It may be noted finally that the ruffian soldiery of the 'Disasters' are wearing French uniform in at least half a dozen plates, and that the original title of the series is uncompromising enough: *Fatales Consecuencias de la Sangrienta Guerra contra Buonaparte, y Otros Caprichos Enfáticos*. They were rechristened *Desastres de la Guerra* by the Royal Academy of San Fernando on publication in 1863. It is not the artist who can be blamed for tact in this particular matter.

A real blot on Goya's record at this period, in the eyes of art-lovers, must be his acquiescence in 1810, when he was ordered with two other painters, Maella and Napoli, to select fifty outstanding examples of Spanish pictorial art for transfer to Paris. For the defence it can be pointed out that Goya and his aides took care to select the least valuable, including fourteen specimens of minor works by Velázquez, Murillo, Zurbarán, and Ribera. Though, as it happened, these paintings were destined never to reach Paris, he was decorated for this business by King Joseph with the ribbon and jewel of a new 'Order of Spain', derisively known as 'The Egg-Plant', but forbore to wear it; with Aragonese sagacity, as it turned out, since immediately after Joseph's final exit this decoration became troublesome to many. On Fernando VII's return numbers of ex-collaborators were combed out and imprisoned on charges of treason. It seems that Goya went into hiding for three months in the house of a friend. When the storm had sufficiently blown over he was able to convince Fernando sufficiently of his innocence to be restored to his official post as First Painter; the King's already-quoted remark concerning what he really deserved had no sequel.

Yet another self-portrait, dated 1815 and now in the Prado in Madrid, reveals the march of time. The greying black hair is still thick and tousled, *au naturel*. The dark coat is defiantly open-necked. The spectacles, that ritual adornment of an older Spanish world which had moved Madame d'Aulnoy to wondering prose, are discarded – for the occasion only, perhaps, since he would now be needing them for work. The artist's features, if this be not too fanciful, express the assurance of a new progressive age about to assert itself in terms of steam engines and balloons; a fine Goyaesque landscape overhung by a most decorative balloon emerges in fact in 1818. The great famine of 1817, the final bequest of five years of invasion, turning the poorer quarters of Madrid alone, with 20,000 dead of hunger, into a nightmare-scene, inspired several etchings of the second Disaster Series. It is

See PLATE XXX pp. 164–65

See pp. 229–39

Self-portrait, about 1815
oil on canvas
$18\frac{1}{8} \times 13\frac{3}{4}$ in. (46 × 35 cm.)
Museo del Prado, Madrid

See PLATES VIII & XXXVII p. 65 & p. 185

PLATE XXX. Saturn
– one of The Black Paintings, 1819–23
fresco transferred to canvas
$57\frac{1}{2} \times 32\frac{5}{8}$ in. (146 × 83 cm.)
Museo del Prado, Madrid

(overleaf)
PLATE XXXI. The Cannibals Prepare the Body of the Archbishop of Quebec and that of his Secretary, to Eat them, about 1815
oil on canvas
$13 \times 18\frac{1}{2}$ in. (33 × 47 cm.)
Musée de Peinture, Besançon

---

[1]The Iroquois who dealt with Pères de Brébeuf and de Lalement (beatified, 1925, with three others), remarks Sánchez Cantón, were not cannibals, and there was no Archbishop of Quebec at the time.

obligatory for justice's sake to recall that in this crisis King Joseph on the eve of his final exit revealed himself a man of humanity and action, organizing and taking the lead, incognito, in the mass-distribution of bread and alms.

Goya had become obsessed meanwhile by a new interest, born in 1815, that of the bullfight as a work of art.

★   ★   ★

Beautiful and terrible, carefully bred, full of ferocity and science, displaying and evoking in his adversaries the highest courage, skill and endurance, the bull in early nineteenth-century Spain was loved and admired as today – a fact difficult to explain to the Nordic sportsman, and especially to hard-men-to-hounds pursuing the fox. In England at this period, one may recall, bulls were chained to a stake at fairs to be attacked by savage dogs; a pitiable and revolting spectacle, since more often than not the bull was covered with half-healed wounds and haggard with previous baitings. Not till the 1840s was this business abolished by law. To the Spaniard, contrariwise, the bull has been for centuries, almost literally, an idol.

See pp. 240–45

Such an attempt at 'situation' seems essential to any grasp of Goya's tauromachy series. One may clearly glimpse Don Francisco on any afternoon during the season in his seat in the Madrid bull ring; on the shady side, very near the president's, seated well forward, scanning every move in the arena, fingering his pencil, sketchbook at hand, as critical of every act below as any *aficionado* on the cheap side sweating in the sun. The trumpets sound. Not all current pageantry was yet established – the mounted *alguacils* in the costume of Felipe IV's time heading the procession of bullfighters towards the presidential box, the ceremonial salutes, the toreros taking their places as the trumpets sound again, the doors of the *toril* flung open, the first bull of the

See p. 69

afternoon charging into the arena and challenging the world. But the spell was the same.

Goya will confine his studies for this new series neither to the metropolitan ring nor to the current corrida. He delves deep into the history and legend of the bullfight and its Moorish origin; a theme which had long since inspired his friend the poet Nicolás Fernández de Moratín to that already mentioned ballad-romance called *Fiesta de Toros in Madrid*, featuring (to adopt film-language, here appropriate) the corrida ordered by the Alcalde Aliatar in honour of the beautiful Zaida, and the gallantry in the ring of the Cid Rodrigo. Goya's handling of his subject at large has not escaped criticism from *aficionados* and artists alike. The fantasy which produced the *Caprichos* and the *Disparates* tends to obtrude at times, jarring on the serious and scientific as would, say, the lyrico-mystical elements of a poem on Association football by Claudel or T. S. Eliot. Some art-critics have considered his interpretation of mass-emotion too vague and fluid. All of them laud his powers of expressing swift and complex violence in action. There can be no cavilling at his

PLATE XXXII. A 'Manola':
Doña Leocadia Zorrilla?
- one of The Black Paintings,
1819–23
oil on plaster transferred
to canvas
57⅞ × 52 in. (147 × 132 cm.)
Museo del Prado, Madrid

The terrible events that took place in the stands of the ring at Madrid, and the death of the mayor of Torrejón (No. 21 of th Bull-fighting series)
etching, burnished aquatint, lavis, drypoint and burin
$9\frac{5}{8} \times 14$ in. (24.5 × 35.5 cm.)
The British Museum, London

The same Ceballos, mounted on a bull, breaks small spears in the ring at Madrid (No. 24 of the Bull-fighting series)
etching, burnished aquatint, drypoint and burin
$9\frac{5}{8} \times 14$ in. (24.5 × 35.5 cm.)
The British Museum, London

The unfortunate death of Pepehillo in the ring at Madrid (No. 33 of the Bull-fighting series)
etching, burnished aquatint, drypoint and burin
$9\frac{5}{8} \times 13\frac{3}{4}$ in. (24.5 × 35 cm.)
The British Museum, London

handling of a moment like the death in the Madrid ring of the illustrious Pepehillo, inventor of the 'flying rush', wrenching at the terrible horns transfixing him. The *mystique* of the bull ring crowd and its swiftly changing moods obviously fascinate Goya powerfully, and he is, as many commentators have noted, especially interested in the difficult and ungrateful role of the *See* p. 70 picadors; in one plate an inextricable tangle of man, horse, and bull on the *See* p. 244 sand is superbly presented.

Since the corrida is not a sport but a rite, any attempt at comparison of Goya's etchings with the work of sporting artists contemporary or modern is impossible. His version of a British fox-hunt would have been, no doubt, enjoyably grotesque; he would not be able to understand to begin with – as any enthusiast would assure him – that the fox enjoys it. Goyaesque playfulness is perceptible in the plate in which the bull, leaping into the ringside-seats at Torrejón, near Alcalá de Henares, has attacked the local alcalde in person. Among the nearest spectators is one strongly resembling the artist. There is no doubt that Goya was a judge of *lidia*, the science, art, and strategy of the bull ring, and was capable of distinguishing a 'noble' bull from one of poor caste very early; likewise of appreciating – though old jealousies may still have burned – the art of Pedro Romero and his two illustrious colleagues. That he owed some of his knowledge to the late Duchess seems likely enough. He was no pedant on the subject. Purists might shake their heads over the conduct of the torero Mariano Ceballos (*El Indio*) who defied all the canons of propriety by employing the banderilla with himself mounted on a bull; a circus-trick, possibly Moorish, appealing to Goya, who duly recorded it, likewise the heresy of another torero vaulting over the bull. Otherwise he respected the dignity of Taurus Africanus. The bulls of the *Tauromaquia* set are elegant and formidable; fit brethren, as Gómez de la Serna remarks, of the historic animal presented by the Duke of Veragua to the Museum of National History.

Had he produced nothing else, this display of vehement tragi-comedy would have proclaimed Goya a master and, incidentally, a pioneer of the study of crowd-psychology in art. 'Are these crowds a presence or an hallucination?' asks Eugenio d'Ors. In some mysterious way Goya has got at the mob-soul more than once; the tension of the spectators is something almost audible, almost fluid, almost visible, like the alleged emanations to be viewed in spiritist photography. Above all throbs the action in the ring for which this series might well be called cinematographic, like the *Dos de Mayo*. One *See* PLATE XXVIII p. 153 plate in colour in which a village arena is divided in halves, each with its own bullfight, is actually bewildering in its complex vitality.

And now, towards 1817, the personal clouds are gathering more densely. Goya is entering on his seventies, more temperamental, more touchy, more morose. The Duchess who bewitched him has been dead fifteen years. His *See* PLATE I p. 33 wife Josefa died in 1811. Of their children only Javier, the comely young buck

(left) Mariano Goya, the artist's grandson, about 1816
oil on panel
$23\frac{1}{4} \times 18\frac{1}{2}$ in. (59 × 47 cm.)
Collection the Duke of Alburquerque, Madrid

(below) SIR PETER PAUL RUBENS
Saturn Devouring a Son, 1636
oil on canvas
$70\frac{7}{8} \times 34\frac{1}{4}$ in. (180 × 87 cm.)
Museo del Prado, Madrid

of the portrait of about 1804, is now in circulation, and apparently in business of some sort in Madrid. Married a few years previously, Javier has a child, Mariano, the alluring portrait (about 1816) of whom, in a tall beaver hat, with a music-score by his side, apparently conducting an imaginary orchestra with another one rolled up, seems evidence that his grandfather cannot have been consistently the glum ageing misanthrope we contemplate at this period.

See p. 31

But the dark days have certainly arrived. Deafness has long since been total, and other disabilities not diagnosed seem to have been increasing; the dizziness, the faintness, mental gloom, pathological crises, an expanding irritability. 'I get so furious at times', he had written to Zapater some time before, 'that I become unbearable even to myself. Then I calm down. . . . But I am very tired.' He ends: 'On Monday, God willing, I am going to the corrida – I'd be glad if you could come too.'

The bulls at length failed Goya also. A distaste for human society, a *taedium vitae* now growing on him, called for the catharsis of a sombre

See PLATES XXX, XXXII, XXXIII, XXXIV, XXXV, p. 163, p. 166, p. 173, p. 175

new series known as The Black Paintings, painted on the walls of his retreat, the Quinta del Sordo, to which we shall come very shortly. The message is more savage and sweeping than that of the *Caprichos*. Goya's target this time is not human folly but the cosmos itself. The kind of hallucinationary fumes exhaled by The Black Paintings continue to inspire a wealth of hermetic abracadabra in art-critics, French and British particularly. Malraux has invented an excellent covering-phrase in 'the corrosive line'. Others have taken refuge, not unnaturally, in psychiatry; The Black Paintings are 'projections of the lonely schizophrenic ego still in conflict with itself', or alternatively, 'communiqués from a mysterious battlefield'.

See PLATE XXX p. 163

The horrific vision called 'Saturn', one of The Black Paintings, evokes natural comparison with the celebrated Rubens canvas on the same theme which Goya had studied in the royal collection. As essays in pictorial sadism go there is not much to choose between them; Rubens's inspiration is perhaps the lusher. The zest with which Saturn leans to suck his struggling offspring's blood as it spurts resembles that of a sturdy Flemish burgher stooping to a roast goose. Goya's Saturn, hoary, glaring, hollow-eyed and mad, is in the midst of his meal, with jaws at work on one of the remaining arms of a gory remnant of the body gripped in his fists, as one wolfing asparagus. It is a less juicy occasion than Rubens's.

The atmosphere of The Black Paintings, unlike that of the *Caprichos*, is unrelieved nightmare, making the witch-gambols of the earlier series look like a dance of housewives. It is simultaneously night and day. The flying monsters, the portents and visions of The Black Paintings, are not of this world. It has proved inevitable to drag in Freud, though, as we may recall, the Viennese master does not seem to know his Goya. The frontispiece of the first English

See p. 172

edition of *Introductory Lectures on Psycho-Analysis* (1921) called 'The Prisoner's Dream', by Moritz von Schwind, is a mild banality which side by side with the least macabre of The Black Paintings looks like an illustration to *Hansel and Gretel*.

Behind the fantastic masquerade of The Black Paintings is a fertility of imagination, a technique, a power of evoking the terrors of the Dark unique in painting. More than one or two of these productions continue to defy all exegesis and lucid explanation. Sadism, hallucination, grotesquerie, fantasy, mockery, comedy, terror, burlesque, nihilism, the darkest and wildest obsessions of the subconscious, the quintessence of the Demonology compose an *olla podrida* cooked, one might almost say, on the hobs of Hell.

★   ★   ★

Whether due to his physical condition or to the phantasms conjured up by a kind of nihilism Goya seems to have suddenly conceived a horror of life. He quitted his house in the Calle del Desengaño in about 1819 and retired to wrestle with his daemon in a hermitage of sorts just outside the capital, on the

(left) MORITZ VON SCHWIND
The Prisoner's Dream, about
oil on board
$19\frac{5}{8} \times 18\frac{7}{8}$ in. (50×48 cm.)
Bayer. Staatsgemäldesamm-
lungen, Munich

(opposite left) Two Monks,
1819–23
– one of The Black Paintings
oil on plaster transferred to
canvas
$56\frac{3}{4} \times 26$ in. (144×66 cm.)
Museo del Prado, Madrid

(opposite centre) Two Women
and a Man – one of The Black
Paintings, 1819–23
oil on plaster transferred to
canvas
$49\frac{1}{4} \times 26$ in. (125×66 cm.)
Museo del Prado, Madrid

(opposite right) The Reading
– one of The Black Paintings,
1819–23
oil on plaster transferred to
canvas
$49\frac{5}{8} \times 26$ in. (126×66 cm.)
Museo del Prado, Madrid

banks of the Manzanares near the Segovia bridge. It was here that he began to occupy himself with The Black Paintings.

His retreat, shared for a time only by an old manservant, was what the French call a *pavillon*, on rising ground surrounded by a garden entirely enclosed by trees. An existent print shows a long low house, agreeable enough; large windows on both storeys; a tiled roof; part of a flower garden with trees and a fountain. Till the 1870s the house was known locally as the Quinta del Sordo, 'Deaf Man's Villa'; its remains are now part of a branch railway station and unrecognizable. Here, on the plastered walls of the living-room and the studio, and apparently in the intervals of gardening, the ageing Goya painted in oils the fourteen productions, covering some thirty-five square yards, which Baron Emile d'Erlanger was to rescue nearly sixty years later, in the very nick of time.

Following a recently-published analysis of The Black Paintings by two

See PLATE XXXIII p. 175

current authorities, it would be more than absurd to attempt anything of the kind in these pages. One may however attempt to set down something of their impact on the amateur. 'Black' here concerns the mood. Only two of the series are dominantly so in terms of colour; one being a study of a stone-deaf bearded ancient accompanied by a demoniacal character bellowing into his ear, the other a caricature of the return from the annual local pilgrimage of San Isidro; a gallimaufry of idiotic and ghoulish faces with gibbering mouths. Figuratively speaking the epithet 'black' covers them all. Of the devils now possessing Goya those of total deafness, increasing ill-health and loneliness, dead passion, the bitter dissatisfaction of success, the disillusion of fame, weariness of life, above all the onset of old age, with its inevitable effects on brain, eyes, and hands – though he was to be spared any failing of his power till the very end – these enemies Goya may have challenged singly and *en masse*.

'Every moon is atrocious, every sun bitter' – perhaps only Rimbaud can adequately convey the mood in which Goya covered the walls of the Quinta; Rimbaud with, perhaps, a dash of the Yeats of the late 1920s:

> What shall I do with this absurdity –
> O heart, O troubled heart – this caricature,
> Decrepit age that has been tied on me
> As upon a dog's tail?
> > Never had I more

173

Excited, passionate, fantastical
Imagination, nor an ear and eye
That more expected the impossible . . .[1]

(above) PLATE XXXIII. The
Festival of San Isidro – one of
The Black Paintings (detail),
1819–23
oil on plaster transferred to
canvas
55⅝ × 172½ in. (140 × 438 cm.)
Museo del Prado, Madrid

(centre) PLATE XXXIV. The
Witches Sabbath – one of
The Black Paintings, 1819–23
oil on plaster transferred to
canvas
55⅝ × 172½ in. (140 × 438 cm.)
Museo del Prado, Madrid

(below) PLATE XXXV. Fight with
Clubs – one of The Black
Paintings, 1819–23
oil on plaster transferred to
canvas
48⅜ × 104¾ in. (123 × 266 cm.)
Museo del Prado, Madrid

Possibly some of Goya's devils were exorcised for a time by painting them. One may imagine him doggedly at it day after day, covering blank walls with nightmare shapes till dusk or weariness compelled a halt. His only recreation at this period, it appears, was the gardening into which he flung himself – and his manservant – with zest.

There is something impressive in the thought of the old man eating his lonely dinner with such self-created ghoulishness surrounding him. Saturn wolfing his offspring; two desperate ruffians fighting with clubs, sinking knee-deep into a bog or quicksand; a congress of witches addressed by their dread lord the Goat; fantastic, vulturish, and prophetic figures of flying men; figures with animal faces or livid, gibbering masks; several mysterious inexplicable shadow-scenes, such as that of a dog's head gazing skywards: Judith, deliverer of Israel, swinging an immense bloody sword. Even from the walls of the Prado they radiate a chill on the sunniest day.

O the mind, mind has mountains; cliffs of fall
Frightful, sheer, no-man-fathomed. Hold them cheap
May who ne'er hung there . . .[2]

The most enigmatic of these murals is, oddly enough, neither fantastic nor diabolic. It represents simply a *manola*, a woman of the Madrilene majority, leaning on one elbow against a rock on which may be seen the square railing of a tomb. She wears the ritual black skirt, bodice, and mantilla. Her expression, gazing ahead and to the left, is one of pensive melancholy. Attempts to identify her with the late Duchess of Alba seem a trifle far-fetched; neither the features, the pose, nor the aura is reminiscent. The figure might have possibly some allegorical significance.[3] In a Victorian picture-gallery it would be labelled 'Memory Brooding Over the Tomb of Love', or something of the kind. Its impact on the viewer of The Black Paintings, one might venture to suggest, involves the surprise value of a piece of simple Christmas Annual sentiment appearing cheek-by-jowl with so many complicated exercises dictated by Bogey; the fact that the tomb-railing is somewhat reminiscent of that of a nursery cot of a past generation may even heighten this contrast. As a production of the master Goya in satanico-misanthropic mood *La Manola* is certainly puzzling.

See PLATE XXXII p. 166

[1] *October Blast*, 1927.

[2] Gerard Manley Hopkins, *Carrion Comfort*.

[3] An alternative theory that it is a portrait of Leocadia Weiss has been suggested. That it is simply an abstract impersonal tribute to a dead passion is adjudged equally feasible. Dr. Xavier de Salas thinks the portrait of a plump lady in black (Bauer, Harris, Swiss Cot.) may be that of Leocadia.

5 Retreat at sundown

See PLATE XXXII p. 166

THE somewhat formidable figure of Doña Leocadia Weiss, born Zorrilla, now enters Goya's life, to remain in it as housekeeper and mistress till the end.

No portrait of her exists, unless indeed she is the original of 'La Manola' of The Black Paintings. She was apparently a middle-aged distant relative of somewhat shaky virtue, married to a German merchant born in Madrid. Four years after marriage her husband, Isidor Weiss, had tried unsuccessfully to secure a legal separation on the grounds of her unfaithfulness – *la conducta y trato ilícito de su mujer* – and her temper. She descended on the Quinta del Sordo with a young child christened Maria del Rosario and known by her pet-name, 'Rosarito'. A much older son was in the background. When Doña Leocadia's husband applied a second time, again unsuccessfully, for a separation, a year before Rosarito's birth, her mother was already Goya's housekeeper. This has seemed to some an indication that he might be Rosarito's father, which would account for his notable and unceasing affection for the child.

In 1819 Goya was seventy-three, stone-deaf, lonely, misanthropic, but still in command of splendid faculties. He needed someone to look after him, preferably a woman of mature experience. Apparently Señora Weiss possessed this qualification, with something of a shrewish tongue, the temper already noted, and advanced opinions, derived belike from Weiss. These were a notable German predilection of the period. Frau Marx had just given birth to tiny Karl, and German taverns were full of philosophers of the Teufelsdröckh pattern emitting transcendental socialism and the Hegelian Absolute through their whiskers with every puff of tobacco-smoke, over steins of the beer called *Gukguk*. To many German exiles in foreign capitals such philosophy would be the voice of the Fatherland.

Whether or not Doña Leocadia's liberalism derived from this source, she was apparently a woman of strong and fixed convictions, and not backward in expressing them. It may be reasonably conjectured that Goya, no thinker without a brush or pencil in his hand, took the line of least resistance in consideration of such benefits as companionship, a hearth, and home-comforts. For a Leocadia Weiss he was easy meat. Whether his deafness would dispose of a feminine urge to lecture at large is a matter for conjecture; no doubt Señora Weiss had soon been able to invent some means of com-

.ATE XXXVI. The Colossus, or
nic, about 1808
 on canvas
 × 41¾ in. (116 × 105 cm.)
useo del Prado, Madrid

The Council of the Philippines,
about 1816
oil on canvas
$114\frac{1}{2} \times 166\frac{3}{4}$ in.
(367 × 443.5 cm.)
Museé Goya, Castres

munication. The presence of the child Rosarito, in whom Goya was delighted
to discover artistic talent, was to make up for a great deal. Like most Spaniards
he loved children. Rosarito became his darling, and in due course, his pupil.

He was still, as the phrase goes, in full production. Between 1812 and 1819
his range of canvases includes the large group-subject in oils known as 'The
Junta of the Philippines', a study of this industrial and mercantile council in
session. Behind the long high table on the dais at one end of a lofty, dusky hall,
lit only by a central ray of sunshine, sit the King, their president, and his
officials, barely recognizable in shadow. On either side below them – at this
moment the secretary is reading a document to Fernando – are the councillors,
seated in various attitudes of attention, inattention, resignation, critical concentration, abstraction. They listen cross-legged, lounging at ease, dozing,
stiffly upright, turning to chat. One or two contemplate the distant ceiling as
if frozen with boredom; another is seemingly asleep and at peace. Evidently
the proceedings have been more long-winded than usual. They will make
little or no difference to the affairs of the Philippines.

The master's satiric eye has viewed in this assembly any one of its kind in
the world; the scene during a contemporary Commons debate in London on
colonial exports would resemble it closely, save that at this period a few
sporting members might be drunk. What is notable in the 'Junta' is the work
Goya has put into it; the varying poses and expressions, the lethargy overhanging all, the light effects, subtle and brilliant. More obviously barbed is a

e Balloon, about 1818
on canvas
$\frac{1}{4}$ × 172$\frac{1}{2}$ in. (140.3 × 438 cm.)
usee, Agen

d Women, about 1817
on canvas
$\frac{1}{4}$ × 48$\frac{3}{8}$ in. (181 × 123 cm.)
lais des Beaux-Arts, Lille

painting of this period entitled 'The Old Ladies'. Two antiquated ex-beauties in fine dress and jewels are gazing into a mirror inscribed on the back '*Qué tal?*' – 'How's everything?' Behind them hovers Father Time, broom in hand. Also at this time, to show his unimpaired versatility, Goya next produced a fine wild landscape under a magnificent sky, with a decorative balloon overhanging it. New portraits include the captivating study of his

See p. 170

little grandson Mariano. Before long he will paint Rosarito as well.

A new domesticity, with recurring intervals of stress and storm, now comforted the ageing master, who may have come by now to regret the loss

See PLATE I p. 33

of patient Josefa and his absorption in the Other.

There was little comfort in the post-war outlook. The despot Fernando was served by a *camarilla* of noblemen universally disliked and despised. There was unrest among the Army generals and the late guerrilleros equally. In the provinces Cadiz was a continuous centre of disturbance; even now a

179

military plot which ripened in 1820 may have been maturing. Simultaneously the huge and for the most part prosperous overseas empire won by the Conquistadores was showing signs of imminent disruption.

It would be as fatiguing to unravel all the causes as to follow the course – under lethal suns, against a background of endless brown pampas, towering sierra, extinct volcanoes, wide, deep rivers, swamps and immense forests full of menace, *adobe* villages, washed blue or brown, Spanish-baroque capitals – of a conflict confusing as a kaleidoscope. Last-ditcher colonists and a small force of Spanish troops are viewed at grips with separatists, Indians, Negroes, halfbreeds, roving bands of irregulars. Rival dictators bob up, fight and fall. A village priest like the celebrated *cura* Hidalgo raises and commands an insurgent Mexican army in the field. A prelate like the Archbishop of Bogotá proclaims Colombia's independence. The vultures and the alligators are busy. One outstanding historical figure emerges from the tumult – that of Simon Bolivar, liberator of Venezuela, whose dictum that 'absolute democratic government is as much a tyranny as despotism' must strike oddly on the ears of a few modern demagogues.

At the root of the revolt, qualified historians seem to agree, was not so much *laissez-faire* and mismanagement from Madrid as the dissolvent influence throughout the colonies – as to some extent in Spain, where even the regular army had its lodges – of freemasonry on the French Encyclopaedist pattern. Vigorous anti-Spanish propaganda had been lately infiltrating the Americas from Europe; moreover Fernando VII's return to absolute rule alienated numbers of colonial loyalists who had supported the mother-country financially and otherwise during the Peninsular War. Among more remote contributory factors Ramiro de Maeztu recalls that the chief concern of one or two early eighteenth-century viceroys had been the paying of their debts, a normal preoccupation of the period. According to an envoy from the United States quoting San Martín, liberator of the Argentine, Chile, and Peru – among other leading rebels he had fought in Spain against Napoleon – insurrection was due not to any oppression by the Spanish Crown but to the 'deplorable necessity' of self-government. By 1825 Mexico, Venezuela, Colombia, Peru, Ecuador, Bolivia, Uruguay, Paraguay, Chile, and the Argentine were self-governing republics. Brazil, having a Portuguese dynasty, remained a kingdom till the 1890s. In the Peninsular War, remarks the historian Manuel Ballesteros Gaibrois, had been forged the spirit of independence of Spanish America. The North American precedent was of course still fresh and impressive.

To Goya, absorbed as ever in his work, the omens at home and abroad may not have been as recognizable as to those in closer touch with affairs, though he can hardly have been spared some of the jubilance of Doña Leocadia. He had no personal complaint against Fernando VII, who had after all overlooked his conduct during the French occupation, restored him to his official post, and even, at his Court Painter's petition, and after Goya's

The Last Communion of St Joseph Calasanz, 1819
oil on canvas
98¾ × 70⅞ in. (250 × 180 cm.)
Escuelas Pías de San Antón, Madrid

See PLATES VIII & XXXVII p. 6 & p. 185

execution of two or three portraits of the King, none of them noteworthy,
increased his pension. One or two of Fernando's *camarilla* Goya painted likewise, without enthusiasm, though the portrait of the Duque de San Carlos,
to be viewed today in Saragossa, is said by connoisseurs to exhale irony of an
unusual subtlety. One can see Goya, if he ever devoted a few moments to
self-examination, dismissing a fleeting discomfort with a shrug. What have
the fiddlings of politicians to do with the artist? Living just before the golden
age of aesthetic punditry, he was not aware (Ruskin *dixit*) that it is the function
of Art to summon the moral energies of a nation to forgotten duties, a directive
which might well have amused Goya's old age. He would doubtless have had
approving growls on the other hand for Whistler's dictum that the artist
paints for his own satisfaction and that it is the duty of everybody else, the
art-critic above all, to mind his own business.

How far he had adjusted himself – could he ever adjust himself? – to the
uneasy new world which had ousted the comforts and securities of the
eighteenth century is difficult to conjecture. To be a liberal under Carlos III
and IV was piquant. To be labelled one under Fernando VII was impolitic
unless you enjoyed trouble; a pleasure strictly for the *engagé*, a label which
can hardly be applied to a man with a mind as divided as Goya's. He had
reasons for a qualm or two. Though there is no evidence that he was ever a
member of any lodge, with the implications such membership then involved
– anti-clerical republicanism, francophilism, subterraneous activities and
what not – he had friends of this kidney, and, being himself the author of a
few choice anti-clerical japes, may well have been suspect.

In 1820 he was summoned to the palace with fellow-members of the
Academy of which he was Director of Painting to take an oath of fidelity to the
Constitution. A surprising return to religious art in the previous year may
have had more motives than a sudden impulse of devotion. Be this suspicion
just or otherwise, he had confounded the critics in 1819 with a painting
entitled 'Christ in the Garden of Olives' which, as has so often been remarked,
a Rembrandt might have signed. Kneeling haggard, against a black sky, with
outspread arms and steadfast eyes, Our Lord receives the angel of the Agony
descending in a beam of spectral light with the chalice of pain. The lighting
of the piece is livid, as of a menacing dawn. The divine Victim is hieratic.
Nothing, save for the unearthly ambiance, could be less Goyaesque.

The same year came another canvas to baffle the quidnuncs – 'The Last
Communion of St Joseph of Calasanz', seventeenth-century founder of the
Escuelas Pías schools for children of the poor, of which the establishment at
Saragossa had afforded Goya his earliest and only education. The canvas, for
which he demanded no fee, is still in the church of San Antón in Madrid for
which it was painted. Not a few critics have discovered in it and proclaimed
another Rembrandtesque or El Grecoesque inspiration, pointing not only to
the ascetic spiritualty of the composition but to an employment of colour
typical of the Hispano-Cretan master. Others perhaps more justly point to an

(above left) Christ in the Garden
of Olives, 1819
oil on canvas
18½ × 13¾ in. (47 × 35 cm.)
Escuelas Pías de San Antón,
Madrid

(above right) SS Justa and
Rufina, 1817
oil on canvas
The Cathedral, Seville

See p. 21

inexplicable mystical streak in himself. It is a fitting counterpart to the previous work; almost an echo. The same mystical ray of light falls on the rapt emaciated kneeling figure at the sanctuary steps of the ninety-two year old saint, to whom the priest is bearing the Host in a ciborium closely resembling the chalice borne by the angel. The dawn-light in the sanctuary is livid as that in the Garden. To style these two works 'pastiche' would be to denigrate. In some mysterious way the seventy-four year old painter of the contemporary Spanish scene, himself usually as far removed from spirituality as could be imagined, has imbibed the very essence of the art of one or other – or both – of a couple of the great ascetic and spiritual painters of all time.

He was to paint one more religious piece at this period – the figures of SS Justa and Rufina, martyrs, patron saints of Seville, in Seville Cathedral. As already remarked, it is difficult for the unenlightened to see in it much more than a pair of Sevillan *majas* gazing skyward in ecstasy and tears, backed by the tower of the Giralda. Nevertheless critics of some penetration have discovered in this painting a 'febrile dynamism' and a 'peremptory agitation'. A 'much-tormented' work, is the rather curious view of Eugenio d'Ors, who adds that it exhales 'a kind of exasperation recalling moods of Cézanne'; which may well be patent to the initiate. Goya was as subject to moods and furies as any other master of his craft, though he never had to suffer rancorous critical attack like (to take a minor example) the Pre-Raphaelites of the 1840s. Had he, like them, been accused of every moral and aesthetic vice, his reaction would doubtless have exhibited a dynamism more than febrile. Actually the Seville canvas was widely acclaimed. It has been pointed out in Goya's behalf that the *maja*-like aspect of both martyrs is historically justified; they were pottery-workers actually of this class. But it seemed that the master received the plaudits with ill-humour and took some calming down by his friends.

Possibly his private judgment differed. Possibly advancing age, the applause of the ill-informed, bad health, and public affairs were combining to make him more touchy. The situation in Spain was becoming distinctly alarming. In 1822 it seemed as if the results of some years of muddle, absolutism, and increasing misery were about to combine and explode in revolution. Within a year, at Fernando VII's urgent appeal, Louis XVIII despatched to Spain an armed force of 100,000 French volunteers – 'Sons of St Louis' – under the Duke of Angoulême to 'preserve the Spanish throne for a grandson of Henri Quatre'. This interlude ended with the escorting of Fernando from Cadiz – where, having proclaimed an emergency regency, he had been practically held in custody – back to Madrid, where an unpredictable populace received him with acclamations and cries of 'Long live absolute monarchy!'. It appeared, Angoulême reported to the King of France, that the whole country would shortly be falling to pieces.

Perceiving that a pogrom of liberals might be soon on the royal agenda, Goya was at last spurred to action. The Quinta del Sordo had already been made over in legal form to his grandson, young Mariano. If he himself were not on the verge of trouble, Doña Leocadia's son Guillermo Weiss certainly was, having joined the late 'Constitutional Militia'. Young Weiss managed, however, to dodge the police and slip over the frontier to Bordeaux, where his mother shortly afterwards joined him with Rosarito. Looking round for an immediate refuge for himself, Goya found one in the house of a friend, an Aragonese cleric of high standing, Canon José Duaso; a royalist but a sympathizer with an illustrious fellow-provincial in difficulties. Here, it seems, Goya lay *perdu* for some months in extreme agitation, incapable of even painting his protector's portrait. To join Doña Leocadia Weiss in France forthwith, a move more than desirable, would mean the loss of his royal post, his pension, and most of his income. The craft of Aragon came shortly to his aid. He was old, celebrated, and infirm, and he had a right to medical treatment. Making application accordingly, in proper usage, he was informed on 30th May, 1824, that his Majesty was graciously pleased to accord his Court Painter leave of absence for six months to take the waters at Plombières-les-Bains in the Vosges, at the time a prominent spa. Goya's doctor – doubtless Arrieta, fainting in whose arms he had four years before

See p. 170

See PLATE XXXIX p. 188

PLATE XXXVII. Fernando VII
oil on canvas
83½ × 57½ in. (212 × 146 cm.)
Museo del Prado, Madrid

PLATE XXXVIII. (overleaf) The Family of Carlos IV (detail), 18
oil on canvas
110¼ × 132½ in. (280 × 336 cm.
Museo del Prado, Madrid

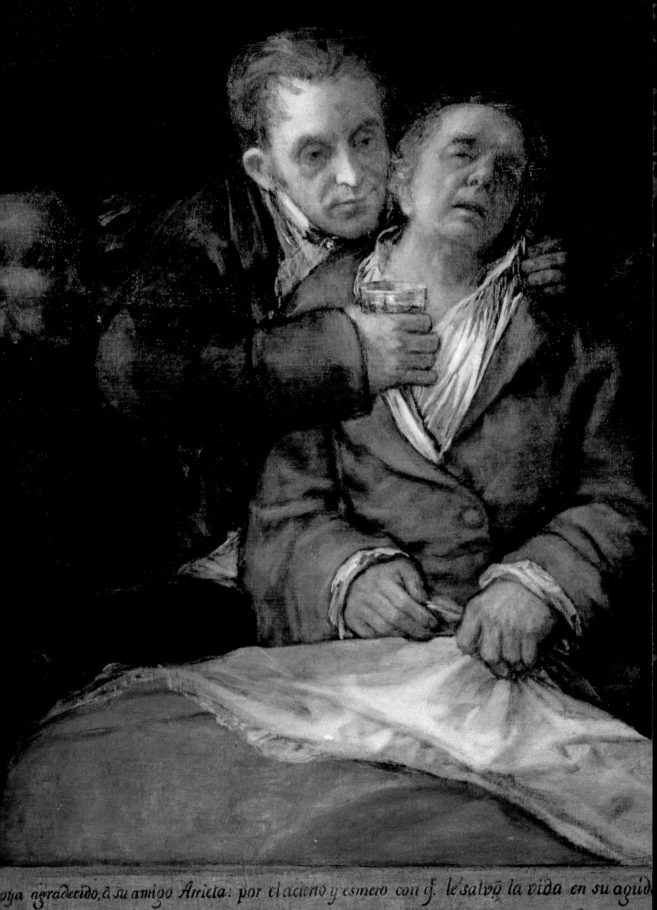

oya agradecido, á su amigo Arrieta: por el acierto y esmero con q. le salvó la vida en su aguda
eligrosa enfermedad, padecida á fines del año 1819. a los setenta y tres de su edad. Lo pintó en

ATE XXXIX. Self-portrait with ' Arrieta (detail), 1820
on canvas
⅓ × 31 in. (115.5 × 78.7 cm.)
ie Minneapolis Institute of
ts, Mineapolis
ie Ethel Morrison van Derlip
ind

depicted himself in a grateful presentation-canvas – had provided the necessary certificate. Within a few days Don Francisco Goya took his seat in a coach bound for the frontier. On the French side he would proceed in another, bound not for Plombières, where he never had any intention of going, but for Bordeaux and thence to Paris.

See PLATES XXXIII & XXX p. 175
& p. 163

The Quinta del Sordo emerges into history again, briefly and finally, forty-five years after Goya's death, being then the property of a M. Caumont, a Frenchman whose nerves were presumably equal to the strain of sipping his claret under the idiot grimaces of the San Isidro pilgrims and the cannibal-glare of Saturn. In 1873 the Ayuntamiento of Madrid decided to clear the site for incorporation in a new cemetery. Just in time a rich connoisseur arrived hotfoot from Paris to buy the Quinta and save The Black Paintings: namely Baron Emile d'Erlanger, of the international banking family. The sequel is not without a pleasant irony. Having had the paintings carefully removed from the walls, mounted on canvas, and transferred to storage in Paris pending presentation to the Louvre, the Baron was inspired to display them beforehand at the Paris Exhibition of 1878. They were received by the critics with furious controversy and by the art-loving public with shudders of distaste. The Black Paintings appeared to Parisian eyes little but a chaotic nightmare. A visiting British critic-pontiff, one P. G. Hamerton, later to come off rather badly in a brush with Whistler, described them with unction in a London journal as 'the vilest abortions that ever came from the brain of a sinner . . . incomprehensible . . . revolting'. Incensed by philistine stupidity, Baron Emile took The Black Paintings back to Madrid and presented them to the Prado, where they remain, displayed with rightful honour.

Crossing the Pyrenees from either side for the first time even by a highroad, even today, is a memorable experience, and must have been so for Don Francisco Goya, who had not been in France for nearly sixty years. The difference in the prospect, so arid on the south side, so lush and gracious on the other; the difference in the skies, the air, the visages, the voices, the costume . . . in Goya's time, when rustic dress still remained more or less national, the change must have been exhilarating. One may justly see a sketchbook lugged out before the coach reached the first French posting-house.

See p. 103

See PLATES VIII & XXXVII p. 65
& p. 185

He was making for Bordeaux not, it seems, in order to rejoin Leocadia Weiss for a space but to meet his liberal friend the poet Leandro Moratín, who had some time before become an *émigré* to avoid Fernando VII's 'rehabilitation' tribunals, and had opened a school there with another exile, one Manuel Silvela. From Moratín we learn that Goya arrived very weary, very weak; incapable of uttering a word of the French he had picked up long before so laboriously; feeling all his seventy-eight years, but restless and impatient to see the world. After two days' stay he insisted on going on, leaving Moratín worried. 'We shall know before long whether the journey

e Duke of Wellington
   on canvas
5¾ × 94½ in. (294 × 239.9 cm.)
e Wellington Museum,
sley House, London

has left him still alive,' he wrote after Goya's departure to a friend in Spain. 'I should be very upset if anything happened to him.' Anxiety was in fact justified. The four-days' coach-journey on to Paris could, even as late as 1824, be an ordeal for a man of Goya's age and infirmities. Moreover he had no contacts in Paris except a friend of Moratín's named Arnao and a painter, not of the first rank: Horace Vernet, a relation of some kind or other. It is a matter for musing to realize that the greatest artist in contemporary Europe was practically unknown outside his own country (though the modern French apparently deny this) till nearly the end of the nineteenth century, save for a few travelled connoisseurs like Emile d'Erlanger. To the Parisians who shuddered a *'Mon Dieu!'* at The Black Paintings at the Exhibition of 1878 he was a morbid half-crazy foreigner.

He got to Paris, probably worn out, and stayed three months. The Paris of 1824 cannot have enchanted him. The Restoration was steadily proceeding under Louis XVIII, a Bourbon of wisdom and intelligence hampered by old age, gout, and bitter memories. The heavy cost of Napoleonic adventure was not yet forgotten or paid. The liberals who had such links with Spain were temporarily under a cloud and allied with a solid mass of prosperous bourgeoisie which wanted no part of the re-Christianization of France, now in progress under Jesuit auspices. State finances had been capably restored and stabilized; 'the budgetry laws of the Restoration', remarks Lucien Romier, 'remain models'. The Press, freed of restriction to begin with, was once more under discipline since the assassination in 1820 of the Duc de Berri by a friend of Progress outside the Opéra in the Square Louvois. Destructive secret societies imitative of the Carbonari of Italy, and equally bound by oath, flourished underground. An anti-regime group of 'Independents' included, naturally, many of the intelligentsia, its mouthpiece being the poet Béranger. Art was entirely respectable.

What contacts Goya made during his stay of three months or so are, if any, not discernible. Wellington, who would probably have remembered him ('Ah, yes – painter fellow – Spaniard – did a couple of damn bad portraits of me'), had left Paris when the Allied occupation, to the genuine grief of the Prussians and the Russians, came to an end six years previously. Art circles in the capital had nothing much to offer a Goya. The aged David, his contemporary, was an exile in Belgium. Goya may or may not have met David's pupil Ingres, Delacroix, or David d'Angers. One may imagine him grunting his way round the recently-established Ecole des Beaux-Arts. 'The old fake-classical stuff, and now this romantic nonsense – *Redios!*'

He would certainly not have missed the opening of the Salon of 1824. Here the familiar sturdy figure, now very grey, may be clearly seen, steered by Vernet unnoticed through the chattering mob of fashionables, dilettantes, critics, professionals, amateurs, dealers, and hangers-on; very glum, peering now and again closely at a wall, with nothing to say apart from an occasional mutter, familiar to his intimates, of '*No es eso!*' – 'That's not it!'. The picture of the year was Delacroix' *Massacres de Chios*, a bravura piece of some dimensions, with Géricault's shipwreck symphony *Le Radeau de la Méduse* as runner-up. Notable foreigners exhibiting were Lawrence, Constable, and Bonington. Doubtless the flaming artist-youth of 1824, running true to traditional form, dismissed all these masters in bulk as *pompiers*. For the polite French painter contemplating a professional brother's latest work there is a well-known non-committal-all-in formula – '*Un beau talent!*'. One cannot hear any Spanish equivalent issuing from the lips of Goya on this occasion. His reaction to the 'wild men' of the period, forerunners of Impressionism like Corot, Rousseau, and Millet, would have been worth recording had he come across them communing with Nature in the forest of Barbizon. Doubtless Goya would have preferred Corot's diaphanous willows to Millet's idealized peasants ('*No es eso!*'). He was, unfortunately, some years too early to encounter Daumier, of whose acid caricatures of the passing scene he would conceivably have approved.

Paris itself may well have struck him as paintable in places, though the capital was rapidly becoming less picturesque. Extensive building was in progress, especially along the Grands Boulevards and in the Etoile quarter. The Champs-Elysées remained a leafy desert, dotted with questionable cabarets. In the Cité and round Les Halles a labyrinth of narrow dark old streets, redolent of crime and revolt, lingered to be swept away after the great cholera epidemic of ten years later. In the fashionable quarters nothing very notable had happened since the assassination of the Duc de Berri. The charms of the new arcades, such as the Passage des Panoramas, so convenient for smart shopping and assignation, were the present talk of the town. A lucrative experiment by a member of the Spanish colony, a Colonel Amoros, who had just opened a million-franc sports-ground in the Grenelle quarter, was interesting his compatriots, though conceivably not Goya. He must have seen some of the experiments in street-gaslighting which were to flower in the successful illumination of the Place Vendôme and the principal boulevards at about this time. Parisian fashion of the moment possibly struck him as ridiculous; the waisted, multi-collared frock-coats, furry tall hats, and tight trousers of the dandies; the huge bonnets, open corsages, and puffed sleeves of the *élégantes*. No, Paris was no place for him.

At the beginning of the autumn Goya returned to Bordeaux, as he had promised Moratín. He had done no painting during his Parisian stay, *See* p. 103 barring one or two portraits of members of the Spanish colony, and since he brought back nothing but a sketch of a couple of large dogs drawing a milk-cart, inscribed 'I saw this in Paris', his visit could hardly be styled inspirational. From a letter in 1825 to Joaquín Maria Ferrer, whom he had painted in Paris, it would seem that a business proposition had suggested itself to him during his stay, in the shape of a re-issue of the *Tauromaquia* set for the French *See* pp. 240–45 market, unsigned, at a cheap rate. A possible sigh at having to reject an even

See pp. 219–28

better idea follows: 'What you say about the *Caprichos* is not possible, since I presented the plates to the King more than twenty years ago . . . nor would I copy them, because I have better plans for a time when they will sell more usefully." The still-existent royal copyright of course made re-sale of the *Caprichos* impossible. And since Goya had, alas, no public in France of any kind, neither scheme would be likely to commend itself to a French business man.

Back in Bordeaux, we learn from Moratín, he took temporary lodgings for himself, Doña Leocadia, and Rosarito in the Rue de Tourny. The move was not immediately auspicious. 'With his seventy-nine years and his chronic ailments', wrote Moratín to a friend, 'he does not know what he hopes for, or what he wants.' In the spring following he fell ill with (to quote an extant medical report) a paralysis of the bladder and a tumour on the perineum. An iron Aragonese constitution prevailed. Within a couple of months Moratín was able to report that he was 'painting away as hard as he can go. . . . He likes the city, the countryside, the food, the independence, and the peace which he can enjoy'. Looking round for a house suitable for setting up a new *ménage* with Leocadia and Rosarito, he found a small but agreeable one, with a garden, in the Rue de la Croix-blanche, renting it in Leocadia's name. Of their resumed relations Moratín was shortly to remark resignedly that they resembled April weather: 'I see no great harmony between them.' And in fact it would seem likely that but for the girl, whom the old man continued to adore, some sudden explosion would have ended the arrangement quite soon, and permanently.

Bordeaux he seems to have accepted at sight. Here was a city an artist and a liberal could live in; a smaller, friendlier, sunnier, more stimulating Paris; the city of Michel de Montaigne, most illustrious of philosopher-mayors, with whose essays Goya may or may not have been acquainted; a city of eighteenth-century comeliness and opulence, of immense luminous skies and good cheer. To the 'period' fragrance exhaled by still-surviving streets with quaint ancient names – The Street of Lost Hopes, the Street of Forgotten Footsteps, Red Hat Row, the Street of the Spirit of the Laws – Goya was doubtless unresponsive, but the splendid piles of the Grand Theatre, barely fifty years old, and the Douane were immediately impressive, and the cathedral was undestroyed. The Esplanade des Quinconces, the parks, the wide Garonne, the cheerful bustle of the riverside, the vivacity of the pavements, the many inviting restaurants, with their often superlative cookery and their classic wines – all these and other attractions, not too far from the frontier, beckoned the traveller to a halt then as now. For any visitor with imagination in Goya's time, moreover, the ghosts of the Girondins massacred in 1793 by the Convention, with some two thousand more all over France, still walked the streets by night.

It would not have taken him long, even without Moratín's guidance, to discover a home-from-home in this pleasant city. The *café-chocolatería* of one Braulio Poch in the Rue de la Petite Taupe, now the Rue de la Huguerie, was the rendezvous of a sizeable colony of Spanish exiles. Poch himself turned out most agreeably to be a fellow-Aragonese and a survivor of the great siege of Saragossa. Here, over chocolate in the Spanish style, thick, hot, velvety, with a chaser of water, a daily assembly presided by Leandro Moratín discussed the gazettes and argued interminably; frequently not without dust and heat, the exiles being of several kinds repelled by successive regimes – republicans, monarchists, freemasons, Catholics, francophobes, francophils: a striking cross-section of Spanish enthusiasms over the previous fifty years. *See* p. 103

We may pause to glimpse the short, square, sturdy, grizzled figure of Don Francisco Goya, Painter to the Spanish Crown, pacing on a fine autumn morning in 1825 towards Poch's establishment. The aged master remains, having exuberated in youth, as Dr Johnson would say, into a beau, a man of fashion still. Since student-days in Rome, of course, he had never cultivated Bohemianism in the Chelsea sense, having so soon entered the world of rank and fashion. Viewed in Bordeaux streets at the end of his life, and undoubtedly owing something to Doña Leocadia's surveillance, Goya might almost be styled a walking Portrait of Successful Artist in Retirement, not that he ever retired; what later journalism might call a Brummell of the Brush. In his present incarnation as recorded for posterity – the waisted dark-brown or plum-coloured frock-coat and 'trowsers'; the snowy well-tied cravat, mounting to the ears; the equally snowy shirt-frill at the bosom; the tall curly-brimmed beaver, of the kind known as a 'Bolivar'; the impeccably-polished shoes; the ebony walking-cane, topped by an ivory ball; the eye-glass dangling from its black ribbon; the thick well-trimmed grey hair, the short curly side-whiskers – he was doubtless a more impressive spectacle than the ruck of Poch's clientele, largely impecunious. But Goya, a Spaniard, was no snob.

One may well see him arrived and seated, as was befitting, in a place of honour, sipping his chocolate under billowing clouds of rank blue cigar-smoke; viewing the sudden disputes, the thumpings on tables, the shaking of fists, the challenges, the incidental breakage, no doubt, of some of Poch's glass and china from time to time; the turbulent entrances, the heated exits. The symposia *chez* Braulio Poch could be, doubtless, as quarrelsome as any others of the kind anywhere, and one may perhaps catch Don Francisco privily sketching, in three or four strokes, some of the orators, whose antics, even if he could hear, would fascinate him more than their Utopias. From the flow of rhetoric deafness mercifully protected him. Sitting there silent, stolid, apparently unreceptive save for the flicker of sardonic eyes observant of every gesture, he would often, no doubt, become totally detached, scanning the newspapers or musing on a myriad other things; at times, again, heartily amused by what would seem to a victim of equal surdity in a later century very like a violent comedy-film of the 'silent' vintage.

Returning home at length, he might well have grunted to Leocadia Weiss, in the words some years later of Browning's Legate, 'I have seen four-and-twenty leaders of revolt.' His own politics, as we have long since gathered, might still be not unfairly summed up in the phrase 'Art and Francisco Goya'. And when the scene at Poch's at length palled on him, there was real and sketchable amusement at intervals in the travelling circuses frequently visiting Bordeaux. The periodical local bullfights probably seemed to him an amateur romp. He nevertheless sketched a few.

For even now he carried a sketchbook, being still at work. While the day's gazette was read aloud and debated at Poch's he would find plenty of material for his pencil. Spanish news items of the period would frequently be provocative of rhetoric. Trouble was looming again over the Peninsula. Oppression under Fernando VII was increasing. What Spanish historians were to See PLATES VIII & XXXVII p. 65 & p. 185 christen 'the Ignominious Decade' had opened in 1823 with the trial and execution, with his chief henchmen, of Colonel Riego, leader three years before of an insurrection in Andalucia proclaiming 'the Constitution of See p. 196 1812'.[1] In 1825 the celebrated 'El Empecinado' was captured, tried, and shot likewise. Goya may have afforded the company at Poch's interesting reminiscences of this hardbitten old fighter, whose whiskers and glare he had immortalized some years before. Other executions included that of a woman, Mariana Pineda, found guilty of embroidering a revolutionary flag and due a century later to be the heroine of one of Lorca's earliest plays. Secret societies See p. 134 and armed bands of malcontents all over Spain were calling to Don Carlos, Fernando's brother, to seize the crown. For poets the glowering Fernando seems, like most tyrants, to have cherished a special malevolence. Though none was shot, at least half a dozen – Moratín, Quintana, Gallego, the Duque de Rivas, Heredia, Espronceda – suffered imprisonment and exile for the Muse. Thus the home front could constantly be relied on to stimulate the talk at Poch's.

If and when this topic was ever exhausted, *pro tem.*, the exiles had plenty of food for debate in the affairs of their adopted country, now enjoying a royalist reaction much favoured elsewhere in Europe. In 1822 the Congress of Verona had offered Louis XVIII a mandate to assist Fernando VII against his rebellious liberals; an invitation bristling with obvious difficulties and rescinded at the behest of a British government which wanted no more French intervention in Spain. In France liberalism was at this moment under a cloud. The demagogues and Utopians had shown their incapacity, and under Charles X arts and letters, if not trade and commerce, were enjoying a renaissance, as likewise was religion. Chateaubriand had published *Le Génie du Christianisme*. Victor Hugo was chanting the sorrows of Louis XVII. Lamartine was engaged on *Harmonies Poétiques et Religieuses*. This state of affairs was not to last long. A majority of the French bourgeoisie was, as

[1]Framed by the self-elected Cortes of Cadiz in that year on French lines, it embraced national sovereignty, division of power, restoration of fundamental liberties, and other obvious demands.

El Empecinado
oil on canvas
Collection Neugebauer, Maracay,
Venezuela

already noted, too anti-royalist and hostile to the re-Christianization movement to endure it. But down to 1830, by which time Goya had ceased to care, Braulio Poch's clientele had plenty to thump the tables about. It was nearly twenty years since some of them had cried with Quintana:

> *En tí su horrible trono*
> *Sentó el numen del mal, Francia culpable!*

> On this thy horrible throne,
> guilty France, I view the Genius of Evil!

Times change. France, their refuge, was now itself in the grip of reaction. What can be called the 'left wing' exiles seem to have had no trouble with the authorities in Bordeaux. Perhaps Poch knew how to soothe the police.

See PLATES VIII & XXXVII p. 65 & 185

In 1826 Goya applied for another extension of leave, journeying to Madrid to do so, and was granted it, after an interview with the King, indefinitely; which speaks not badly once again for Fernando VII, whose only stipulation was that Goya's portrait should be painted by Vicente López.

See p. 199

The respectable result hangs now in the Prado.

See p. 92

That the sessions at Poch's compensated Goya for the steady loss of old friends by death, one of the most melancholy concomitants of increasing age, seems doubtful. He may at times have been missing the unique Zapater, in past years neglected, now gone. The fate of a friend and patron like Godoy, himself now an exile and fallen into poverty, may likewise have afforded him uneasiness at times. Whether they met once more during Goya's visit to Paris in 1824 is not recorded. There would have been no need to climb four pairs of dusty stairs to Godoy's lodging; the ex-Prince of the Peace was to be found any fine afternoon with his friends, the children playing in the Tuileries gardens. Spanish contempt for him, it may be remarked here, had begun to dwindle. By 1838 a group of sympathizers in Madrid would be pledged to his rehabilitation, strongly urged by Ramón de Mesonero Romanos, archivist of the capital.[1] Before long the poet Juan Meléndez Valdés would be publishing a long indignant laudatory ode to his address in time to be freely quoted by Godoy in his forthcoming memoirs, *Cuenta dada de su Vida Política*, an eloquently rhetorical apologia published shortly before his death at eighty-five. But Goya's make-up, however painful the realization by anyone under his spell, seems not to have included much generosity of mind.

He found nowadays, it may be conjectured, no great solace at home save in the company of his beloved Rosarito. Her mother's shrewishness, according to Moratín, was increasing. Quarrels were now frequent. One may well see the old man finding solace in supervising Rosarito's sketching or playing the educative game of *riquitillas* with the girl in the evenings after dinner, dashing down his dots on paper haphazard, defying her gruffly to make anything of them. He would still take Rosarito and her mother to the theatre,

---

[1]An unofficial invitation from the British Government, via Lord Holland, to settle in England had been gratefully declined.

A. Tiburcio Perez
Goya. 1820

The architect Don Tiburcio
Pérez, 1820
Oil on canvas
40¼ × 32 in. (102.2 × 81.2 cm.)
The Metropolitan Museum of
Art, New York
The Theodore M. Davis
Collection. Bequest of Theodore
M. Davis 1915

the cafés, the travelling circuses, for which he had a decided taste, and of course, to an occasional bullfight. The bulls – if involved – of the Camargue, though not gladiators of intelligence comparable with the Vistahermosa or any other aristocratic Andalucian breed, can be formidable enough. The feat of vaulting over their charging horns, deriving, say scholars, from Minoan Crete and – at least down to the First World War – still practised in the Landes, may now have seemed to the connoisseur Goya an unseemly trick, fit only for acrobats, and the whole display perhaps quaintly provincial. *No es eso!* Even so it was more restful than an evening at home. The bustle of the streets gave him much pleasure. His pencil was constantly busy with Bordelais types – loungers, shopkeepers, bourgeois, beggars, the Mid-Lent carnival, the guillotine, all the passing show.

See p. 31
See p. 170

He had long since manifested a strong fondness for his son Javier and his grandson Mariano, now adolescent, in the interests of whose future he was now bestirring himself. 'To produce an income of 12,000 *reales*', he writes to Javier, 'I need 3,000 francs, which will make a permanent property for Mariano and his descendants. . . .' Goya himself maintained a comfortable balance with the banker Galos, refreshing it by a few new portrait-commissions. His latest hobby, lithography, with which he had begun toying in 1819, was yielding him pleasure not unprofitable. In the 1820s lithography was still more or less a novelty, having been developed by Aloys Senefelder in Germany in the late 1790s. Goya may be seen taking keen pleasure in mastering this new difficult technique; the drawing with pencil and brush on the prepared surface of the stone, the laying of the paper, the manipulation of the roller, the final emergence of the print from the press. His work at the easel likewise continued, with the assistance of his pupil Brugada. Those qualified to do so discern a new note in his portraits, suitable to the age; more austerity in treatment; more concentration on revealing personality; a marked sobriety in garb and tint. His clients come now from the solid bourgeoisie and the liberal intelligentsia; the banker Galos, the poet-schoolmaster Moratín, the architect Tiburcio Perez in his shirtsleeves. Their costume is black or dark-blue, their expressions grave, their hair alone unruly.

VICENTE LOPEZ Francisco Goya, about 1826
Oil on canvas
6⅝ × 53½ in. (93 × 75 cm.)
Museo del Prado, Madrid

See p. 103

See p. 201
See p. 98

See p. 200

Being free to travel, Goya returned to Madrid at this time for a space to add to portraits of some five years previous – José Luis Munarriz of the Academy, Juan de Muguiro seated by his writing-table, the actress Rita Luna; this latter a study of a leading lady differing much from that of 'La Tirana' years before, and combining an apparent absence of bust with the soulful tragic eyes of a heroine of Corneille. 'La Luna' is no dazzling spectacle like Doña Antonia Zárate, whom Goya painted twice; in 1810, in the blaze of her opulent beauty, with those magnificent eyes, and again, ten years later, although this painting is now lost.

In his last years his feminine sitters are chiefly ladies of a certain age, very plainly dressed in black, spared nothing of the stigmata of Time. Failing

he actress Doña Antonia
rate de Gil, about 1810
on canvas
⅜ × 33⅛ in. (105 × 84 cm.)
llection Sir Alfred Beit, Bart,
. Wicklow, Ireland

on Juan Bautista de Muguiro,
'27
on canvas
½ × 33⅛ in. (103 × 84 cm.)
useo del Prado, Madrid

See p. 203

eyesight has been held to explain the number of small strokes of the brush visible in these later canvases. Goya has nowadays to stand very close to his work, wearing stronger spectacles, at times reinforced by a magnifying glass. His present clientele is not so opulent or extensive as it used to be. His Court pension, still paid regularly, has lately been increased by 1,000 *reales*; which speaks not badly once more for the detestable Fernando. If Goya is very far from the poverty-line, his art is naturally not the goldmine it was in the days of the Duchess. Hence no doubt that momentary interest in 1825, already noted, in a French edition of selected bullfight-lithographs. It may be that such a preoccupation was due not so much to lack of money as to a marked fondness for it, to which his early letters to Zapater now and again testify; a rustic addiction inherited or acquired. This trait in an artist wedded to his art has been known to wound the highminded. In Whistler's libel action against Ruskin in 1878 for describing one of his nocturnes as 'flinging a pot of

Asensio Julio, 1814
oil on canvas
28⅞ × 22½ in. (73.3 × 57.1 cm.)
Sterling and Francine Clark Art
Institute, Williamstown, Mass.

(above left) Spanish
entertainment, 1825
lithographic crayon and scraper
11⅞ × 16⅛ in. (30 × 41 cm.)
The British Museum, London

(above right) The famous
American, Mariano Ceballas,
1825
lithographic crayon and scraper
12 × 15¾ in. (30.5 × 40 cm.)
The British Museum, London

paint in the public's face', Burne-Jones's evidence establishes that the artist need have no rooted objection to money for 'earnest work', and may take it in fact with a clear conscience. The jury, awarding Whistler one farthing damages, seemingly agreed.

Goya's charge for the original published set of the *Caprichos* we know. His fees for portraits, mostly unknown, were of course much higher. Fifty-odd years of supremely successful practice had earned him sufficient – he was apparently not a lavish spender – to keep the wolf appreciably far from the door in old age. His attitude towards money will be seen to differ from, say, that of British statesmen who normally, as Chesterton remarked at the time of the Marconi shares scandal, keep their eyes fixed on the further stars and receive their salaries with a start of surprise. Goya's fixed approach, so far as is discoverable, was that of the girl's refrain in Quevedo's sardonic *Letrilla*:

> *Poderoso caballero*
> *es Don Dinero*
>
> A powerful beau
> is old Don Dough.

See p. 18

See PLATES VIII & XXXVII p. 65
& p. 185

Such, to judge by more than one remark to Martin Zapater, had been the lifelong sentiment of Don Francisco Goya, whose average income over half a century must have been high. Only one rebel against his fees seems to be on record – General José de Palafox, hero in chief of the Saragossa siege, who sat for an equestrian study shortly after his triumphal entry into Madrid with Fernando VII in 1814. On receiving the artist's bill the warrior promptly repudiated his portrait. A protesting note from Goya quoting the high current price of oil and colour had no effect, and the canvas remained on Goya's hands thenceforth. Some little time after his death Javier Goya offered it *See* p. 31 again to Palafox at the same fee, with the same result. As a French critic has *See* p. 18 surmised, the hero of Saragossa was doubtless of the opinion that bloodshed for one's country was enough. Such seems not to be the view down the ages, generally speaking, of the professional artist.

Among the portraits he painted in these final years, mostly of fellow-*émigrés*, the last of them all, that of Don José Pío de Molina, is usually singled out as representing Goya's final phase of sobriety and realism at a peak. Against a black background the pallid, heavy-lidded features and white neckcloth of the ageing Molina, black-haired and black-clothed, provide the only light. In Whistlerian terms the portrait might almost be called a Decomposition in Black and White. The sitter could indeed be watching the shuffling approach of Death up a long avenue; impassively, inscrutably, a stoic awaiting the end rather than a Christian awaiting the beginning. It is an immensely powerful study, displaying what has accurately been called a *supertécnica*. The prevailing colour-key seems to have some significance. If an earlier portrait, that of Don Francisco de Mazo, is an authentic Goya (this has apparently been queried), the possibilities of black as the dominant in portraiture must have appealed to Goya as far back as 1820 or thereabouts. This particular canvas might almost, were the language of Sunday journalism permissible, be styled a 'symphony in sable' – hair, eyes, brows, costume, against a lighter background. The thought, possibly a trifle baroque, suggests itself that in the final productions of a lifetime Goya seems to be expressing essential *hispanitas*, the Iberian Thing, in a foreign land.

Black might be called the third Spanish national colour. What Velázquez, to whom Goya obviously owed something, could express with it all the world knows. The favour still accorded it by the Spaniard of both sexes derives undoubtedly from the high Renaissance, Spanish and Italian, at which period Castiglione in his classic manual of manners at the court of Urbino observes, like Prince Hamlet, 'methinks a black colour hath a better grace in garments than any other'. And indeed a typical hard-eyed bashaw of Elizabeth Tudor's court – Raleigh, say, or Dudley – bedizened like a peacock and plastered with jewels, would have seemed, side by side with some hidalgo of the period garbed in unrelieved sable save for the narrow white *golilla*, a vulgarian. Of the dignity black vesture lends to the wearer Goya was well aware, and many nineteenth-century mandarins outside Spain were sensible enough to employ it when sitting for their portraits. If a black coat could not do much for, for example, the eyes of the eminent historian Froude, it at least confers on him a general veneer of decency – what would that faker have looked like in pepper-and-salt?

PLATE XL. Don José Pío de Molina, 1828
oil on canvas
Collection Oskar Reinhart, Winterthur, Switzerland

PLATE XLI. (overleaf) The Danc of San Antonio de la Florida (detail) – tapestry cartoon, 1791–92
oil on canvas
$107\frac{1}{8} \times 116\frac{1}{8}$ in. (272 × 295 cm.)
Museo del Prado, Madrid

6 'I keep learning...'

See p. 103

S o pass Goya's last years, with no visible diminution of his artistic powers. His domestic life seems to have continued chequered. In 1827 Moratín writes to a friend somewhat dubiously: 'It seems to me that peace now reigns in that household.' It is not difficult to hear at intervals shrill cries and responsive growls. The master cannot have been the easiest person to live with, and Doña Leocadia's temper, as Herr Weiss could have testified, could apparently be formidable. Towards Rosarito, now nineteen and studying painting at a Bordeaux academy under a director who had served his apprenticeship with David, Goya continued to be an affectionate and indulgent acting-grandfather. Her ripening talent for miniatures on ivory delighted him. Having made her (it is believed) his model for the charming *See p. 211* 'Milkmaid' now in the Prado, his very last canvas, he seems to have devoted himself chiefly to his pupil Brugada, to whom he would bequeath his palette.

He had made and registered his will at Madrid in 1811, jointly with his late wife, deceased in that year:

PLATE XLII. The Repentant Peter, about 1824–25
oil on canvas
29 × 25½ in. (73.6 × 64.7 cm.)
The Phillips Collection,
Washington, D.C.

In the name of God the All-Powerful, Amen. We, Don Francisco Goya, by profession painter, and Doña Josefa Bayeu, married woman, both inhabitants of this city; I, Don Francisco, being a native of Fuendetodos in the kingdom of Aragon and the archbishopric of Saragossa, and son in lawful wedlock of Don José Goya and Doña Grazia [Engracia] Lucientes, both deceased, formerly natives of the city of Saragossa; and I, Doña Josefa, being a native of the said city and lawful daughter of Don Ramón Bayeu and Doña Maria Subias, both dead, natives of the said city:

Being in good health and sound in mind, judgement, memory, and understanding, as accorded us by the Divine Majesty, we firmly believe and confess the mystery of the Holy Trinity, Father, Son, and Holy Ghost, three Persons and one God; likewise all mysteries and sacraments which our holy Mother the Catholic, Apostolic, and Roman Church believes and confesses; in which true faith and belief we have lived and in which we intend to die, as befits Catholics and faithful Christians aware of death, which is most certain for every creature. Desiring to be thereto prepared with a will and testament, we have made and ordered the same in the form following:

For what may remain of all our goods, possessions, furniture . . .

See p. 31 Everything is left to Don Francisco Xavier (or Javier) de Goya, 'our lawful son', with God's blessing and theirs. Since settling in Bordeaux Goya had begun and kept up a fairly regular correspondence with Javier, now resident in Madrid with a wife and child. His letters to *querido Javier*, as usual notable neither for graces, spelling, nor style, are concerned largely with his settlement on young Mariano. A note of true affection may increasingly be discerned: See p. 170

> To Don Francisco Javier de Goya,
> Calle de Valverde 15, Madrid.
> Thursday, 17th January
>
> My dearest Javier,
>   I was much gratified with satisfaction (*loco de contento*) at getting your last, with notes on Gibraltar during your travels. The days go by and you will get this a little late, but never mind – when you [plural] come here to spend a couple of years, when you can, I shall be very content. . . . I take it, as is only right, that you will stay with me the whole time you are in Bordeaux between going to and returning from Paris; at least that is my impression, and I am already looking after everything concerned with your arrival and stay. You must tell me exactly when you leave Barcelona and so forth. Take all precautions and let nothing escape you – you know what we have in Galos' bank, and that this is all yours. Yesterday I heard that Gallardo has been assassinated, which disturbed me a lot. . . .
>   Give Don Rafael Esteve a thousand wishes from me.
>
> Frco. de Goya

A month later he wrote to his son:

> Bordeaux, 26th February 1828
>
> Drst. Javier,
>   I am impatiently and anxiously expecting my dear travellers; all that you said in your last about staying with me longer after leaving Paris gives me the greatest pleasure you could possibly have given. Your stay here will be the greatest of pleasures, and if you come this summer, that will be everything I could desire.
>   On Saturday at Monsieur Galos' place I received the two months' instalment you sent me. I still have the other note for 979 francs, and if you send me the two months' I propose putting it in the Funds towards that 12,000 *reales* a year which will make a permanent income for Mariano and his descendants – is this all right?
>   I feel much better and hope to remain as I was before the attack. I owe this recovery to Molina, who was telling me about taking powered valerian. I am well content at being recovered sufficiently to welcome my dear travellers. Goodbye from your father,
>
> Fr. de Goya

On 1st April, having announced to his father his imminent arrival, Javier – then in Barcelona – received a reply in a very shaky hand:

> My dear Javier,
>   I can say no more than that such a great happiness has made me ill and I am in bed. May God grant you come and pick them [his wife and son] up. My happiness will then be complete.
>
> Your father, Francisco

Above this was a scrawl by Mariano, who had arrived on 28th March with his mother:

> Dear Father, Grandpapa is writing four lines at the end of my letter, which will show you he is still alive.

The end was near. A month beforehand the old man had suffered a stroke leaving him partly paralyzed. He had been found lying unconscious, brush in hand, on the studio floor. In the night of 14th April he roused from torpor feebly to raise the hand which had done so much for him, looking at it for a moment and – according to Leocadia Weiss – muttering something about a will.

See PLATE XL p. 205

He died calmly in the early hours of 16th April, a fortnight after his eighty-second birthday, in the presence of his daughter-in-law, his grandson, his friend Molina, and his pupil Brugada; Doña Leocadia having retired under strain.[1]

The manner of his passing is not known, or whether he received the last sacraments; or whether, again, he was vested for burial, according to agelong Spanish usage, in the Franciscan tertiary habit specified for himself, as for his wife, in their joint will of 1811. Matheron reports that his friends had the customary Mass of requiem said for him in the church of Notre Dame, near the Grand Theatre. Javier later supplied a tablet engraved 'R.I.P.' Goya's personal attitude to the Four Last Things tends perhaps to be misconstrued by the celebrated etching which portrays a corpse pushing up the lid of a tomb marked *Nada*, 'Nothing'. Widely interpreted as a denial of the after-life, this could of course be equally conveying the nothingness of human existence, a theme for many saints down the ages. Here Goya may certainly be given the benefit of the doubt.

See p. 31

See p. 12

Since he left no will but that of 1811 we find Doña Leocadia and her daughter left in a parlous condition, judging by an hysterical letter from Leocadia to Moratín within a fortnight of Goya's death:

> Grandson and daughter-in-law arrived here on the 28th of last month. On the 1st [of April] we lunched together; it made him [Goya] ill, and on April 2 he remained without speech till 5 o'clock, when he recovered, but had paralysis in his side. This lasted thirteen days. He recognized all of us. About three hours before he died he raised his hand, but feebly, and said he wanted to make a will in our favour, but his daughter-in-law said this was already done. His weakness prevented him from understanding what was being said ... In this state he remained thirteen days, and died between the 15th and 16th at 2 in the morning. It is enough to tell you that I continue to exist for the sake of my poor daughter. I am in a complete state of exhaustion and at the end of my tether. [Six more lines elaborating this omitted.]
>
> Molina left for Madrid on the 19th. He is concerned about our fate, and has taken upon himself to find out if there is anything in the will of 1811, and he will speak to the son ...

After asserting that Javier Goya had told her that he had secured her, to begin with, a thousand francs and all the furniture and clothing in the house, Leocadia ends:

> Such is my situation, my friend. The house was paid to the end of the month.

he Milkmaid, about 1827
l on canvas
9⅛ × 26¾ in. (74 × 68 cm.)
Iuseo del Prado, Madrid

RANCISCO DE LA TORRE
joya on his deathbed, 1828
encil
ibliotéca Nacional, Madrid

[1] 'After twelve o'clock I could no longer stay by his bed,' she wrote to Moratín, then in Paris. Her incoherence at this period is marked.

I left it, Molina having said he would spare me the arrangements for the funeral. I am now looking for somewhere to live. Meanwhile I remain in the greatest anxiety to hear from you and in the deepest sorrow, though helped by friends. Today the son and his wife are returning to Madrid. I can say no more. Regards from my poor Rosarito.   Leocadia Zorrilla

She writes to Moratín again on 13th May, expressing rather confusedly an *See* p. 103 unexplained desire to be put in touch with 'Mr Hoogen, who was secretary to Lord Wellington when that gentleman was ambassador in Paris', and mentioning offers of help from a German friend of her husband's father. The most interesting part of this letter is the final paragraph:

My Rosarito, who is sad for a thousand reasons, since she needs to give four months' more pianoforte lessons, though she gives no lessons and has no piano, which was hired, and to which she was devoted, is made more miserable, having no distractions, by this uncertainty we are in, despite her talent. . . . They still have not written from Madrid nor put the inscription on the tomb. . . . But nothing afflicts me so much as the fate of my poor daughter. Pardon me the liberty of sending you the attached [letter] so that my friends Melón and Doña Luisa may do for me what I think they can. This favour will be eternally grateful to your melancholy friend.

Thus the sunset of genius is followed by the murkiest of clouds. It is difficult to believe that Goya knowingly left the companion-helpmate of his later years, shrew as she may have been, and her – possibly his – daughter, whom he sincerely loved, in such a predicament. But as a great Mayor of Bordeaux had remarked more than two centuries before him, *homo sapiens* is changeful and elusive as flowing water, and it is difficult to form any judgement on him. For Doña Leocadia it is possible to feel a fleeting sympathy. No doubt she was disliked by more people than Goya's son and daughter-in-law; by Moratín undoubtedly; also, it may be, by a few others of Braulio Poch's clientele allowed to visit the house in the Rue de la Croix-blanche. One might even see her descending on Goya *chez* Poch in full conclave and creating an embarrassing scene before taking him home. Assuredly memories of a more gracious bondage must have returned to him more than once before the end of his life.

So, shrilly complaining, perhaps not without a trifle of justice, Doña Leocadia Weiss fades from the scene and is no more heard of. Javier Goya, if *See* p. 31 she was telling the truth, shows up none too well in this business. He was now well off, apart from his 3,500 *reales* a year from the Duchess of Alba's will and the previous 2,000 granted him by Carlos IV in acknowledgment of the copyright of the *Caprichos*. The sale of some of his father's canvases in 1834 must have been not unprofitable likewise. If moreover the young Goyas found Leocadia detestable, her daughter had considerably brightened the old man's last years.

It is pleasant to record for Rosarito Weiss – judging by 'The Milkmaid', a *See* p. 211 charming creature – a modest success with the miniature-painting in which Goya had encouraged and assisted her. Her talent had developed sufficiently by study at the Prado a few years after his death to secure her the post of drawing-mistress to Princess Isabella, daughter of the Regent Maria Cristina and later Queen Isabella II; possibly this sinecure was not attributable entirely to Rosarito's art. Had she not been carried off by fever at twenty-six she might conceivably have figured with Rosa Bonheur on the brief roll of nineteenth-century women painters. Goya seems to have slightly overestimated her gifts. 'This astonishing child', he wrote to his friend Ferrer after his return from Paris, 'wants to paint miniatures, which is what I want, too. What she can do at her age is the biggest phenomenon in the world.' He was even thinking at the time of sending her to Paris. 'I'd like you to look after her as if she were my daughter.' This was in 1825, a year after he had taken to miniature-painting himself.

Leocadia Weiss herself may be given her due. Though she can claim no place with such starry handmaids of genius as Dante's Beatrice, Petrarch's Laura, Wagner's Mathilda, or Heine's Camille, she cooked Goya's dinners, starched his linen, polished his shoes, tied his cravats, supervised his wardrobe, listened – or did not listen – to his diatribes, endured his bad temper, and generally made him in old age some sort of home-life, for thirteen years. He was infuriatingly deaf, actually and doubtless in any case on principle, to her views on the Cosmos. The affection of her talented daughter would make up to him for much acrimony and boredom. Goya might have done something for Rosarito at least. Whether Doña Leocadia could possibly have been involved in the disappearance of the master's skull has not, so far as can be gathered, been an issue with anyone interested. As a liberal freethinker in financial straits, and in a bitter fury, she would possibly have no great qualms over assisting the march of Science in this way. The thought may nevertheless be unjust, and an apology due to her *manes*.

See p. 170 As for the master's surviving offspring, Javier, left with a comfortable fortune, died in 1853 with no history. Mariano, developing apparently into a highly temperamental character, lost most of his subsequent inheritance by speculation, married twice, and died in 1874, being then styled Marqués de Espinar, a title apparently authentic.

International celebrity came slowly to Goya. Outside Spain, where the cream of his immense production is now concentrated in the Prado, he continued merely – save for a few coteries in France – a name for the best part of a century. A French Baedeker guide to Spain dated 1900 sums up the Goyas in the central salon of the Royal Academy, Madrid, in two lines:

> Several witty (*spirituelles*) sketches by Goya; bullfights, madhouses, carnival and Inquisition-scenes.
> One proceeds by way of the corner salon (etc.)

The Prado display, not yet what it is today, merited seven lines:

> 731 and 732, portraits of King Charles IV and his wife, Maria Luisa. 734, Madrilenes shot by Murat's soldiers. 735, Combat between Spaniards and

(left) A scene from *El Hechizado por Fuerza* ('Bewitched Perforce') by Antonio de Zamora, 1798
oil on canvas
$16\frac{3}{4} \times 12\frac{1}{8}$ in. (42.5 × 30.8 cm.)
The National Gallery, London

(right) I keep learning, after 1800
lithograph pencil
$7\frac{1}{2} \times 5\frac{1}{2}$ in. (19 × 14 cm.)
Museo del Prado, Madrid
(Prado No. 416)

Mamelukes; two large pictures illustrating scenes of the rising of May 1808 against the French, and remarkable for the vigour and actuality of the impression conveyed. 736, Charles IV surrounded by his family. 737–743, portraits of the Royal family.

It is true that the introductory review of Spanish art down the ages in this same handbook does the master more justice ('the satiric observation of a Hogarth, the feeling of a Teniers for popular humour, and a chaos of spectres seemingly escaped from the sorcerers' sabbats of a Bosch and a Bruegel. In the *Dos de Mayo* he has illustrated with the power of genius terrible moments in the War of Independence, in his sinister 'Disasters of War' he has faithfully rendered war's horrors, etc.'). A flood of scholarly exegesis since that day makes such an introduction even for tourists look meagre enough. The first foreign critic to probe Goya's 'this-ness' was undoubtedly Baudelaire, whose salute to his *diableries* in the oft-quoted verse of the 1850s may be said to have raised the curtain, if only on one aspect of a multiple phenomenon. In his art-critic phase, it is true, Baudelaire went further, finding in this *génie sombre et fantastique* something of Rembrandt, Hogarth, Callot, and Watteau. A critic of our own time, Chabrun, has remarked more accurately that Goya is not one great artist but at least twenty, all separate and clearly defined.

Seclusion behind that formidable barrier of which Louis XIV inaccurately remarked '*Il n'y a plus de Pyrenées*' undoubtedly explains why Goya figured so long in the eyes of artistic Europe as merely the exponent of fantastic diabolism: in Baudelaire's words, 'a melancholy, sceptical Cervantes turned Voltairean'. This was not very surprising, since most of Goya's major works were to be viewed in the private galleries of Spanish royalty and nobility or in quarters equally inaccessible, the paintings sold by Javier Goya in 1834 included. Hence he remained until relatively recent times the creator of the *Caprichos* and The Black Paintings exclusively, earning a poor press thereby

See PLATE XXVIII p. 153
See pp. 229–39

See p. 31

See pp. 219–28

See PLATES XXX, XXXII, XXXIII, XXXIV, XXXV, p. 163, p. 166 p. 175, p. 173

from decent critics. We have seen the kind of reception given to the latter at the Paris Exhibition of 1878. The art-critics of Europe, the art-critics especially of Great Britain . . . but let us meditate a moment on an epic contribution from one of the brotherhood quoted by Whistler in *The Gentle Art of Making Enemies*. It is from one of the leading provincial newspapers in England in the 1880s:

> Under the same roof with Mr Whistler's strange productions is the collection of animal-paintings done by various artists for the proprietors of the *Graphic*, and very refreshing it is to turn into this agreeably lighted room and rest on comfortable settees whilst looking at 'Mother Hubbard's Dog', or the sweet little pussy-cats in the 'Happy Family'.

Doubtless no French critic could rise to these heights. But even in France Goya had no *afición*, barring Baudelaire, Victor Hugo, Manet, and a few other eccentrics, till well into the present day.

The reverberating success of the Goya Exhibition (December 1963–March 1964) at Burlington House, London, opened British eyes at length. Of the one or two Goyas already hung in the National Gallery and Apsley *See* PLATE XXIX p. 154 House the admittedly-mediocre Wellington portrait attracted little notice until it was recently stolen, for some reason still unexplained, to be recovered four years later, and the masterly and amusing 'Bewitched Perforce' was merely a puzzle-picture to the average British spectator. At Burlington House a skilfully chosen wide-range display drew daily crowds and established the artist's name – already attached to a brand of perfume – once and for all with a large cultivated public, whereas it had been previously known chiefly to connoisseurs able to afford those volumes *de luxe* of reproductions, criticism, and appreciation obtainable in Bond Street or the Charing Cross Road,[1] In the United States, where more than one gallery boasts a Goya, his art is said to be still the admiration of a coterie; such a situation should be easily remediable on the London pattern. By and large the missing skull seems entitled to the traditional grin.

Taking our leave of Goya, it is lawful to surmise that the prospect of post-mortem fame would not greatly have astonished him. During a long life of ceaseless work, productive of at least three hundred and fifty portraits and even more drawings, etchings, drypoints, aquatints, and lithographs, he had had a surfeit of it. In one of his last drawings, made at Bordeaux in his eighties, an old man hobbles along with the aid of a crutch and a cane; below, Goya has written *Aún aprendo* – 'I keep learning', a statement echoed by the aged Renoir some time later. That Goya meant it is indisputable. He possessed, with all his Aragonese self-assertion, that fundamental humility discernible in so many of the truly great. If it is difficult to share all the implications of Eugenio d'Ors' conviction that he 'died of joy', those last thirteen days of

[1]The latest of these, at the time of writing is *Goya and the Black Paintings*, by J. J. Sánchez Cantón, Director of the Prado, with an appendix by Xavier de Salas, Sub-Director.

immobility may indeed, unless more urgent matters for reflection intervened, have afforded him a review of the past yielding undiluted satisfaction.

Untroubled by rivals of his stature anywhere – Blake, Goya's almost exact contemporary, being a phenomenon inhabiting a different universe, and David in France being submerged in a frigid neo-classicism – Goya had all the vibrant life and colour of a traditional Spain to draw upon, nor had he ever lacked influential admirers and clients from royalty down. Intermittent sickness, frustrated passion, deafness, and old age alike had no weakening effect on his powers. After his execution of the *navet*-to-order for which he won a 'mention' at Parma he was never infuriated by art-critics; a major boon, since he would have been incapable of dealing with them *à la* Whistler. He knew neither early struggles for recognition nor sitters (Wellington and *See* p. 190 perhaps Palafox excepted) presuming to query his interpretation of their *See* p. 18 ego; they took what they got and were grateful.

Few artists in history could look back on such a sustained blaze of glory. He had achieved a long and profitable pre-eminence in at least three or four media, and his politics had not affected either his productivity or his fame. Even that accommodating episode under the French occupation had done him no harm. So far as any genius can be happy Goya was that genius, being able to transmute his blackest moods into enduring art and forget them – for presumably the late Somerset Maugham's dogma on this theme concerning the sister-art of letters applies equally to painting. But who can say such satisfaction prevails to the end?

> *Breve suspiro y último, y amargo*
> *es la muerte, forzosa y heredada ...*

> A short sigh, the last, and a painful one,
> is implacable and inherited Death.

Perhaps Quevedo's concluding line may have come to Goya's help as the death-sweat began:

> *Mas si es el ley y no pena, qué me aflijo?*

> But if it is the law, and no punishment,
> why do I afflict myself?

OS CAPRICHOS

1 *Franco Goya y Lucientes, Pintor*
2 *El si pronuncian y la mano alargan Al primero que Llega*
3 *Que viene el Coco*
4 *El de la rollona*
5 *Tal para qual*
6 *Nadie se conoce*
7 *Ni asi la Distingue*
8 *Que se la llevaron!*
9 *Tantalo*
10 *El amor y la muerte*
11 *Muchachos al avío*
12 *A caza de dientes*
13 *Estan calientes*
14 *Que sacrificio!*
15 *Bellos consejos*
16 *Dios la perdone : Y era su madre*
17 *Bien tirada está*
18 *Ysele quema la Casa*
19 *Todos Caerán*
20 *Ya van desplumados*
21 *¡Qual la descañonan!*
22 *Pobrecitas!*
23 *Aquellos polbos*
24 *Nohubo remedio*
25 *Si quebró el Cantaro*
26 *Ya tienen asiento*
27 *Quien mas rendido?*
28 *Chiton*
29 *Esto si que es leer*
30 *Porque esconderlos?*
31 *Ruega por ella*
32 *Por que fue sensible*
33 *Al Conde Palatino*
34 *Las rinde el Sueño*
35 *Le descañona*
36 *Mala noche*
37 *Si sabrá mas el discipulo?*
38 *Brabisimo!*
39 *Asta su Abuelo*
40 *De que mal morira?*
41 *Ni mas ni menos*
42 *Tu que no puedes*
43 *El sueño de la razon produce monstruos*
44 *Hilan delgado*
45 *Mucho hay que chupar*
46 *Correccion*
47 *Obsequio á el maestro*
48 *Soplones*
49 *Duendecitos*
50 *Los Chinchillas*
51 *Se repulen*
52 *Lo que puede un Sastre!*
53 *Que pico de Oro!*
54 *El Vergonzoso*
55 *Hasta la muerte*
56 *Subir y bajar*
57 *La filiacion*
58 *Tragala perro*
59 *Y aun no se van!*
60 *Ensayos*
61 *Volaverunt*
62 *Quien lo creyera!*
63 *Miren que grabes!*
64 *Buen Viage*
65 *Donde vá mamá?*
66 *Allá vá eso*
67 *Aguarda que te unten*
68 *Linda maestra!*
69 *Sopla*
70 *Devota profesion*
71 *Si amanece; nos Vamos*
72 *No te escaparás*
73 *Mejor es holgar*
74 *No grites, tonta*
75 *¿No hay quien nos desate?*
76 *¿Está Umd ... pues, Como digo ... eh! Cuidado! si no! ...*
77 *Unos á otros*
78 *Despacha, que despiertan*
79 *Nadie nos ha visto*
80 *Ya es hora*
Sueño de la Mentira y la ynconstancia

LOS DESASTRES DE LA GUERRA

1 *Tristes presentimientos de lo que ha de acontecer*
2 *Con razon ó sin ella*
3 *Lo mismo*
4 *Las mugeres dan valor*
5 *Y son fieras*
6 *Bien te se está*
7 *Que valor!*
8 *Siempre sucede*
9 *No quieren*
10 *tampoco*
11 *Ni por esas*
12 *Para eso habeis nacido*
13 *Amarga presencia*
14 *Duro es el paso!*
15 *Y no hai remedio*
16 *Se aprovechan*
17 *No se convienen*
18 *Enterrar y callar*
19 *Ya no hay tiempo*
20 *Curarlos, yá otra*
21 *Será lo mismo*
22 *tanto y mas*
23 *Lo mismo en otras partes*
24 *Aun podrán servir*
25 *tambien estos*
26 *No se puede mirar*
27 *Caridad*
28 *Populacho*
29 *Lo merecia*
30 *Estragos de la guerra*
31 *Fuerte cosa es!*
32 *Por qué?*
33 *Qué hai que hacer mas?*
34 *Por una navaja*
35 *No se puede saber por qué*
36 *tampoco*
37 *Esto es peor*
38 *Bárbaros!*
39 *Grande hazaña! Con muertos!*
40 *Algun partido saca*
41 *Escapan entre las llamas*
42 *Todo va revuelto*
43 *Tambien esto*
44 *Yo lo vi*
45 *Y esto tambien*
46 *Esto es malo*
47 *Así sucedió*
48 *Cruel lástima!*
49 *Caridad de una muger*
50 *Madre infeliz!*
51 *Gracias á la almorta*
52 *No llegan á tiempo*
53 *Espiró sin remedio*
54 *Clamores en vano*
55 *Lo peor es pedir*
56 *Al cementerio*
57 *Sanos y enfermos*
58 *No hay que dar voces*
59 *De qué sirve una taza?*
60 *No hay quien los socorra*
61 *Si son de otro linage*
62 *Las camas de la muerte*
63 *Muertos recogidos*
64 *Carretadas al cementerio*
65 *Qué alboroto es este?*
66 *Extraña devocion!*
67 *Esta no lo es menos*
68 *Que locura!*
69 *Nada. Ello dirá*
70 *No saben el camino*
71 *Contra el bien general*
72 *Las resultas*
73 *Gatesca pantomima*
74 *Esto es lo peor!*
75 *Farándula de charlatanes*
76 *El buitre carnívoro*
77 *Que se rompe la cuerda*
78 *Se defiende bien*
79 *Murió la Verdad*
80 *Si resucitará?*
81 *Fiero Monstruo!*
82 *Esto es lo verdadero*
Infame Provecho

LA TAUROMAQUIA

LOS PROVERBIOS

The Caprices

Plates 1–80 The British Museum, London

Francisco Goya y Lucientes,
Painter

2 *They say 'I will' and give their
hand to the first that comes along*

3 *The Bogey man is coming*

4 *Nanny's boy*

5 *Two of a kind*

6 *No one is recognised*

7 *And even so he does not recognise her*

8 *So they carried her off*

9 *Tantalus*

10 *Love and Death*

11 *Get ready, boys!*

12 *Hunting for teeth*

13 *It's hot!*

14 *What a sacrifice!*

15 *Pretty advice*

Dios la perdone. Y era su madre.

May God forgive her! – and it was her mother

Bien tirada está.

17 It fits nicely

Ysele quema la Casa.

18 And he burnt down his house

Todos Caerán.

They will all fall

Ya van desplumados.

20 They have been stripped clean

¡Qual la descañonan!

21 And they pluck her!

Pobrecitas!

Poor things!

Aquellos polbos.

23 As you sow...

Nohubo remedio.

24 There was no remedy

221

Si quebró el Cantaro.

25 *He broke the jug*

Ya tienen asiento.

26 *They have taken their seats*

Quien mas rendido?

27 *Who is the more devoted?*

Chiton.

28 *Ssh!*

Esto si que es leer.

29 *This is really reading!*

Porque esconderlos!

30 *Why hide them away?*

Ruega por ella.

31 *She prays for her*

Por que fue sensible.

32 *Because she was easily moved*

Al Conde Palatino.

33 *To the Count Palatine!*

La vinte el Sueño.

4 *Sleep subdues them*

Le desuñona.

35 *She is giving him a close shave*

Mala noche.

36 *A bad night*

Si sabrá mas el discipulo?

7 *Is the pupil any wiser?*

¡Brabisimo!

38 *Bravo!*

Asta su Abuelo.

39 *As far back as his grandfathers*

De que mal morira?

What sickness will he die of?

Ni mas ni menos.

41 *Neither more nor less*

Tu que no puedes.

42 *You who are unable...*

223

43 *The sleep of reason produces Monsters*

Hilan delgado.

44 *They spin fine*

Mucho hay que chupar.

45 *There is a lot to suck*

Correccion.

46 *Correction*

Obsequio á el maestro.

47 *Offerings to the master*

Soplones.

48 *Tale-bearers*

Duendecitos.

49 *Hobgoblins*

Las Chinchillas.

50 *The Chinchilla's*

Se repulen.

51 *They smarten themselves up*

Lo que puede un Sastre!

52 *What a tailor can do*

Que pico de Oro!

53 *What a golden beak!*

El Vergonzoso.

54 *The bashful one*

Hasta la muerte.

Until death

Subir y bajar.

56 *Rise and fall*

La filiacion.

57 *Her family credentials*

Tragala perro.

Take it, dog!

Y aun no se van!

59 *And still they don't go!*

Ensayos.

60 *First attempts*

225

61 *The bird has flown*

62 *Who would believe it?*

63 *Look how important they are!*

64 *Have a good trip!*

65 *Where is Mummy going?*

66 *Look out! There it goes!*

67 *Wait till they've finished grea-sing you!*

68 *A good teacher!*

69 *What next!*

70 *Devout profession*

71 *When day breaks, we shall go*

72 *You won't get away*

73 *It's better to do nothing*

74 *Don't scream, stupid!*

75 *Is there no one who can untie us?*

76 *You understand, Sir?... for, as I say... Eh? Look out! or...*

77 *First their turn, then the others'*

78 *Hurry, they're waking up!*

79 *No one has seen us*

80 *Now it's time*

First plate for plate 23
Bibliothèque Nationale, Paris

Woman in prison
The British Museum, London

Old woman and a gallant
Bibliothèque Nationale, Paris

Dream of lies and inconstancy
Biblioteca Nacional, Madrid

Women weeping over an injured dog
Biblioteca Nacional, Madrid

The Disasters of War

Plates 1–82 The British Museum, London

Sad forebodings of the events to come

2 With reason or without

The same

4 The women show courage

... and are like wild beasts

6 That serves you right

7 *What courage!*

8 *It is always happening*

9 *They do not desire it*

10 *Neither do these*

11 *Nor these*

12 *For this you were born*

13 *Bitter presence*

14 *It is a hard step*

5 ... and there is no way out

16 They take advantage from it

7 They cannot agree

18 Bury and be silent

9 There is no time now!

20 Treat them, and then on to others

1 It is just the same

22 So much – and even more

23 *The same in other parts*

24 *They will still be able to serve*

25 *... and so will these*

26 *It is not possible to look*

27 *Charity*

28 *The mob*

29 *He deserved it*

30 *Ravages of war*

31 *It is a hard thing!*

32 *Why?*

33 *What more can one do?*

34 *Because of a knife*

35 *One will never know why*

36 *... nor in this case*

37 *This is worse*

38 *Barbarians!*

39 *What heroism – with the dead!*

40 *He gains some advantage*

41 *They escape through the flames*

42 *All is confusion*

43 *... and here also*

44 *This I saw*

45 *... and this as well*

46 *This is bad*

47 It happened like this

48 Merciless grief!

49 A woman's charity

50 Unhappy mother!

51 Thanks to the wild beans

52 They do not arrive in time

53 He died – there was nothing else for it

54 They cry out in vain

235

55 *The worst is to beg*

56 *To the cemetery*

57 *The hale and the infirm*

58 *It is useless to cry out*

59 *Of what use is a cup?*

60 *No one can help them*

61 *They are of another race*

62 *The beds of Death*

63 *The dead gathered in*

64 *Cart-loads to the cemetery*

65 *And what commotion is this?*

66 *What strange devotion!*

67 *And this is no less strange*

68 *What madness!*

69 *'Nothing!' That is what it says*

70 *They do not know the way*

237

71 *Against the common good*

72 *The final outcome*

73 *Feline Pantomime*

74 *The worst is this!*

75 *A charlatan show*

76 *The carnivorous vulture*

77 *The rope is breaking*

78 *He defends himself well*

Truth has died

80 *But will She rise again?*

Ferocious monster!

82 *This is Truth*

nfamous gain
he Museum of Fine Arts, Boston

The Bull-fighting series

Plates 1–33 The British Museum, London

1 *The way in which the Spaniards in ancient times hunted bulls on horseback in the open country*

2 *Another way of hunting on foot*

3 *The Moors, settled in Spain, take up the sport ignoring the proscriptions of the Koran, and spear a bull in the open country*

4 *They play another bull with the cape in a closed arena*

5 *The courageous Moor Gazul was the first to spear bulls according to rules*

6 *The Moors play the bull in the ring with their burnouse*

240

The origin of the darts or banderillas

8 *A Moor caught by the bull in the ring*

A Spanish knight kills a bull after losing his horse

10 *Charles V spearing a bull in the ring at Valladolid*

The warrior El Cid spears another bull

12 *The mob hamstring the bull with spears, crescents, banderillas and other arms*

A Spanish knight breaking small spears in the ring without the help of the assistants

14 *The very skilful student of Falces, wrapped in his cloak, taunts the bull by his body movements*

15 *The famous Martincho planting the banderillas on the bull as he turns*

16 *He now throws the bull with his hands in the ring at Madrid*

17 *The Moors using donkeys as a barrier to defend themselves against the bull which has its horns tipped with balls*

18 *Martincho's recklessness in the ring at Saragossa*

19 *Another foolhardy act of his in the same ring*

20 *The agility and daring of Juanito Apiñani in the ring at Madrid*

21 *The terrible events that took place in the stands of the ring at Madrid, and the death of the mayor of Torrejón*

22 *The celebrated Pajuelera displays her manly courage in the ring at Saragossa*

242

23 *Mariano Ceballos, nicknamed El Indio, kills the bull from his horse*

24 *The same Ceballos, mounted on a bull, breaks small spears in the ring at Madrid*

25 *Dogs are set on to the bull*

26 *A picador falls from his horse under the bull*

27 *The celebrated picador Fernando del Toro tempts the beast forward with his pike*

28 *The valiant Rendón stabbing a bull with his pike, the pass which caused his death in the ring at Madrid*

9 *Pepehillo making the recorte pass*

30 *Pedro Romero killing a bull that has halted*

243

31 *Banderillas with flares*

33 *The unfortunate death of Pepehillo in the ring at Madrid*

B *A horse thrown by the bull*
Biblioteca Nacional, Madrid

D *A bullfighter, mounted on the shoulders of an assistant spearing a bull*
The British Museum, London

244

32 *Two teams of picadors thrown one after the other by a single bull*

A *A Spanish knight breaking small spears with the help of the assistants*
The British Museum, London

C *Dogs are set on to the bull*
The British Museum, London

E *Death of Pepehillo (2nd composition)*
The British Museum, London

Death of Pepehillo (3rd composition)
Biblioteca Nacional, Madrid

G *Fighting the bull from a carriage drawn by two mules*
The British Museum, London

...ring of Martincho in the bull ring at Saragossa
...ertina, Vienna

Torero going in to kill, using a hat instead of the cape
Biblioteca Nacional, Madrid

...riano Ceballos mounted on a bull, breaking spears
...lioteca Nacional, Madrid

A skilful fighter calling the bull with his back turned
Biblioteca Nacional, Madrid

245

The Proverbs

All Proverbs plates The British Museum, London

1 *(It weighs more than a dead donkey)*
(Feminine folly)

2 *(Do not through fear lose your honour)*
(Folly of fear)

3 *(To go among the branches)*
(Ridiculous folly)

4 *(Fornication follows vice)*
(Buffoon)

5 *(Reject the friend who embraces you with his wings and*
tears you with his beak)
(Flying folly)

6 *(God made us, and we marvel at His work)*
(Furious folly)

246

(She who is ill wed never tires of saying so)
(Folly of confusion)

8 *(Much may be hidden beneath the sackcloth)*
  (Men in sacks)

(The claws of a cat and the habit of a saint)
(General folly)

10 *(A woman and a horse, may another break them in)*
   (Equine abductor)

(Two heads are better than one)
(Poor folly)

12 *(If Marina dances, she must take what she finds)*

(Where there's a will there's a way)
(A way to fly)

14 *(Enjoy the Easter Carnival, for tomorrow will be Lent)*
   (Carnival folly)

247

15 *(To commend oneself neither to God nor the Devil)*
   (Clear folly)

16 *(Wounds will heal, but not cruel words)*

17 *(He who does not like you will defame you in jest)*
   (Loyalty)

18 *(God created them and they join with their like)*
   (Birds of a feather flock together)

(Two to one, so put straw in your breeches)
(Known folly)

(Dancing on a slack rope)
(Exact folly)

(Who will bell the cat?)
(Animal folly)

(Give a clear path to the bull and the wind)
(Folly of little bulls or *Folly of Fools)*

Bibliography

In the last forty years there has been a considerable output of studies of Goya, concerned chiefly with his art. Among authorities consulted during the writing of this book are, in addition to those quoted in the text:

Almagro, Antonio: *Constantes Históricas del Pueblo Español*, 1951

Baroja, Julio Caro: *Las Brujas y su Mundo*, 1961

Bertrand, Comte Henri-Gratien: *Mémoires*, Vol. I, ed. Fleuriot de l'Angle, 1953

Caballero: *En el Centenario de Jovellanos* (Revista de Estudios Políticos, IX, 1944)

Chabrun, Jean-François: *Goya*, 1965

De Arteche, Gómez: *El Reinado de Carlos IV*, 1959

De Maeztu, Ramiro: *Defensa de la Hispanidad*, 1920

De La Serna, Ramón Gómez: *Goya*, 1950

De Salas, Xavier: *La Familia de Carlos IV*, 1959

D'Ors, Eugenio: *Goya*, 1928

Dubech, Lucien, et d'Espezel, Pierre: *Histoire de Paris*, 1926

Ezquerra del Bayo, Joaquín: *La Duquesa de Alba y Goya*, 1959

Gaibrois, Manuel Ballesteros: *Historia de España*, 1962

Godoy, Manuel: *Cuenta Dada de su Vida Política, por el Principe de la Paz*, ed. Peters, 1904

Guazzo, Fra Francesco Maria: *Compendium Malificarum*, 1608: tr. Ashwin, ed. Summers, 1929

Holland, Lord: *Foreign Reminiscences*, 1850

Malraux, André: *Saturne*, 1950

Menéndez y Pidal, Ramón: *Estudios Literarios*, 1938

Oliver-Martin, Felix: *L'Inconnu; Essai sur Napoléon Bonaparte*, 1952

Remy, Nicolas: *Demonolatry* (Demonolatreiae libri tres), 1595; ed. Summers, 1930

Ruíz, Angel Salcedo: *La Epoca de Goya*, 1924

Sánchez Cantón, F. J.: *Goya* (Les Maîtres d'Autrefois), 1930. *Goya and the Black Paintings*; with an appendix by Xavier de Salas (English ed. 1965)

Soler, Blanco: Pascual, Piga; y Petinto, Perez, Drs: *La Duquesa de Alba y su Tiempo*, 1949. (Report of the autopsy of 1945)

Photographic credits and acknowledgements

Graphisches Samm. Albertina, Vienna: p. 245

The Duke of Alburquerque, Madrid: p. 170

Ampliaciones y Reproducciones Mas, Barcelona: p. 14, p. 19 (left), p. 31, p. 51, PLATE V, PLATE VI, PLATE VIII, PLATE XV, PLATE XVII, p. 181, p. 183, PLATE XXXVII, p. 196

Walter C. Baker: p. 29 (left)

Banco Urquijo, Madrid: p. 28

Bayer. Staatsgemäldesammlungen, Munich: p. 172

Sir Alfred Beit, Bart: p. 200

Biblioteca Nacional, Madrid: p. 30 (right), p. 80 (left), p. 130, p. 211, p. 228, p. 244, p. 245

Bibliothèque Nationale, Paris: p. 228

Bibliothèque Royale, Brussels: p. 126

The Bowes Museum, Barnard Castle, co. Durham: p. 64 (top)

The British Museum, London: p. 12, p. 24, p. 25 (top left and right), p. 25 (right), p. 30 (left), p. 38, p. 72, p. 109, p. 111, p. 112, p. 113, p. 120, p. 122, p. 168, p. 203 (top), pp. 219–56

Ets. J. E. Bulloz, Paris: PLATE XXXI

Mrs D. David-Weill, Paris: p. 23

Editions d'Art Albert Skira, Geneva: PLATE XL

Fratelli Alinari, Florence: p. 125 (right)

John R. Freeman, London: p. 12, p. 24, p. 25 (top left and right), p. 29 (right), p. 30 (left), p. 38, p. 72, p. 109, p. 111, p. 112, p. 113, p. 120, p. 122, p. 168, p. 203 (top), pp. 219–56

The Frick Collection, New York: p. 160 (mid)

John Hadfield, London: PLATE XXX

The Hispanic Society of America, New York: PLATE XII

David Manso (Fotógrafo Oficial del Museo del Prado): p. 18, p. 19 (right), p. 21, p. 25 (below), p. 28, PLATE I, PLATE II, p. 35, p. 41, PLATE IV, PLATE V, PLATE VII, p. 57, p. 60, p. 61, p. 62, p. 63, p. 64 (mid), PLATE IX, p. 67, p. 69, p. 70, p. 73, PLATE XI, p. 79 (below), p. 80 (right), p. 82, PLATE XIII, PLATE XIV, p. 92, p. 96, p. 97, p. 99, p. 100, p. 101, p. 103, p. 104, PLATE XVI, p. 110, PLATE XVII, PLATE XVIII, PLATE XIX, PLATE XX, p. 125 (left), p. 134, p. 135, p. 136, PLATE XXIII,

PLATE XXIV, PLATE XXV, p. 148, PLATE XXVII, PLATE XXVIII, p. 156 (left), p. 162, PLATE XXXIII, p. 171, p. 173, PLATE XXXIII, PLATE XXXIV, PLATE XXV, PLATE XXXVI, PLATE XXXVIII, p. 199, p. 201, PLATE XLI, p. 210 (right), p. 214 (right)

The Metropolitan Museum of Art, New York: p. 46, p. 64 (below), p. 198

The Minneapolis Institute of Arts: PLATE XXXIX

The Duke of Montellano, Madrid: p. 85, PLATE XIII, p. 104

Museo Lázaro Galdiano, Madrid: PLATE XVII

The Museum and Art Gallery, São Paolo: p. 121

The Museum of Fine Arts, Boston: p. 68, p. 239

The National Gallery, London: PLATE X, p. 79 (top), p. 83, PLATE XXIX, p. 214 (left)

The National Gallery of Art, Washington, D.C.: PLATE XXVI

The National Gallery of Prague: p. 157 (top)

The Phillips Collection, Washington, D.C.: PLATE XLIII

Photographie Giraudon, Paris: PLATE III, p. 95, p. 156 (right), p. 178, p. 179

Oskar Reinhart, Winterthur, Switzerland: PLATE XL

The Royal Academy, London: p. 200

The Marquis of Santa Cruz, Madrid: p. 156 (mid)

Peter C. Scheier, São Paolo: p. 121

Sterling and Francine Clark Institute, Williamstown, Mass.: p. 202

The Duke of Sueca, Madrid: PLATE XV

Szépművészeti Múzeum, Budapest: p. 161 (top and below)

Fernando Sanz Vega, Madrid: PLATE XXI, PLATE XXII

The Victoria and Albert Museum, London (Crown Copyright): p. 190

The William Rockhill Nelson Gallery of Art – Atkins Museum of Fine Arts, Kansas City: p. 157 (below)

Derrick Witty, London: PLATE X, PLATE XXIX

Index